CASSELL STUDIES IN PASTORAL CARE AND PERSONAL
AND SOCIAL EDUCATION

AFFECTIVE EDUCATION

Books in this series:

R. Best (ed.): *Education, Spirituality and the Whole Child*

R. Best, P. Lang, C. Lodge and C. Watkins (eds): *Pastoral Care and PSE: Entitlement and Provision*

M. Calvert and J. Henderson (eds): *Managing Pastoral Care*

G. Haydon: *Teaching about Values: A Practical Approach*

P. Lang (ed.): *Affective Education: A Comparative View*

P. Lang, R. Best and A. Lichtenberg (eds): *Caring for Children: International Perspectives on Pastoral Care and PSE*

O. Leaman: *Death and Loss: Compassionate Approaches in the Classroom*

J. McGuiness: *Teachers, Pupils and Behaviour: A Managerial Approach*

J. McGuiness: *Counselling in Schools*

L. O'Connor, D. O'Connor and R. Best: *Drugs: Partnerships for Policy, Prevention and Education*

S. Power: *The Pastoral and the Academic: Conflict and Contradiction in the Curriculum*

P. Whitaker: *Managing to Learn: Aspects of Reflective and Experiential Learning in Schools*

J. Ungoed-Thomas: *Vision of a School: The Good School in the Good Society*

CASSELL STUDIES IN PASTORAL CARE AND PERSONAL
AND SOCIAL EDUCATION

AFFECTIVE EDUCATION

A Comparative View

Edited by
Peter Lang with Yaacov Katz and Isabel Menezes

CASSELL

London and New York

Cassell
Wellington House
125 Strand
London WC2R 0BB

370 Lexington Avenue
New York
NY 10017-6550

www.cassell.co.uk

First published 1998

British Library Cataloguing-in-Publication Data
A catalogue record for this book is available from the British Library.

ISBN 0–304–33988–1 (paperback)
 0–304–33987–3 (hardback) ✓

Typeset by Ruth Noble, Peebles
Printed and bound in Great Britain by Biddles Limited, Guildford and King's
Lynn

Contents

PART 3
Examples of European Research and Initiatives in the Affective Domain

PART 4

Series Editor's foreword

Perhaps all ages are ages of paradox. This one certainly is. The rich have never been richer – whether we speak of individuals or nations – but the poor remain poor. Nations too impoverished to feed all their people find the money to test nuclear weapons. The age of the 'global village' has arrived, yet what has come to be known as 'ethnic cleansing' splits communities and separates neighbours as much as (if not more than) ever. State control of education in the countries of the former communist bloc is relaxed and a new era of intellectual freedom proclaimed, yet in the Western democracies, the state continues to tighten its control on school curricula. Nations have more to learn from one another than ever yet many remain insular and suspicious of others who are 'different'.

This book provides an important opportunity for those concerned with education in its widest sense to learn from one another. In focusing upon affective education rather than academic outcomes or technological competence, it is somewhat at odds with the trend. Paradoxically, the intriguing and often subtle differences in policy and practice which follow from distinctive cultures are accompanied by a shared commitment to the education of the whole person. Approaches differ in emphasis and interpretation from society to society, yet in every case the authors identify strands in educational provision which embody the shared values of personal development and social harmony.

It is right and proper that, as we approach the millennium, this series should include a book which brings together diverse European perspectives on pastoral care and personal-social education, yet re-emphasizes the core values which, at some level, they all espouse. I commend it to teachers, students, researchers and policy-makers everywhere.

Ron Best

Notes on contributors

François Audiger worked for 12 years in colleges and lycées and directed a number of research projects into the teaching of history and geography before taking over responsibility for research and didactics in history, geography and civic education at the Institut National de Recherche Pédagogique in Paris. In this capacity he has directed a number of research projects into such areas as human rights and civic education. For eight years he acted as expert for the Council of Europe in his special areas. He has convened a number of colloquia, produced a number of reports and published widely.

Ron Best is Professor of Education and Dean in the Faculty of Education at Roehampton Institute, London. He is author and editor of several books and many papers on aspects of pastoral care and personal and social education. He is a founder member of the National Association for Pastoral Care in Education and executive editor of the journal *Pastoral Care in Education*.

Ad Boes began his career as a primary teacher. Since 1969 he has been a lecturer in pedagogics at Drenth University and at the primary teacher training college De Eekhorst in Assen. He is involved in Jena-plan education, one of the reform movements (progressive education) that are well developed in the Netherlands, at different levels. He has published a number of books and articles, most of them about Jena-plan education.

Bártolo P. Campos is a professor in the faculty of psychology and education at the University of Porto and at the Portuguese Catholic University. He has worked and written widely in the area of education, including affective education, psychological development and intervention and career guidance.

Úna Collins is Head of the Post-Primary Department in the Marino Institute of Education in Dublin. The institute provides in-career development and re-training for secondary teachers. She has been a key figure in the development of pastoral care in Ireland over a number of years. She is author of *Pastoral Care: A Teacher's Handbook* and *Pastoral Care Programmes for Students*. She has also co-edited, with Jean McNiff, *A New Approach to In-Career Development for Teachers in Ireland*.

Maria Teresa Crucillà works in Rome, where she was awarded her first degree in psychology at La Sapienza University. She also has a specialist qualification in family counselling from the Catholic University and completed an internship in the adolescent department of the Rome Neuropsychiatric Hospital. After 20 years teaching in state primary schools she moved in 1990 to the third University of Rome, where she is engaged in teacher training and in research projects concerned with health education and youth alienation.

Reinhold Fess has been a comprehensive school teacher in Saarland since 1983. In 1986 he became involved in a state-wide school reform, as an in-service teacher trainer and chairperson of a curriculum development committee. Since 1994 he has been a member of the management team of the Riegelsberg Gesamtschule, responsible for didactic and pedagogical issues and in-service training.

Donata Francescato gained an MA in French Literature before taking a PhD in clinical psychology at the University of Houston. She is now Professor of Community Psychology at La Sapienza University, Rome. She is interested in research and training in empowering individuals, small groups, organizations and networks and in women's studies.

Anne Ghysselinckx-Janssens teaches didactics of psychology at the University of Louvain and developmental psychology at the Institut Libre Marie Haps in Brussels. Her studies of children's left–right role-taking have been published in the *European Journal of Psychology of Education* and in *L'Ecole fondamentale*.

Victoria Gordillo is Professor of Counselling in the Education Department at the University Compultense of Madrid. Currently she is working as an adviser for the Spanish Ministry of Education. She has written over twenty books on a range of educational topics. She is director of a collaborative project on education and AIDS prevention with the universities of Coimbra and Palermo.

Rea Karageorgiou-Short is a registered drama therapist with a background in pre-school education and special education. She teaches drama and story-telling in education in the postgraduate teacher training programme Anima and also undertakes freelance work.

Yaacov Katz is currently the Director of the School of Education, Bar-Ilan University and Head of the Department of Educational Studies. He is also the Director of the Institute for Community Education and Research. Prior to his current appointments he served as Director of the Division of Educational Counselling in the School of Education. His main teaching and research interests are affective education, educational counselling, and attitudes in Israeli society in general and in the Israeli school system in particular, topics on which he has published a number of papers. He has recently edited a book on pedagogical and psychological implications of the use of information technology in the learning process.

Alkistis Kondoyianni is a specialist in drama in education. She has taught this and puppet theatre from 1989 to 1994 in Athens University Department of Early Childhood Education and from 1994 in Athens University, Department of Theatre Studies. She has written 37 books for children and 8 for teachers. Since 1992 she has been President of the Greek section of the World Organization for Early Childhood Education.

Niels Kryger is Associate Professor in Educational Research at the Royal Danish School of Educational Studies. He participated in a nationwide evaluation of the Danish class teacher tradition. He has researched the school's role in building masculine identities and is currently researching new media in school and leisure activities.

Peter Lang is based at the Institute of Education at the University of Warwick. He has been involved in teaching, writing and research in the area of affective education for 20 years. For over 10 years he has been concerned with developing international perspectives on this area. He has edited several books on aspects of affective education and written many papers, and has a particular interest in pupil perspectives and the issue of how schools can develop shared values. He is currently involved in comparative research into the attitudes of European teachers and pupils to affective education and also into the differing practices described as circle time.

Manuel Marroquín is Director of the Counselling Department and Vice-Dean of Postgraduate Studies as well as a professor in the Faculty of Psychology at the University of Deusto, where he teaches counselling psychology and humanistic psychotherapy. Apart from a PhD in psychology from the University Compultense in Madrid he holds a masters in counselling from Loyola University, Chicago. He has published a large number of papers and several books.

Ana Martínez Pampliega teaches in the Faculty of Philosophy and Educational Science at the University of Deusto, where she teaches a range of psychological courses. She has specialized in clinical psychology and has researched the influence that families with low mental adjustment have on their children's health.

Isabel Menezes teaches in the Faculty of Psychology and Education at the University of Porto. She has been working in the area of personal and social education, civic education, values and moral education, and affective education. She is currently co-ordinating the Portuguese participation in the IEA international project on civic education.

Alex Minaev is based at Krasnoyarsk State Educational University in the Faculty of Foreign Languages. His interests include adolescent alienation and the contribution that psychological courses can make to overcoming this.

Daniel Motta worked for 15 years in colleges and lycées before joining the staff at the Institut National de Recherche Pédagogique in Paris, where he works in the area of the pedagogy of physical and sports education. His research areas are physical, sports and arts education and his work involves approaches through dance and theatre to aspects of affective education relating to health.

Margarita Popova is Head of the Department of Educational Development at a Federal Centre of Vocational Guidance and Psychological Support. She also teaches at a Federal Teachers' Retraining Institute. Her interests include the development of textbooks for schools and the effect of teaching psychology to pupils on their personal and social development.

Kirsten Reisby is Associate Professor at the Aarhus branch of the Royal Danish School of Educational Studies. She has research interests in theoretical and empirical studies within gender, democracy and education. From 1997 to 2001 she will be director of a qualitative research project on gender barriers and carriers in higher education. She is co-editor of the *Journal of Nordic Educational Research* and associate editor of *Teachers and Teaching: Theory and Practice* and *NORA: The Journal of Nordic Research on Gender*.

Athena Sideri is Associate Professor in Psychology (Special Education and Ethnic Minorities) at the University of Athens. She teaches in the area of special educational needs and runs programmes for ethnic minority groups. She has research interests in the integration of ethnic and religious minorities and their affective education.

Christiane Vandenplas-Holper is a professor at the Université Catholique de Louvain where she teaches developmental psychology. Her research interests concern children's socio-cognitive and socio-emotional development, parents' and teachers' implicit developmental and educational theories and lifespan developmental psychology. Among her many publications is *Education et développement social de l'enfant* (Paris, 1987).

Klaus Winkel gained his doctorate with a thesis on school reform. From 1972 to 1983 he worked with the university co-ordinators of the comprehensive school of Göttingen-Geismar on the development, implementation, and evaluation of the Team/Small-Group Model. From 1983 to 1986 he was engaged in the first phase of teacher preparation at the University of Paderborn. Since 1986 he has been director of the In-service Training to Accompany the Development of the Comprehensive School project. He is a department director at the Saarland Institute of Pedagogy and Media, and a lecturer at the University of Saarbrucken. His special interest is in school reform and development as well as the professionalization of the work of teachers.

Yuri Zabrodin is General Director of the Federal Centre of Vocational Guidance and Psychological Support, Head of Department of Professional Education and Development of Human Resources at the Ministry of Labour and Social Development and Head of the Department of Social Psychology at Moscow State City University. His research interests are in the area of theoretical and applied psychology, psychology of education and the elaboration of educational and social technologies. He has written extensively and worked in higher education for more than thirty years.

Acknowledgements

The editors would like to thank Ron Best for his very helpful comments on the final manuscript.

PART 1

Introduction

CHAPTER 1

Towards an understanding of affective education in a European context

Peter Lang

INTRODUCTION

This book might have been subtitled 'Pupils can be people too.' This would have signalled two of its central concerns. Both involve aspects of schooling which do not always get the attention and resources that they deserve. In the first place, that pupils are in fact also people is something that is often forgotten or ignored in many of the current debates on school effectiveness, economic competitiveness and classroom pedagogy. The fact that pupils are people with many of the same emotions and feelings as those who teach them needs emphasis not just because respect and care for the individual should be a fundamental concern of all democratic societies, but also because where their importance is recognized and responded to there is a probability that the more academic side of the education process will be more effective as well. The second idea is that a key aim of education is not just to produce academically processed pupils but autonomous people capable of contributing to their societies and leading fulfilled lives in ways that go well beyond that facilitated by basic skills and academic knowledge.

That the kind of education described above is not just a recent fashion or only part of the most liberal and progressive educational approaches is illustrated by Albert Camus' description of an Algerian-French elementary school teacher in his unfinished novel *The First Man* (1996). In his description of this teacher he is clearly talking of one of his own teachers. This was someone who inspired him through far more than traditional teaching, though working in the most traditional of systems early this century.

> No, school did not just provide them an escape from family life. At least in M. Bernard's class, it fed a hunger in them more basic even to the child than to the man, and that is the hunger for discovery. In their other classes, no doubt they were taught many things, but it was somewhat the way geese are stuffed: food was presented to them and they

were asked please to swallow it. In M. Bernard's class, they felt for the first time they existed and that they were the objects of the highest regard: they were judged worthy to discover the world. And even their teacher did not devote himself just to what he was paid to teach them; he welcomed them with simplicity into his personal life, he lived that life with them, told them about his childhood and the lives of children he had known, shared with them his philosophy but not his opinions, for though he was for example anticlerical, like many of his colleagues, he never said a word against religion in class, nor against anything that could be the object of a choice or a belief, but he would condemn with all the more vigour those evils over which there could be no argument – theft, betrayal, rudeness, dirtiness.

The value of what Camus describes is poignantly underlined by two letters included in an appendix. These, written some thirty years after Camus' elementary schooling, show that he still corresponded with and valued the opinion of the teacher who was the basis of the description above. Today, when education seems increasingly to follow the 'stuffing geese with food' model, it is hard not to be concerned for the Camus of tomorrow.

The dimension of education described above can be identified by the word 'affective', and in this book the term 'affective education' is used. In the view of its contributors, this should be seen as meaning a significant dimension of the educational process which is concerned with the feelings, beliefs, attitudes and emotions of students, with their interpersonal relationships and social skills. This dimension is likely to involve a concern for their moral, spiritual and values development. It is more indirectly concerned with the same areas in relation to teachers and parents. Affective education operates on at least three different levels and has objectives involving different time scales. These different levels are those of:

- the individual, attention directed to individual students, their self-esteem, emotional literacy, study skills, their life and career plans;
- the group, attention to the nature and quality of interactions within the groups in which students work and relate;
- the institution, a concern for the quality of the climate and ethos of the school itself, the guidance and support it offers students, its care and concern in relation to their welfare.

Work at these different levels may be seen to have both short- and longer-term goals. Thus it is suggested that the development of good interpersonal relationships within student groups leads to the creation of a better learning environment. A positive school ethos with which the students can engage can lead to greater motivation and decrease the likelihood of alienation in the longer term, while the development of emotional literacy and maturity is likely to affect the quality of the student's adult life as well as the student's life in school.

This book has been produced because of a belief that the area described above is essential to the full and effective education of future Europeans, a belief shared by all of its contributors. Such a book is needed because it deals with an area that often receives support only of a rhetorical kind, and one that tends to be overshadowed by more utilitarian concerns, particularly of an economic nature. It is also an area that is neglected in terms of the preparation of teachers and the allocation of resources. This book reflects a belief that this is a quite unsatisfactory state of affairs and that the success of even the most utilitarian economic aim will be more likely if this imbalance is redressed.

The dimension described here exists to some extent in all the education systems of Europe (and of course elsewhere; see Lang, Best and Lichtenberg, 1994). However, the degree to which it exists and the manner in which it is articulated vary significantly. It is also the case that the terminology used to identify it varies from one country to another.

A number of the chapters in this book were presented either as they are reproduced or in earlier versions at a seminar held in May 1994 at the University of Warwick. The participants at this seminar were drawn from ten European countries. Each had a particular interest in aspects of the dimension of education described above. Indeed, it was possible at that time for those involved to confirm that a shared concern existed and to agree that the most appropriate term to describe it was 'affective education'. This term was chosen because it was both understood by, and acceptable to, all those involved at the time even though it did not enjoy popular usage in any of the countries represented. A working definition was also developed, as a basis for analysis and refinement:

> By 'affective education' is meant that part of the educational process that concerns itself with attitudes, feelings, beliefs and emotions of students. This involves a concern for the personal and social development of pupils and their self-esteem or as it is perhaps more appropriately expressed in French as regards each student, that 'Je suis bien dans ma peau'. A further important dimension goes beyond the individual students and concerns the effectiveness of their relationships with others, thus interpersonal relationships and social skills are recognized as central to affective education. Related to this view of the affective dimension of education are two further points: that it often involves both the provision of support and guidance for students and that the affective and cognitive dimensions of education are interrelated. Students' feelings about themselves as learners and about their academic subjects can be at least as influential as their actual ability.

There are, of course, problems about definitions of this kind, when what is described is both positive and rather general in nature. Once such definitions have been drawn up they attain a validity of their own and there is a danger that descriptions of systems are distorted to fit the definition rather than that the definition is modified in the light of empirical data.

One purpose of this book is to draw attention to the significant common ground that exists in terms of the theory, policy and practice of affective education in a European context. This common ground manifests itself in a multiplicity of ways and in no case is it suggested that there are complete parallels between any two countries. The emphasis on the shared aspects of the affective dimension of education in Europe has at least two important purposes. First, there is a conventional awareness of the differences between education systems and this is frequently invoked to make political points, usually that other systems that do things differently from one's own achieve better results. There tends to be less awareness of similarities, so these need highlighting. Second, every contributor to this book has a strong commitment to affective education and its development. This development is likely to be promoted by a greater shared understanding of the concerns of colleagues in other European countries and of the work that is done in the pursuit of common objectives.

The first section of the book contains a number of chapters which provide an overview of the situation in particular European countries. They illustrate some of the various ways in which affective education has developed and been articulated in different countries. In some cases (e.g. England and Denmark), it has a history going back into the last century; in others (e.g. Italy, Spain and Portugal) its development has been relatively recent. In such countries the growth of affective education has often been accompanied by specific legislation. In a few countries, affective education in one particular guise may be observed in virtually all schools. In Denmark it is to be found in the role of the class teacher; in England it is manifested in what is known as Pastoral Care; in Israel it is identified with counselling. In other countries it is developing but has yet to affect the majority of schools. This is the situation in Portugal, where Personal and Social Education has been introduced through national legislation but is being developed only in a limited number of schools. There are also countries (e.g. France and Germany) where its influence is still very limited.

These chapters also illustrate that in the broadest terms, all manifestations of affective education stem from shared concerns that all pupils should gain the most from their education, that their time in school should not only be academically profitable but also enjoyable and secure and should encourage their development both cognitively and affectively. All manifestations seem also to include a focus on encouraging the development of pupils which will allow them to take their place as contributing, mature and worthwhile members of a democratic society.

The second section comprises chapters that relate to a number of these countries, offering examples of specific research, investigations or projects which focus on aspects of affective education within that particular national context. These chapters illustrate some of the many ways in which a concern to improve and understand the affective dimension has been pursued. In some cases an affective issue has been addressed through a systematic research methodology as in the case of the Spanish study of altruism in young children. In others a more hands-on approach has been adopted as with circle time in Italy, and the German case-study approach.

THE NEED FOR FURTHER INVESTIGATION

The approaches described in this book are not exhaustive of the forms affective education takes in the countries represented. Nor are the countries not represented necessarily without any form of affective education.

According to the Swedish Ministry of Education:

> The paramount task of the school is to stimulate every pupil's learning and development. Active learning requires a school environment in which all adults co-operate to this end. Schools have a special responsibility towards pupils with difficulties of various kinds.
>
> Pupil welfare comprises all measures taken for the well-being of pupils in school, and it is therefore an integral part of the work of schools. The conduct of pupil welfare is the joint responsibility of the home room teacher, head teacher and special pupil welfare staff. There are also special teachers for pupils requiring special educational support. School activities must, moreover, be designed in accordance with basic democratic values. The Education Act 1994 (new curriculum) makes it the duty of all active members of the school community to endeavour to prevent any efforts by pupils to subject others to degrading treatment.
>
> (Swedish Ministry of Education Information Broadsheet)

The curriculum guidance which elaborates this Act includes a great deal which has an affective element. For example under *Fundamental Values* we read:

> The task of the school is to encourage all pupils to discover their own uniqueness as individuals and thereby actively participate in social life by giving of their best in responsible freedom.
>
> Understanding and Compassion
> The school shall encourage understanding of other people and the ability to empathize. It shall also actively resist any tendency toward bullying or persecution. Xenophobia and intolerance must be actively confronted with knowledge, open discussion and effective measures.
>
> (Curriculum for Compulsory Schools, Swedish Ministry of Education and Science, 1994)

Indications of the possible development of affective education are to be found in the re-emergent European countries. In a survey of approaches to values education in Estonia the following point is made:

> There are not many subjects oriented towards values education in the curriculum. Among those in which values are explicitly examined, Civics, Ethics, Family Education and Psychology can be mentioned ... Civics, being a compulsory subject, is taught at grade 9 (age 15–16) one hour per week. Psychology, Family Therapy and Health Care are compulsory subjects at secondary level each for one hour per week. An optional subject, Ethics, is taught at secondary level.
>
> (Taylor, 1994)

In Poland too the fundamental values of affective education are to be discerned in the concept of *wychowanie*, which is mentioned later in this chapter.

It is clear that there is much more to be investigated regarding the extent and nature of affective education in Europe. However, the editors of this book believe that it provides a very significant advance in terms of knowledge and understanding of this area within a European context. It illustrates not only the common ground that exists but also how this is expressed in a wide range of different ways both between countries and within them.

COMPARISON AND CONTRAST

The chapters in this book illustrate at least three important points about affective education in a European context.

- the existence of 'common ground', an area of shared understanding in relation to the ideas covered by the term 'affective education'
- a developing body of research activity which supports this
- significant differences in relation to the actual conceptualization and practice of affective education in individual countries.

The existence of an area of shared understanding

Demonstrating the existence of common ground in relation to education in the affective domain is one of the central aims of this book. Common ground in this instance means the existence of some parallel or common aims, understandings and practice in a selection of European countries. That there is common ground is evidenced by the fact that although the contributors work in over 12 different European countries and are involved in significantly different educational systems and cultures, none has found difficulty in producing a contribution that both reflects their own situation and relates to the broader idea of affective education. Of course, the perspective from which each has been able to write varies, so in cases such as Ireland, Portugal and Spain the contributions have involved discussion of initiatives in affective education which are actually in progress, whereas at the other extreme the main focus of the German and French contributions is the relatively limited role afforded to affective education in the ideas, policy and practice of those countries. In several countries such as Denmark, England and Israel a significant affective dimension has been in place for many years.

A developing research area

There exists in a number of European countries a growing body of research activity which focuses on areas which have a significant affective aspect. The examples included in this book are an indication of this research interest. Nevertheless, though not all countries represented by chapters in Part 2, which deals with affective education in general, are represented in Part 3 on research, there is clear evidence that similar research is being undertaken in most of the countries represented, and indeed in some of those not included. Thus the *European Educational Research Yearbook* for 1994/95 lists research in the Czech Republic at both Charles University, Prague and at the University of West Bohemia, Plzeň into teacher–pupil relationships, how teacher personality may affect these and how to improve the quality of pupil–pupil interaction in the education process (EUDISED, 1996).

Significant conceptual and practical differences
Despite the existence of common ground and related research, there are very significant differences between countries at the levels of concept, theory, policy and practice. The contrasting approaches of the all-embracing Danish Folkeskole with the centrality of the class teacher role and the differentiated secondary system of Hauptschule, Realschule and Gymnasium of neighbouring Germany provides an example of this. However, it is difficult to assess the real significance of such contrast for affective education: to what degree are these differences fundamental and to what degree only superficial? This problem has been exacerbated by both the lack of awareness and the inattention that until very recently have characterized attitudes to the affective elements of European education. Some eight years ago Dockrell (1987) drew attention to this when he commented on the limited amount of research that could be identified internationally which specifically focused on the affective dimension of education. This neglect has meant that there have been few attempts at conceptual analysis or model building which might inform comparisons of affective education across Europe or indeed on a broader international front.

However, more recently the existence of a wide range of examples of different approaches to affective education in a number of countries internationally has begun to be documented (see for instance Lang, Best and Lichtenberg, 1994 and Lang, 1995). This book seeks to add a specifically European perspective, and breaks new ground with the inclusion of chapters focusing specifically on research.

WIDER EUROPEAN PERSPECTIVES

As has already been suggested, there is evidence that in a number of European countries which are not covered by this book the affective dimension is significant. This is an important point as inevitably with all initial comparative investigations the identification of examples is somewhat fortuitous. For example, the writer's initial inquiries to the education sections of a number of European embassies in London drew a complete blank: nothing appeared to be known about an affective dimension to education in the countries concerned and it was felt certain that none existed. It is a significant fact that almost all the countries approached at that time are represented in this book. It is not suggested that this book offers a definitive survey, a point underlined by the following examples.

Hungary provides an example of a well-developed philosophy corresponding to our notion of affective education. Since 1990 a new statutory curriculum has been established for all pupils between the ages of 6 and 16 (there is a separate curriculum for 3- to 6-year-olds).

The ideas that inform this curriculum are:

- that it should only be presented at policy level in a broad and general way with individual schools being responsible for developing their own specific curriculum
- that education has two almost equally important aims, academic achievement and personal and social education

The objectives of the personal and social dimension of the curriculum include enabling pupils to:

• learn to respect and value themselves and others
• appreciate the benefits of resolving conflict by non-violent means
• learn to tell the difference between intention and action
• learn tolerance and the need to take responsibility for their own behaviour

The new curriculum is not without antecedents. In recent years a number of alternative schools have been established in Hungary including those associated with Waldorf, Freneit, Montessori and Rogerian approaches. At the same time some innovative teachers have developed affective programmes in traditional schools.

Teacher training now includes work to encourage the development of students' own communication skills, conflict resolution skills and self-esteem, methods for developing communication and conflict resolution skills among their pupils.

Hungary has a fairly long and successful tradition of class teacher – a teacher responsible for the class, and concerned with the children's welfare. The class teacher acts as a go-between or mediator between the class and other teachers. There is a weekly form lesson in which a curriculum covering a wide range of issues is covered. This includes topics such as friendship, the family, tolerance, co-operation, behaviour in relation to older children and those with disabilities, prejudice, prejudice-reduction, different cultures and moral dilemmas.

Though French-speaking Belgium is represented in this book the Flemish-speaking region is not. However, in 1995 Marie Bouverne De-Bie of the University of Ghent wrote:

> In the debate in Flanders on education, guidance is a live issue of growing interest. This interest is seen as making up for the fact that, on the one hand, education makes a priority of transmitting knowledge and, on the other, that schools generally take little interest in their pupils' wider needs for self-fulfilment. Interest in guidance is accompanied by arguments in favour of including broader care of pupils in the definition of the duties of teachers and of schools. It is also argued that those responsible for education and for various forms of social welfare should co-operate more closely.
>
> (Bouverne De-Bie, 1995)

Though currently more at the level of debate than practice, Bouverne De-Bie's article makes it clear that affective education is very much a live issue in Flanders.

Two particular issues need to be addressed in relation to comparative analysis of affective education within a European context. The first of these is the issue of terminology and conceptualization. The second is the possibility of developing a model which might assist us to progress beyond the simple acknowledgement of common ground to a situation where it is actually understood. This may provide a starting point for collaboration between countries at both a practical and research level.

THE ISSUE OF MEANING

I have already considered the issue of meaning and the wide range of terminology used in relation to different examples of the affective elsewhere (Lang, 1995), so will only touch these issues as they specifically relate to the use of the term 'affective education' in a European context.

To what degree does even an agreed umbrella term such as 'affective education' ensure that the common ground as explained earlier is really adequately mapped? An extract from a recent letter to the writer from Lennart Vriens (Professor of Peace Education at the University of Utrecht) illustrates the sort of issues involved:

> In my studies I always stress that learning is not in the first place a cognitive process, but that it starts with the experience of values and norms which provide the basic conditions for further learning. I do not use the same words as you do, but I think that there is a close connection between values and norms and the affective domain.

Again as Nathan Deen has pointed out in relation to the same country:

> In the Netherlands the concept 'pedagogical' and 'pedagogy', are used to indicate the style (including norms and values) parents and teachers use in the interaction between them and their children or students. This style may be called 'pedagogical atmosphere'.
>
> (Deen, 1995)

Lennart Vriens was already aware of the existence of the notion of 'affective education' and able to measure his ideas against it. Nathan Deen provides us with enough information to suggest that in the Netherlands the concept of pedagogy is likely to incorporate affective elements. However, it seems likely that there will be cases where very significant activities might not be easily identified with affective education because of different terminology or indeed because of the strength of their conceptualization within a particular cultural framework.

A case in point is the Polish concept of *wychowanie*, which was only identified by the writer as the result of a chance conversation with a Polish postgraduate student. Its affective nature in an educational context was not apparent until a very detailed discussion had taken place.

In the Polish context the concept of wychowanie is nearest to that of 'the affective', but it has two distinct and related meanings. The first (and wider) one is close to that of education in an English context, as the following definitions from the Polish literature illustrate:

> *Wychowanie* – purposeful activity of some people aiming to cause permanent changes in other people's personalities through interaction.
>
> (Muszynski, 1977)

> *Wychowanie* takes place when a mature person engages in the process of development of the other, less mature person. *Wychowanie* may be conscious or unconscious, in fact it may be both, and this is most often the case.
>
> (Sujak, 1979)

> *Wychowanie* can be understood as a process of changes in an individual person that comes from the conscious activity of other people.
>
> (Wroczynski, 1985)

Clearly even at this more general level there are potential parallels with the approach we describe as affective education.

The second, more specific meaning of wychowanie is closer to the concept of 'the affective'. It has been defined as:

> The full range of endeavours undertaken to form human beings in physical, intellectual, moral and spiritual ways as well as preparing for life among others: in the family, the fatherland and the world.
>
> (Sikorski, 1989)

It is concerned not so much with formal education as with the whole process of shaping personality. It describes the process of discovering and internalizing the language of culture, meanings and symbols and traditions of family, church, and those which are common nationally. Wychowanie in this sense involves not only the (cognitive) understanding of values but, more importantly, the emotional relationships which accompany them and the behaviour that expresses them in actual life.

The concept of wychowanie provides an illustration of where what is at issue goes a good deal further than simple terminology and semantics. Wychowanie is not simply affective education under another name; it is a multifaceted concept which, in its Polish context, may assume an affective dimension when related to education. Wychowanie's complexity makes comparing it with and relating it to affective education a difficult undertaking. Nevertheless, this is precisely the kind of analysis which is now needed if the nature of affective education in Europe is to be fully understood.

One important outcome of the identification of common ground and conceptual and semantic differences has been the recognition of the need to undertake research which focuses on the actual attitudes and understandings of teachers, pupils and parents in relation to those things that have been identified as falling under the umbrella of 'affective education'. Important from a practical perspective is clarification of the nature and extent of the parallels and differences that exist between European countries. Currently, collaborative research is being undertaken which will seek to produce some understanding of this.

MAKING SENSE OF WHAT IS HAPPENING

Ways of analysing and comparing the ideas and the practice of affective education remain both fairly general and of necessity tentative. This is true of the working definition given earlier, and we are reminded that the term 'affective education' is adopted not because of its conceptual power but because it is the term that made some sense to all the European countries involved in the collaborative work of which this book is one outcome. It has always been recognized that both the terms we use and their definition are likely to require development and refinement. One way of doing this is through the development of models which map the area and in so doing offer a framework for identifying and comparing situations which involve some affective elements. The writer has developed one model that could provide a starting point for such developments.

A THREE-LEVEL MODEL OF AFFECTIVE EDUCATION

Reaction / cure:

Doing something after the problem has arisen, e.g. offering counselling to pupils who have had problems, referring pupils with problems to social services or other outside agency, supporting a child who has been bereaved, discussing and mediating after a fight. Telling a pupil to take more serious attitude to her/his work. Reacting to child abuse. Exhortations in assembly about honesty after a theft.

Proaction / prevention:

Doing something before the event by preparing people to cope with anticipated situations, e.g. assertiveness training; drugs and Aids programmes, discussing the issue of death and loss with the class, perhaps in relation to the death of pets. Providing opportunities to explore and express feelings. Study and decision-making skills. Problem- and conflict-resolution skills. Providing opportunities for moral reflection and developing one's own code of conduct.

Enhancement:

Positive encouragement of development, not primarily 'driven' by the desirability of prevention, but by the aim of developing the whole person, e.g. role play, interpersonal skills, work decision-making opportunities in class, working on self-esteem, offering praise and encouragement. Encouraging a positive and effective approach to study through involvement in own learning. Providing spiritual experience in a wide sense.

This three-level model can be seen as possessing an historical dimension in that it reflects the order in which different aspects of affective education developed in many educational systems; that is, starting with reaction and extending to proaction when the relative ineffectiveness of a purely reactive approach is recognized, and culminating in programmes of enhancement when the intrinsic value of coping skills is grasped. There are alternative models that could be developed. Maslow's classic model of the hierarchy of needs provides the basis for most analysis and assessment of affective education (Maslow, 1968), but this should not be allowed to discourage the search for fresh perspectives. What is important is that the challenge is taken up by those concerned with affective education in Europe, and that research, debate and analysis are encouraged. In this way we may create a repertoire of concepts and models to underpin that greater understanding and more purposeful collaboration which leads to more effective practice.

Making sense of practice

Where some degree of clarity with regard to the meaning of 'affective education' in a particular context has been achieved it should be relatively easy to identify whether and how this is articulated in the policy and practice of that particular system. Since policy becomes practice in the roles we play, the role of the teacher is the obvious place to begin.

An initial analysis of the situation in a number of European countries shows that there are in fact a number of different roles that teachers are expected to perform in relation to the affective dimension of education. In some systems, affective education may be exclusive to one of these; in some others, several roles may be pertinent. The main roles that have been identified to date are:

- The teacher as carer, the person responsible for the support and welfare of pupils, normally a particular group or class. There is an expectation that among other things this teacher will undertake individual work with some or all pupils for whom they are responsible. In many cases it is also expected that some of the in-class and extra-curricular activities that the teacher promotes should contain an affective element. (This dimension is found in the role of teachers in the UK, Denmark, Spain and to some extent in the Benelux countries.)
- The teacher as subject specialist, who includes an affective dimension in her/his approach to subject/classroom teaching. (Again, this is found in the UK but also in Spain and Italy and in some Gesamtschulen in Germany.)
- The teacher as deliverer of a special programme of PSE. (Again, this is common in the UK but also in Portugal and to some extent Spain, Italy and Russia.)
- The teacher in a specialist supportive role, as counsellor, for example (found in a significant number of European countries and Israel).
- The teacher in a managerial role, managing others who are concerned with aspects of affective education. This is something which appears to be almost unique to the UK, where in secondary schools such roles as head of year and pastoral deputy are very common. However, some project work in Italy and Portugal increasingly involves teachers in quasi-managerial/organizational roles.
- Where teachers have significant teaching responsibility for a particular group, either because they teach them for most of the time or because they have a long-term relationship with the group (or both), it is generally assumed that they will have at least some caring and developmental responsibilities for the group. This situation mainly applies to teachers working with children of the primary/elementary age range, but there are situations where it applies to older pupils.

The way the teacher's role is understood is affected by the perception of affective education as either an area that ought to be within the competence of the majority of teachers or as something which requires specialized skills. Where it is seen as a generalist role within the competence of most teachers it is expected that most teachers should be involved. Where it is seen as a more specialized activity much of the work is undertaken by a limited number of individuals, frequently based outside the school who are seen as having the requisite special skills.

In most cases the way that teachers' roles are perceived has its roots in the particular cultural and historical development of the country concerned. However, it is also possible to view teachers' roles in terms of the way educational institutions are organized in relation to the affective dimension. From this a categorization of types of organizational approach might be derived which might well show that it is the organizational approach which has determined the nature of the role rather than historico-cultural traditions *per se*. However, in some countries it seems that the relationship between the school as an institution and the teacher's role is more of a symbiotic one. Though it is not always the case that the way roles are conceived ultimately determines the way an organization develops (see for example Lang, 1984), some of the role types described above appear to exist in every system investigated, so the identification of causation is a complex matter. Moreover, our understanding of practice is still at an early stage, and much systematic work is needed both to draw out the subtleties of the situation in each country and to develop the tools adequately to compare them.

This book offers a significant starting point but only if it provides the impetus for further work, work which is not only systematic but undertaken on a shared basis where a number of countries are involved so that a European rather than a particular national perspective is maintained.

NOTE

I am indebted to Dr Katalin Horváth Szabó of Pázmány Péter Catholic University for the information on which the section on Hungary above is based.

REFERENCES

Bouverne De-Bie, M. (1995), 'Guidance in Secondary Education: The Flemish Experience', *Pastoral Care in Education*, Vol. 13, No. 2.

Camus, Albert (1996), *The First Man*, London: Penguin.

Deen, N. (1995), 'Schools Make People Grow: Notes on a Supportive School', *Pastoral Care in Education*, Vol. 13, No. 3.

Dockrell, D. (1987), 'The Assessment of Children's Affective Characteristics', *British Journal of Educational Research*, 13(1), 3–13.

EUDISED (1996), *European Educational Research Yearbook 1994/95*, London: K. G. Saur.

Lang, P. (1984), 'Pastoral Care: Some Reflections on Possible Influences', *Pastoral Care in Education*, Vol. 2, No. 2, pp. 136–46.

Lang, P. (1995), 'International Perspectives on Pastoral Care (Affective Education)', in Best, R., Lang, P., Lodge, C. and Watkins, C. (eds), *Pastoral Care and Personal and Social Education: Entitlement and Provision*, London: Cassell (pp. 266–84).

Lang, P., Best, R. and Lichtenberg, A. (eds) (1994), *Caring for Children: International Perspectives on Pastoral Care and PSE*, London: Cassell.

Maslow, A. H. (1968), *Toward a Psychology of Being* (2nd edn), New York: Van Nostrand.

Muszynski, H. (1977), *Zarys teorii wychowania*, Warsaw: PWN (Polskie Wydownictwo Neukowe).

Sikorski, T. (1989), *Slownik teologiczny*, Katowice: Ksiegarnia Sw. Jacka.

Skolverket (1995), *Pupils' Welfare*, Stockholm: Swedish Ministry of Education and Science.

Sujak, E. (1979), *Zycie jako zadanie*, Warsaw.

Swedish Ministry of Education (1994), *Curriculum for Compulsory Schools (Lpo 94)*, Stockholm: Swedish Ministry of Education and Science.

Taylor, M. (1994), *Values Education in Europe*: Volume 8, Slough: NFER.

Wroczynski, R. (1985), *Pedagogika spoleczna*, Warsaw.

PART 2

How the Affective Dimension of Education Is Manifested in Different European Countries

CHAPTER 2

Affective education in French-speaking parts of Belgium: a brief overview

Christiane Vandenplas-Holper

In Belgium, affective education – a concept with many facets (see Peter Lang's chapter) – is implemented in many different forms and in many places, both inside and outside schools. This chapter gives a brief outline of some of the institutions in which affective education takes place, of the many facets of its content and of some studies which have recently been conducted.

Affective education takes place mainly in the family and in schools. Belgium has been a federal state since 1994. Formal education is organized on an autonomous basis in each of the three 'communities' – the Flemish-speaking, the French-speaking and the German-speaking which, in decreasing order of population size – make up the federal state.

Overall trends in these three communities are very similar. Many children attend day care centres. From three years on, the majority of children are enrolled in nursery school and kindergarten. Primary education starts at age 6 and is organized in six grades. Secondary education is organized in six further grades and has been compulsory up to the age of 18 since 1984. Secondary education offers several tracks: the classical general orientation which gives access to university, a more technically oriented track and a professionally oriented track. Higher education is available in a variety of institutions which offer 'short' and more technically oriented curricula of two or three years and 'long' curricula of mostly four or five years, mainly organized in universities. 'Special education' (Education spéciale) is provided in many schools to pupils who suffer from different kinds of physical or mental handicaps or from personality disorders. Teachers in charge of nursery school, kindergarten, primary school and the first years of secondary school are trained in teacher training colleges which offer three-year curricula. Teachers in charge of the last years of secondary education are trained in the universities.

Belgium is not only divided into three 'linguistic' communities. Formal education is also organized in three different 'networks'. The 'official' network is organized in the French-speaking part of the country by the government of the French-speaking community. The 'free' network is organized mainly by the Fédération de l'enseignement catholique. Another network is organized by the town councils.

Despite the similarity of formal and informal education in the different parts of Belgium and given the complexity of affective education in different settings, this chapter refers only to curricula, programmes and interventions which are conducted in the French-speaking part of Belgium.

AFFECTIVE EDUCATION IN SCHOOLS

Day care centres, nursery schools, kindergartens, primary and secondary schools do not only focus their efforts on cognitive development and scholastic achievement, but affective education is recognized as an important part of the curriculum. As an example, the Conseil central de l'Enseignement primaire catholique stated as early as 1973 (pp. 10–14) that among the objectives of primary school, pupils should learn to co-operate by helping their peers and by explaining to them what they have not understood. Further objectives concern being sensitive to the needs of others, listening to other persons, not always imposing one's own views. Also in the early 1970s, the former Ministère de l'Education nationale et de la Culture française (no date, pp. 10 and 20) stressed the necessity to foster both cognitive development and social sensitivity in boys as well as in girls. These objectives remained the same in the 1990s. In a training manual for teachers of early adolescents, the second edition of which has been published recently in a French translation (Caroll and Resnick, 1995), techniques are presented in order to stimulate youngsters to communicate effectively, to express their feelings, to interact efficiently with family and friends and to think critically.

In the late 1970s, a number of schools introduced the '5–8 cycle'. This educational structure brings together children aged from five to eight years in mixed-age learning groups. Teaching and organization of group activities are carried out by a team made up of a pre-school and two primary school teachers. Children are supposed to cope more easily with the transition from pre-school to primary school, to benefit from social interaction in 'vertical groupings' and to acquire the basic scholastic skills in a more flexible and individual way than in age-segregated classes, in which specific skills are assessed on a general schedule applying to all pupils in the same way. In 1990, it was estimated that approximately a hundred schools were using the 5–8 cycle. Some forty other schools used a similar mixed-age grouping for children aged eight to ten (Meuris, 1992, pp. 107–8).

Parents' associations exist in each of the different networks and at different levels. The goals of the Confédération (nationale) des associations de parents for instance are many. The association aims to help parents to clarify their child-rearing attitudes and to understand their child better, to help teachers to reflect on their teaching methods and the educational climate of their class and finally to represent parents in negotiations at the political decision-making level. Some of the parents' associations are concerned with specific disabilities. The Association de parents et de professionnels autour de la personne polyhandicapée, for instance, groups families and professionals concerned with multi-handicapped persons. They co-operate on problems concerning health, nursing, instruction and teaching of the handicapped child, adolescent or adult.

AFFECTIVE EDUCATION OUTSIDE SCHOOLS

'Psycho-medico-social centres (Centres PMS) are closely related to schools in each of the different networks and at each of the age levels. The personnel of a PMS centre includes, at a minimum, a psychologist, a psycho-educational counsellor, a social worker, a paramedical auxiliary and a medical doctor. The goal of the PMS centres is 'to optimize the psychological, educational, medical, paramedical and social conditions of the pupil and his or her surroundings in order to provide the best opportunities for a harmonious development of his or her personality and his or her individual and social well-being' (*Centres PMS libres*, 1993, p. 15). PMS centres assess children on a group basis several times in their educational curriculum and on an individual basis whenever necessary. They provide information and advice to pupils, their parents and their teachers concerning scholastic, personality and vocational development. Children's individual and classroom behaviour is also observed. Teachers are advised on how to handle problems concerning teacher–pupil relationships, scholastic assessment and remedial teaching. Health records are also updated on a regular basis. All of these actions aim at stimulating autonomous and responsible decision-making by the pupils, their parents and the schools (*Centres PMS libres*, 1993, p. 16; Meuris, 1992, pp. 108–9).

The Office de la Naissance et de l'Enfance (ONE) of the French community and the Fondation Roi Baudouin are public organizations, which implement many programmes of affective education. The Oeuvre nationale de l'Enfance, as ONE was called until 1983, was created at the beginning of the 20th century in order to protect pregnant women, mother and child and the family. At a moment when infant mortality was very high, ONE's initial mission concerned mainly medical and hygienic care. This mission has been progressively enlarged to take into account the well-being of the child, the mother and the family. ONE organizes medical consultations for pregnant women and infants. During these consultations, women are also given psychological, educational and administrative information and advice. Furthermore medico-social workers visit mothers at home after the birth of the child and more often if necessary. ONE also co-operates with day care centres which attend to a larger number of infants and toddlers while their mothers are working and with private childminders who take care in their home of only a few babies. ONE also helps families to cope with difficult situations and co-operates with homes which care for children who have been temporarily separated from their families, most of which are of low socio-economic status (Office de la Naissance et de l'Enfance, 1993). Finally, ONE funds several action-research projects concerning, for instance, educational counselling, health education, severely deprived families, psychotherapy with pregnant women in prison, counselling of substance-dependent mothers, and prevention and treatment of various kinds of child abuse (Office de la Naissance et de l'Enfance, 1992, pp. 86–7).

The Fondation Roi Baudouin was set up in the 1970s as a gift to the nation by King Baudouin. The foundation implements a large number of programmes devoted to the well-being of the nation. Among these programmes, some concern the protection of the environment, socio-economically disadvantaged persons, prostitution, and 'solidarity between generations', a programme which aims at stimulating contacts between children and elderly persons.

Affective education is also conducted in a variety of non-profit-making organizations and has applications to all stages of life.

Some libraries specializing in youth literature give advice on the educational value of stories and some ludothèques – toy libraries – give advice on the educational value of toys. Such facilities are offered for instance by the Centre de Littérature de la Jeunesse and the Centre de Recherche du Jeu et du Jouet of the University of Louvain. Some hospitals give special attention to children who are admitted in the paediatric service. Booklets explain to them how their stay at the hospital will develop and help them to cope with fear of illness, of doctors and of operations (Thomas-Van Moerbeke and Puyts, 1984). In some paediatric services, clowns visit hospitalized children, bringing tenderness, fun and personal words of encouragement for each of them.

Some centres address problems faced by adolescents. Infor Jeunes, for instance, helps adolescents and their families with problems of running away, drug use or depression. The Centre d'Information, de Documentation sur les Etudes, les Professions et l'Emploi helps students to make their career choices, to cope with their studies and to find a job.

Adults are offered a variety of programmes which aim at enhancing the educational competence of parents and educators or at enhancing their personal growth. The Ecole des Parents et des Educateurs provides a wide variety of programmes concerning, for instance, conducting meetings, creativity, personal growth by assertiveness training or relaxation, coping with the death of a loved one. A very popular programme for kindergarten and primary school teachers is PRODAS (Programme de développement affectif et social) which aims at stimulating effective communication, expression of feelings, mutual comprehension, acceptance of differences and uses circle time as one of its methods (see Chapter 1, by Peter Lang). The Ligue de l'Enseignement et de l'Education permanente organizes programmes which help participants to reflect on education that leads to respect for human rights or to tell their life story and reflect on their goals and potential for personal development. A similar programme based on narratives and focusing on teachers' past education, professional training and career development, is also provided by the Faculté ouverte pour Enseignants, Educateurs et Formateurs d'Adultes of the University of Louvain (Cockx, Gallez and de Villers, 1986). Unemployment is widespread in Belgium as in other European countries. The Centres d'Accueil et d'Orientation de la Formation professionnelle en

Communauté française help the unemployed to elaborate plans for reorienting their professional lives and to cope with the requirements of interviews for job selection.

Affective education is provided for people throughout their lives. The Université des Aînés, which has its headquarters in Louvain-la-Neuve and is active in about ten cities across the French-speaking community, provides a very large array of conferences and workshops on history, philosophy, religion, politics, economics, medicine and the exact sciences. Several workshops focus on creative expression through drama, painting, photography and on personal development through yoga, relaxation or preparation for retirement. Affective education even concerns elderly people who suffer from Alzheimer's disease. In the Hôpital Psychogériatrique le Péri in Liège, they learn to live as independently as possible and to enjoy many facets of social life. Support groups are also organized for their families.

The theoretical framework which underlies these interventions is very diverse. It feeds on humanistic psychology, psychoanalysis, life-span developmental psychology, cognitive psychology and the systems approach. In many institutions, several theoretical orientations co-exist very peacefully.

A WEALTH OF PUBLICATIONS

Scholars working in the French-speaking universities are very active conducting fundamental and applied research on almost all of the topics which have been outlined.

Some of the publications report results of emprical studies. Pourtois (1979), for instance, carried out an educational study concerning the manner in which mothers teach their five-year-old children. Piérart and Harmegnie (1993) conducted a psycholinguistic study concerning mothers who told a story to their dysphasic or to their normally developing child. Other recent publications concern, for instance, juvenile delinquency (Born, 1983), the effect of day care attendance of young children on their cognitive and affective development (Quoirin-De Ridder, 1991), the narrative approach to moral development (Day and Tappan, 1996), self-direction (Van Rillaer, 1992) and cognitive-behavioural therapies (Van Rillaer, 1995). There are also books that present overviews and research on such topics as teacher representations as well as the cognitive and socio-affective implications of scholastic failure (Crahay, 1996), a general framework for clinical psychology (Huber, 1993), the clinical and educational implications of adoption and the new medical technologies in the field of pregnancy (Gillot-de Vries, 1988), and the psychological, sociological and legal aspects of step-families (Steichen and de Neuter, 1995). Educational materials and programmes are designed for health education (Coppé, Schoonbroodt and Noël, 1992) and prevention of the crisis of adolescence (van Meerbeeck, 1996). Several educational programmes concern children with special needs, such as deaf children (Lepot-Froment and Clerebaut, 1996), people with various handicaps (Montreuil and Magerotte, 1994) or abused children (Born, 1996; Pourtois, 1995).

My own publications include one examining the child's social development in relation to child-rearing techniques (Vandenplas-Holper, 1987) as well as parents' and teachers' implicit developmental and educational theories (Vandenplas-Holper, 1991). I have also conducted a series of studies of the relationship of cognitive development assessed in the Piagetian tradition to problem-solving in triads of five- to eight-year-old children, each of whom belongs to a different level of cognitive development (Vandenplas-Holper, 1994). These studies simulated in a laboratory setting the interactions which take place in mixed age groups in the '5–8 cycle'. Two of my studies concern the enhancement of children's prosocial development by telling and discussing children's stories (Vandenplas-Holper, 1987, pp. 111–15; see also Chapter 16 by Victoria Gordillo in this book). They are featured in a two-hour educational video based on the concept of implicit educational theories (Vandenplas-Holper, 1986; Vandenplas-Holper, 1986/1988). Designed for a large audience of teachers, educators, psychologists, and heads of youth libraries, the video presents different tasks. People watching the video are first asked to rely on their naïve and implicit theories. These are further expanded by the concepts and observations presented as the video progresses. Some of the sequences concern the main features of conducting a discussion in small groups of children; other sequences refer to the development of children's prosocial moral reasoning.

Children's stories and films designed for children (see Chapter 19, by Vandenplas-Holper and Ghysselinckx-Janssens) are fascinating material which can be used to stimulate affective development. My interest in children's stories in relation to prosocial behaviour and reasoning has expanded to other types of stories. In a series of studies concerning children's fears, classical fairy-tales (both 1995) and children coping with the separation or divorce of their parents (in preparation), I have devised a series of frameworks for the content analysis of stories. These analyses should help parents, teachers and counsellors to reflect on the educational value of stories they are going to tell to their children, pupils or clients and to analyse the content of the discussions they are conducting with the children in order to stimulate their personal growth.

This brief outline is far from being a complete picture of all that is being done in the French-speaking part of Belgium with respect to affective education. I hope nevertheless that it gives a good idea of interventions which are implemented in some places.

REFERENCES

Scientific publications

Born, M. (1983), *Jeunes déviants ou délinquants juvéniles?*, Brussels: Mardaga.
Born, M. (1996), *Les abus sexuels*, Brussels: Mardaga.
Cockx, B., Gallez, D. and de Villers, G. (1986), 'Récit de vie et formation', in M. Finger and Ch. Josso (eds), *Pratiques du récit de vie et théories de la formation*, Cahier 44, pp. 53–71, Geneva: University of Geneva.

Coppé, M., Schoonbroodt, C. and Noël, A. (1992), *Guide pratique d'éduca-tion pour la santé. Réflexion, expérimentation et 50 fiches à l'usage des formateurs*, Brussels: De Boeck University.

Crahay, M. (1996), *Peut-on lutter contre l'échec scolaire?*, Brussels: De Boeck University.

Day, J. and Tappan, M. B. (1996), 'The narrative approach to moral devel-opment: from the epistemic subject to dialogical selves', *Human Development*, 39, pp. 67–82.

Gillot-Devries, F. (1988), *Les nouvelles parentalités: un enfant à tout prix*, Brussels: Presses Universitaires de Bruxelles.

Huber, W. (1993), *L'homme psychopathologique et la psychologie clinique*, Paris: Presses Universitaires de France.

Lepot-Froment, Ch. and Clerebaut, M. (1996), *L'enfant sourd. Communi-cation et langage*, Brussels: De Boeck University.

Meuris, G. (1992), 'Elementary school education for young children in Belgium', *International Handbook of Early Childhood Education*, pp. 105–9, New York: Woodill G. A.

Montreuil, N. and Magerotte, Gh. (1994), *Pratique de l'intervention indi-vidualisée*, Brussels: De Boeck University.

Piérart, B. and Harmegnies, B. (1993), 'Dysphasie simple de l'enfant et langage de la mère', *L'Année Psychologique*, 93, 227–68.

Pourtois, J.-P. (1979), *Comment les mères enseignent à leur enfant (5–6 ans)*, Paris: Presses Universitaires de France.

Pourtois, J.-P. (1991), *Innovation en éducation familiale*, Brussels: De Boeck University.

Pourtois, J.-P. (1995), *Blessure d'enfant. La maltraitance: théorie, pratique et intervention*, Brussels: De Boeck University.

Quoirin-De Ridder, C. (1991), 'Effets du séjour en crèche sur le développe-ment du jeune enfant. Recherches comparatives entre enfants élevés en crèche et enfants élevés dans d'autres contextes éducatifs. Bilan des connaissances actuelles', *Bulletin de Psychologie*, XLIV, 400, 264–76.

Steichen, R. and de Neuter, P. (1995), *Les familles recomposées et leurs enfants*, Louvain-la-Neuve: Academia.

Vandenplas-Holper, Ch. (1986), 'La narration et la discussion de récits pour enfants', in M. Fauquet (ed.), *Un défi à la formation des éduca-teurs: l'environnement audiovisuel*, Brussels: Association for Teacher Education in Europe (ATEE), pp. 38–50.

Vandenplas-Holper, Ch. (1987), *Education et développement social de l'en-fant*, 2nd enlarged edition, Paris: PUF.

Vandenplas-Holper, Ch. (1986, 1988) with Crivisqui-Linares, C., Ghysselinckx-Janssens, A. and Jates, N., *La narration et la discussion de récits pour enfants*. Donner comme le Petit Prince – Aider comme Micha. 1. Micha et le Petit Prince: leur perspective et la tienne. 2. Réalisation technique: Centre Audiovisuel de l'UCL. Two 55-minute videos plus manual of 65 pp. Louvain-la-Neuve: CIACO, Collection 'Cours et Documents de la Faculté de Psychologie et des Sciences de l'Education'. Distributed by ARTEL, Place Baudouin 1er, B – 5004 Namur.

Vandenplas-Holper, Ch. (1991), 'Implicit developmental and educational theories. Perspectives for counseling and teacher education', in B. P. Campos (ed.), *Psychological intervention and human development*, Porto: Instituto de Consulta Psicologica, Formaçao e Desenvolvimento, pp. 123–35.

Vandenplas-Holper, Ch. (1994), 'Action, interaction and cognitive development: Process-oriented research with 5- to 8-year-old children', in A. Vijt, H. Bloch and M. H. Bornstein (eds), *Early Child Development in the French Tradition. Contributions from Current Research*, Hillsdale, N. J.: Lawrence Erlbaum Associates (pp. 149–66).

Vandenplas-Holper, Ch. (1995), 'Les contes classiques, supports de l'éducation socio-émotionnelle de l'enfant: au-delà de Bettelheim', in Y. Prêteur and M. de Léonardis, *Education familiale, image de soi et compétences sociales*, Brussels: De Boeck University, (pp. 92–110).

Vandenplas-Holper, Ch. (1995), 'The educational value of stories concerning children's fears: a training study with second-year psychology students', *Scientia Paedagogica Experimentalis*, XXII, 1, pp. 97–126.

Vandenplas-Holper, Ch. (in preparation), 'La séparation et le divorce des parents dans les récits pour enfants: un cadre de référence pour l'analyse de contenu et l'intervention', in A. M. Fontaine and J. P. Pourtois, *(Ré)inventer la famille*, Brussels: Matrice.

van Meerbeeck, Ph., Bardos, A., Deschamps *et al.* (1996), *Le mal d'être moi. Abords pluriels de l'adolescence*, Brussels: De Boeck University.

Van Rillaer, J. (1992), *La gestion de soi*, Brussels: Mardaga.

Van Rillaer, J. (1995), *Les thérapies comportementales*, Paris: Editions Morisset.

Reports of organizations

Fédération des Centres PMS Libres (1993), *Livre blanc des centres PMS libres*, Rue Philippe Baucq, 18, B 1040 Brussels.

Office de la Naissance et de l'Enfance (1992), *Rapport d'activité*, Brussels.

Office de la Naissance et de l'Enfance (1993), *Tout savoir sur l'ONE*, Brussels.

Curricula and educational materials

Carroll and Resnick (1995), *Clefs pour l'adolescence. Méthodologie*, 2nd edition, translation of *Skills for Adolescence*, Quest Europe: Merelbeke.

Conseil Central de l'Enseignement Primaire Catholique (1973), *Pour une rénovation de l'enseignement fondamental. Objectifs de l'école chrétienne primaire et maternelle*.

Ministère de l'Education Nationale et de la Culture Française (no date), *L'initiation sociale des enfants de 6 à 12 ans. Programme provisoire*, Brussels.

Ministère de l'Education Nationale et de la Culture Française (1974), *La réforme de l'enseignement préscolaire. L'accueil et l'éducation des enfants de 18 mois à 7 ans*, Brussels.

Thomas-Van Moerbeke, R. M. and Puyts, M. L. (1984), *Avec Tintin, découvre la pédiatrie*, Cliniques Universitaires St. Luc, 1200 Brussels and Brussels: Editions Casterman.

Organizations implementing affective education programmes

Association de Parents et de Professionnels autour de la Personne Polyhandicapée, Chemin des Noces, 8, B 1410 Waterloo.

Centre d'Information et de Documentation sur les Etudes, les Professions et l'Emploi (CID), Place de l'Université, 16, B 1348 Louvain-la-Neuve.

Centre de Littérature de la Jeunesse; Centre de Recherche du Jeu et du Jouet, Place du Cardinal Mercier, 10, B 1348 Louvain-la-Neuve.

Centres d'Accueil et d'Orientation de la Formation Professionnelle en Communauté Française, Boulevard de l'Empereur, 5, B 1000 Brussels.

Confédération Nationale des Associations de Parents (CNAP), Rue Belliard, 23 a/1, B 1040 Brussels.

Ecole des Parents et des Educateurs de Belgique (EPE), Place des Acacias, 14, B 1040 Brussels.

Fondation Roi Baudouin, Rue de Brederode, 21, B 1000 Brussels.

Hôpital Psychogériatrique Le Péri, 4 bis, Montagne Sainte Walburge, 4000 Liège.

Infor Jeunes, Grasmarkt, 27, B 1000 Brussels.

Ligue de l'Enseignement et de l'Education Permanente, Place Rouppe, 29, B 1000 Brussels.

Office de la Naissance et de l'Enfance (ONE), Avenue de la Toison d'Or, 84–86, B 1060 Brussels.

Université des Aînés, Sentier du Goria, 8, B 1348 Louvain-la-Neuve.

ACKNOWLEDGEMENT

A preliminary version of this article was presented at the Warwick Conference on Affective Education in Europe which took place in May 1994. The sabbatical leave which had been granted to me by the Université catholique de Louvain and the financial support provided by Peter Lang facilitated my attendance at this conference. During her training as a research student, Chantal Scharff made a valuable contribution in gathering information concerning this overview. I gratefully acknowledge these various forms of help.

CHAPTER 3

Affective education in Germany. Existing structures and opportunities: are we using them effectively?

Reinhold Fess

INTRODUCTION

This chapter seeks to provide a general overview of affective education in Germany. Because schooling is the responsibility of the individual states, it is impossible to make any generalizations which apply consistently across the board. Nevertheless I will try to convey a general impression of the conditions in which affective education is imbedded.

In the first section I present an outline of the present German school system. I have not attempted to make it complete, as my purpose is merely to indicate the areas within the system in which affective education can (or could) effectively take place. The second section discusses some research on 'climate' or 'environment' in the classroom, a concept which I feel directly addresses many concerns of the affective domain. In the third section I have described to the best of my knowledge the nature and extent of affective education actually found in schools in Germany.

I conclude with some critical points regarding the situation of affective education in Germany today.

SCHOOLING IN GERMANY

In this section I present a very brief and simplified scheme of the German educational system, always keeping in mind the question: Where and how could affective education take place?

Kindergarten

The educational system starts for many children at the age of three, with kindergarten. It is not compulsory and quite a few parents have difficulties finding a kindergarten with room to take their three-year-olds – and in rural areas kindergarten attendance is much less common than in urban areas. For these reasons not every child benefits from the skills taught in kindergarten. Nor can the elementary school build on the work done in kindergarten. Aside from practical objectives, such as learning to manage in the world around them, social objectives primarily are pursued, such as group behaviour.

In addition there are psychomotor and sensory objectives such as motor skills and the encouragement of perceptual skills. The focus is always on the development of the whole personality of the child (Klein, 1995). Nevertheless, the transition to the elementary school represents an abrupt change in the child's scholastic career.

Elementary school

Elementary school is the only school in Germany which is compulsory for every child, regardless of academic performance, social status, or place of residence. Every child is required to attend the local elementary school for four years, generally from age six to ten (in Berlin there are six years of elementary school).

Affective education in elementary school takes place in the sense that personal relationships between teachers and children are fostered. When entering the elementary school the children are grouped into a class which is assigned one classroom and one teacher. Throughout all four years of elementary school this bond remains intact – the group of children, the room and the teacher. In general, all instruction is given by the same teacher, but it can also happen that a few subjects, such as German, arithmetic and science, may be covered by others later on.

Unfortunately the selective effects of the following secondary school system trickle down into the final year of elementary school. Elementary teachers are required at least to recommend the type of secondary school they feel is best suited to each of their pupils, who are grouped accordingly into high, middle, and low achievers. In some cases the high achievers are even prepared for the Gymnasium, the most demanding type of school. They are therefore given more attention, while low achievers are often neglected. Another effect is that the over-emphasis on achievement in this last year undermines the social skills acquired in the first years.

Secondary schools

The secondary school system is very complicated and varies from state to state. In all states the Gymnasium is the school which demands the highest academic performance and confers the highest leaving certificate, the *Abitur*. Some states have a dual school system based on the Gymnasium and a second type of school. Other states offer up to five different types of secondary school. In all states school attendance is mandatory until the age of 16. If schooling ends prior to that or a pupil drops out, a vocational school may fulfil that requirement.

In the secondary schools the general framework for affective education also exists, in that a group of pupils forms a class, which is 'taken care of' by a class teacher in a classroom where the majority of instruction takes place. (The exception is found in the upper classes of the Gymnasium where the class system evolves into a course system as pupils begin to specialize in various disciplines. Every pupil has a different schedule, and instead of a class teacher there is a career counsellor.)

However, this class/classroom/class teacher system is not followed as rigorously as it has been. It may last the duration of the whole school cycle, especially in those schools which choose to make it a priority. It can also happen, however, that class teachers are replaced, that the classroom is changed from year to year, or that the class itself is split up and regrouped. This has serious consequences for the affective aspect of the pupils' education. Mutual acceptance among members in a group increases with the duration of their association and the frequency of their interactions, and this needs time (Graumann and Kruse, 1976).

In general, it can be said that more affective education takes place in those schools committed to pedagogical reforms (comprehensive schools and so-called reform schools) and in those schools where the low achievers and underprivileged pupils are concentrated (Hauptschulen and special schools for children with learning disabilities) (based on Dreesmann, 1982). In conservative schools such as the Gymnasium, the Realschule, or those newly created types which recruit their staff from the traditional school system, affective education plays a minor role compared to academic training. Here the class teacher might limit his or her efforts to filling out lists for the class, while a class teacher at a comprehensive school might take over the full responsibility for his or her pupils' welfare and school career. An excellent example of the importance of caring class teachers is the subject of the chapter by Klaus Winkel in this book, which describes the career of a pupil at risk in a team/small group model (TSGM) school. Such schools base their pedagogy almost exclusively on social learning and an intense and stable relationship among pupils and between pupils and teachers (Schlömerkemper and Winkel, 1987).

Vocational and technical schools
On leaving one of the lower level secondary schools after the 9th or 10th form pupils may attend various vocational technical schools for the completion of their education. In these schools the acquisition of knowledge about various professional fields is the main objective. It has been found that selective influences in vocational and technical schools (such as examinations and performance pressures) diminish the degree of significance that the pupils themselves attach to the classroom climate (Achtenhagen et al., 1979).

Empirical measurement of affective education
Is affective education measurable? Can its objectives be tested as to whether they have been achieved or not, or to what extent they have been achieved?

A very promising approach is the concept of classroom environment. Dreesmann offers three different perspectives of it (Dreesmann, 1982):

- the objective environment (such as the number of pupils, learning material, observable behaviour)
- the individual subjective reality (how the individual pupil perceives and assesses the objective environment)

- the collective subjective reality (that part of individual experience which is shared by all or most others)

Both the individual as well as the collective subjective realities are of great importance for affective education. Pupils must be given a chance to express their perceptions and feelings and to share their realities with others. This is the basis of the learning process.

There are many dimensions of the instructional climate (a sub-category of the educational environment) which were found in factor-analytic studies to be important for the subjective reality of pupils (according to Dreesmann, 1982):

- pupil–teacher relations:
  - co-operation between pupils and teachers
  - teacher neglect of some pupils
- pupil–pupil relations:
  - comradeship
  - competitive attitude
- personal development:
  - intellectual
  - affective
  - increase in self-esteem
  - identification with the lesson, whether the pupils feel they'd 'get something out of it'
  - realistic judgement
  - development of personal responsibility:
  - autonomy in decision-making and independence of the pupils' activities in the lesson
  - setting one's own objectives
  - assuming responsibility for one's own behaviour
  - chances of success for one's efforts
  - achievement

Dreesmann draws the conclusion that 'the personal relations between the pupils in the class and their teacher as well as pupil interrelations are of great importance for pupils while the teaching subject and its instruction play a secondary role' (Dreesmann, 1982, p. 98). He also found that the academic performance of a pupil correlates strongly with the way he or she perceives the lesson. Fend found in his studies that low and average achievers are more dependent on the learning environment than high achievers (Fend, 1976). The results of a recent study show that the classroom climate created by the class teacher also has an effect on the class members' assessment of the learning environment in subjects taught by other teachers (Dawo, 1996).

There can be no doubt therefore that affective objectives are of significance, not only for the well-being of the pupils, but for their academic performance as well. But there are no subjects called 'personal development' or 'relating to others'. How are these objectives taught?

THE PRACTICE OF AFFECTIVE EDUCATION IN GERMAN SCHOOLS

Social learning always takes place, but it should not be governed merely by subject matter, the topic at hand, and the situation as defined by didactic and methodological considerations, and certainly not by evaluation rituals, but rather by the behaviours deemed necessary for society and a humanitarian school.

(Winkel, 1990)

To provide some overview of how objectives such as social learning are taught, I shall refer to two main tendencies which have had a lasting influence on German education.

The first considers the child an independent learner and has its roots in reform pedagogy going back to the first half of this century. The ideas of Maria Montessori, Peter Peterson, Rudolf Steiner and Célestin Freinet influenced many teachers, though the strict state-regulated German school system did not give these reform ideas much chance to prosper as the underlying ethos of a school. 'Reform pedagogy is a semantic corpus of great continuity flexible enough to react to new types of development in society ... The language and model assumptions of "reform" have extended their range of influence and gain increasing public acceptance.' (Oelkers, 1994) One finds reform-pedagogical concepts realized only in some special private schools, but teacher-independent study, learning according to an individual weekly plan, free learning, open instruction or workshop learning are conceptual items implemented in many elementary schools and increasingly in schools at the secondary level. Comprehensive schools and private schools especially work in this manner.

The second tendency is based on a holistic view of the child, who is more than a mere learner of facts and disciplines. Social learning takes place in encounters with others and in reflection and talking about these encounters and the feelings they have caused. This tendency has its roots in the experience and practice of humanistic psychology (Karmann, 1987), in Alfred Adler's individual psychology, in Fritz Peris' Gestalt pedagogy, in the person-centred, non-directive pedagogy of Carl Hogers and in the communication psychology of Paul Watzlawick and Friedemann Schulz von Thun. A central role is played by the concept of living learning (*Themenzentrierte Interaktion* or TZI in German) developed by Ruth Cohn (Cohn and Farau, 1991; Reiser and Lotz, 1995). The work of these psychologists caused an attitude change in many teachers. The pupils are regarded as full partners, as people not only with duties but with needs and rights as well, with distinguishable and unmistakable personalities. These teachers not only teach, they also work with children.

Furthermore, there are many publications which relay methods developed in psychology or even psychotherapy for use in the classroom (e.g. Burow, 1987; Gudjons, 1983; Heimlich, 1988; Kochan, 1981; Vopel, 1986). Class council, circle time, doubling, empty chair, feed back, 'I' messages, interaction plays, role plays and so on are methods based on humanistic psychology. They are used for conflict-solving, improving self-esteem, consolidating a group or relating to others, with the aim of making the individual and collective subjective realities of the pupils as positive as possible.

CRITICAL REMARKS ON AFFECTIVE EDUCATION IN GERMANY

Considering the potential for affective education offered by the German school system and considering its historical background and the powerful influences of reform pedagogy and humanistic psychology, it is astounding that the concept of affective education is not more pervasive. Academic achievement is still what counts most for many teachers and parents, and it is still the case that everything else that happens in the school is subordinated to the acquisition of knowledge about the various disciplines. This is compounded by a school system that is determined to select and exclude pupils rather than integrate and support them.

Against this work only a few reform schools and comprehensive schools dependent on the personal commitment of their administrators and teachers offer greater range for a child-centred, holistic pedagogy. A good example is the team/small group model, which Klaus Winkel describes in more detail elsewhere in this book. It is based on a pedagogically grounded theory (which has as its core the goals of affective education) and twenty years of pedagogical practice (Keim, 1996). Although this model, established in the comprehensive schools of Köln-Holweide and Göttingen-Geismar in 1976, has not only inspired numerous imitator schools in Germany but has also stirred great interest in the USA and Australia (Ratzki, 1996), it has failed to cause a general rethinking in Germany much less a nationwide change in pedagogical practice. This is due, in my view, to the fact that the implementation of the objectives of affective education is left to chance.

In pre-service teacher training instructional content of this type is hardly ever found. The instruction of methods and didactics is restricted to that of the disciplines; newcomers to the profession must learn the tasks of a class teacher, the possibilities for interaction with pupils, parents, and colleagues, by picking them up for themselves or observing colleagues. In-service training alone offers an increasing number of courses, in keeping with increasing demand for improving teachers' expertise in areas of affective education.

Nevertheless, it is left up to the individual teacher trainers whether they choose to cover the area of affective education with their student teachers or not. It is left up to the individual new teachers whether they acquire elements of affective education during their training or not, and it is left up to individual teachers whether they avail themselves of in-service training or not. It is also left up to administrators to decide the extent to which they incorporate social learning objectives and teacher-independent learning into their school programme. There is scarcely any incentive to do so, except for the personal satisfaction of feeling in harmony with oneself and the world through one's work.

Yet in the task of preparing the next generation for their lives in society, nothing should be left up to the individual or even to chance, especially when it is a matter of instilling dialectical values such as individuality and public spirit, self-actualization and solidarity, assertiveness and co-operation. Klaus Schwarz concluded his contribution to *Affective Education in Europe* with the argument:

> A lot of children see their world threatened and threatening. A lot of children do not feel sheltered, they feel unsafe, mistrust the future, are confused. Pupils do not suffer permanently in this society, but sometimes their genuine, real life problems overlay their learning problems. It is then when they really need solidarity from other pupils and their teachers. They need people who listen to them, care for them, give advice. They need a school that helps them to overcome their learning and life problems.
>
> (Schwarz, 1994)

And I would like to add that it is now that we must create the school that our children need, instead of reforming and deforming our children until they fit into the present school.

REFERENCES

Achtenhagen, F., Sembill, D. and Steinhoff, E. (1979), 'Die Lehrerpersönlichkeit im Urteil von Schülern', *Zeitschrift für Pädagogik*, 25, pp. 191–208.

Burow, O. A. (1987), *Gestallpädagogik in der Praxis*, Salzburg: Otto Müller Verlag.

Cohn, R. and Farau, A. (1991), *Gelebte Geschichte der Psychotherapie*, Stuttgart: Klett-Cotta Verlag.

Dawo, O. (1996), *Prima Klima? Der Einfluss von Geschlecht und Leistungsstatus auf die Wahrnehmung des Schulklimas an einer Gesamtschule*, thesis, University of Saarbrücken.

Dreesmann, H. (1982), *Unterrichtsklima: wie Schüler den Unterricht wahrnehmen*, Weinheim: Beltz Verlag.

Fend, H. (1976), *Sozialisationseffekte in der Schule*, Weinheim: Beltz Verlag.

Graumann, C. F. and Kruse, L. (1976), 'Die Klasse als Gruppe', in C. F. Graumann *et al.*, *Pädagogische Psychologie*, Beltz-Lehrgang, IV, Weinheim: Beltz Verlag.

Gudjons, H. (1983), *Spielbuch Interaktionserziehung*, Bad Heilbrunn: Klinkhardt Verlag.

Heimlich, R. (1988), *Soziales und emotionales Lernen in der Schule*, Weinheim: Beltz Verlag.

Karmann, G. (1987), *Humanistische Psychologie und Pädagogik: psychotherapeutische und verwandte Ansätze. Perspektiven für eine integrative Pädagogik*, Bad Heilbrunn: Klinkhardt Verlag.

Keim, W. (1996), 'Außenansichten eines Insiders – Theoretische Grundlagen und pädagogische Praxis des TKM', in A. Ratzki *et al.*, *Team-Kleingruppen-Modell Köln-Holweide*, Frankfurt: Peter Lang Europäischer Verlag der Wissenschaften.

Klein, G. (1995), 'Kontinuität und Herausforderung. Über den Wechsel vom Kindergarten in die Grundschule', *Die Deutsche Schule*, 87, pp. 218–27.

Kochan, B. (1981), *Rollenspiel als Methode sozialen Lernens*, Königstein: Athenäus Verlag.

Oelkers, J. (1994), 'Bruch und Kontinuität, zum Modernisierungseffekt der Reformpädagogik', *Zeitschrift für Pädagogik*, 40, pp. 565–83.

Ratzki, A. (1996), 'Netzwerk Team-Kleingruppen-Modell', in A. Ratzki *et al.*, *Team-Kleingruppen-Modell Köln-Holweide*, Frankfurt: Peter Lang Europäischer Verlag der Wissenschaften.

Reiser, H. and Lotz, W. (1995), *Themenzentrierte Interaktion als Pädagogik*, Mainz: Mathias-Grünewald Verlag.

Schlömerkemper, J. and Winkel, K. (1987), *Lernen im Team-Kleingruppen-Modell*, Frankfurt: Peter Lang Europäischer Verlag der Wissenschaften.

Schwarz, K. (1994), *Affective Education in the Team-Small-Group-Model Comprehensive Schools in the Saarland (Germany)*, Paper presented at the seminar on Affective Education in Europe, University of Warwick, May 1994.

Vopel, K. W. (1986), *Interaktionsspiele*, Hamburg: Isko-Press.

Winkel, K. (1990), *The Objectives of Social Learning / Ziele solidarischen Lernens*, unpublished.

CHAPTER 4

'Fiche bliain ag fás'
(Twenty years a-growing)
Úna Collins

INTRODUCTION

If the mythical Martian were to arrive in the Republic of Ireland to investigate the dominant activity of its citizens she or he might be forgiven for assuming that its principal industry is education. The figures show that nearly one third of the population (968,457 people) are engaged in full-time education (Department of Education, 1992). In addition to these, a considerable body of workers provide a service to these students, teachers, lecturers and others in the administration of the educational system. When one takes into consideration that for each of these students there are also parents and often family members supporting or monitoring their progress through the system, one can reasonably conclude that education is a central institution in Irish society.
(Drudy and Lynch, 1993)

This chapter addresses that central institution, and, in particular, focuses on how that institution addresses itself to affective education. The basic argument is that a formal recognition of affective education has been growing in the Irish educational system, specifically since the early 1970s.

In 1994 there took place what was described as 'an unprecedented democratic event in the history of Irish education' (Coolahan, 1994). This event was the National Education Convention held in Dublin Castle in the autumn of that year. The Convention brought together representatives from 42 educational bodies, parents' associations, and the Minister for Education and her Department officials, to engage, in a structured way, in a discussion on the key issues of Irish educational policy. This chapter shows how this Convention, among other considerations, might be termed a milestone in the public awareness of affective/pastoral education in the Irish secondary school system.

A BRIEF HISTORY OF THE IRISH EDUCATIONAL SYSTEM

Firstly, let us take an overview of Ireland, its people, and, in particular, its educational system, and briefly explain why this education convention was so significant in Irish educational history. Ireland, geographically, is a small island on the far west of Europe, and, since the development of the British/French 'chunnel', the only member state cut off from its European family by sea. Despite this geographical separation, Ireland and the continent have close historical links.

'Two hundred years of Western World change has happened in thirty years in Ireland' (Ryan, 1993). As a humorous illustration of this, Liam Ryan, a leading sociologist in Maynooth University, tells a story of a farmer driving his cows along a country road in his Mercedes car with the window down and using an old golf club! Ten per cent truth and ninety per cent Irish humour! On a realistic level we know that new wealth, the media, national debates and referenda on social/family issues such as divorce, contraception and abortion, have propelled our people in a short space of time from the vision Éamon de Valera framed in our Constitution (1937) which values freedom, spirituality, family and 'frugal comfort' to a situation which is very different. Today, the vision inspiring those values has been at worst, shattered, at best severely challenged.

Ireland, currently, has one of the best economic prospects of the European states and the best it has itself experienced for over thirty years. Unfortunately, this prospect is not translating quickly enough into job creation. We have, proportionately, the largest population under 21 in Europe. Over 93 per cent of our 16-year-olds, and 75 per cent of 17-year-olds participate in schooling. Within this rapidly changing society, our post-primary/secondary school sector is itself undergoing profound change as it responds to family and societal change, and as it finds itself held responsible, by society, for addressing the negative outcomes of the changes.

The population of the country is three and a half million, and one whole section of the island, the north east, is still politically part of the United Kingdom. Our history from the 12th century to the early 20th was one of political and social deprivation. For eight hundred years, there were few opportunities to decide our own destiny in the normal spheres of life. The Irish were very good at rebellion! Two core values were, however, claimed and developed, the values of religion and education. One might postulate that these values became synonymous, for the Irish, with freedom and identity.

Within the eight hundred years of Irish/English history there are parallel stories of positive and negative influences by England on Irish institutional development. The educational system was influenced as part of the institutional life. There are some differences. Though adopting the English language in the 19th century, the majority of the Irish people have studied the native Gaelic language in their primary and secondary schooling and there are specific schools in many parts of the country where Gaelic is the first language. Our Irish/Gaelic literature, music, dance and games survived with remarkable success, and are currently experiencing a very lively renaissance.

In developing the frame for this chapter, one might be tempted to say that all education is affective, and that any worthwhile teacher or school is consciously addressing the affective dimension. It is also true to say that education in Ireland was always rooted in the affective, in the reverence with which Irish people held learning. The Irish education story includes chapters on the early bards and poets, the monasteries (influencing the rest of the civilized world), of hedge schools which kept education alive, of emigration to the Catholic universities of Europe, of new religious orders of men and of women, providing education for the poor, and it is always a story of valuing learning, faith, literature, music, and especially valuing the person.

> For the Irish this question serves to anchor a concern for knowledge and education which has been a persistent part of our cultural tradition over millenia and countless generations ... At times the concern for the provision of formal education reached great heights as for instance during the golden age era when Ireland was acclaimed 'The Island of Saints and Scholars'. At other times during periods of harsh political and economic conditions, for example the 18th century, the appetite for learning remained remarkably alive.
>
> (John Coolahan, 1987)

THE FORMAL EDUCATION SYSTEM IN IRELAND

To contextualize this chapter, affective education in secondary schools in Ireland, it is appropriate to span briefly the three formal education structures within the national system.

The formal education system was developed in the 19th century when the whole of Ireland was still part of the United Kingdom. The struggle between the United Kingdom government and the Church (Roman Catholic) is central to the 19th century development. Today's symbiotic relationship of Church and State control reflects this history. Most schools are non-denominational in law and are largely financed by the state but are denominational (predominantly Roman Catholic) in terms of ownership and management. The fact that the majority of the Roman Catholic schools, primary and secondary, were largely staffed as well as managed by the religious sisters, brothers and priests from the early and middle 19th century to the middle of the 20th century influenced the development of affective education in the formal system.

A state-supported primary education system was established in 1831 (forty years earlier than a similar system in England). The state did not formally support secondary education until 1878, and free secondary school education came into the Irish education system in the 1970s. Ireland dates the foundation of its first university to the end of the 16th century but free third-level education was not introduced until February 1995.

The development of schooling in Ireland, as a cultural and socializing agency, is closely linked to each of these dates. When Ireland was part of the United Kingdom, schools were used to promote Anglicization, especially through the use of the English language and the discouragement of Roman Catholicism. Following the establishment of the Irish Free State in 1921, the promotion of Irish culture and the Irish language assumed prime educational importance. Irish language became a compulsory curriculum subject, and religious education came to occupy a central position. It is in this context that affective education has most often been formally addressed. Being Irish, Catholic and educated were key targets in the system and until the 1960s there was no clear adjustment of that system to economic factors. The 1960s witnessed the emergence and pursuit of major aims of social policy affecting education. 'These areas have been identified as economic (increased productivity in economic growth), egalitarian (equalisation of opportunity), and humanitarian (the relief of poverty and the provision of minimum education for all)' (Kennedy, 1975).

Ireland has a larger proportion of its total population (about 23 per cent) at school than has any other country in the EU. The whole education system is centralized.

FIRST LEVEL EDUCATION

At primary level there are eight grades. The aim and functions of the primary school curriculum (Curaclam Na Bunscoil) 1971 are:

- All children are complex human beings with physical, emotional, intellectual, and spiritual needs and potentialities.
- Because each child is an individual he deserves to be valued for himself and to be provided with the kind of variety of opportunities towards stimulation and fulfilment which will enable him to develop his natural powers at his own rate to his fullest capacity.

If he is to know and value himself and form objective standards of judgement and behaviour ('Más áil leis aithne agus meas a bheith aige air féin'), he must learn through experience to live and to co-operate with other children and with adults, and gradually to become familiar with the complexity, and evolution of the society of which he is part. Effective education for citizenship requires that each individual be enabled to feel that he is an integral part of the community deriving satisfaction from his full participation in its common life.

In the section on the teaching of English in this primary curriculum we read: 'The development of the child's personality through language will be the teacher's first concern'. On learning poetry: 'He will have gone a long way towards the understanding of poetry and towards his own personal enrichment ... The characters and themes should be central to the life of the child.' (The writer has 'affective' difficulties with the exclusive language used here ('he', 'his'), but is in admiration of the principles being expressed!) The terms 'pleasure', 'enjoyment', 'interest', 'appreciation', 'allowed to choose' and 'natural desire' are frequently found in the text of the New Primary School Curriculum.

The background to this chapter is that of professional life in the post-primary (secondary) section of the Irish national system, therefore assessment of the affective education in the primary school is necessarily limited. However, one can claim that the aims and principles, and, generally, the practice in that sector are directed towards educating the affective. Equally it must be acknowledged that the word 'affective' is not found in the official literature, in the teacher's handbook, nor is it assessed in the curriculum.

THIRD LEVEL

At third level, affective education is addressed and assessed much as it is in other EU countries. There are student support services. There are professional courses in the behavioural and human sciences. One of the most interesting developments has been the introduction and expansion of Equality Studies in University College, Dublin. Postgraduate courses include: the politics and sociology of development, women in Irish society, sexuality, and the structure and legitimization of power. These are welcome educational challenges for third level affective education.

SECOND LEVEL

Focusing on the secondary sector of Irish education, and considering pastoral care/affective education in this sector, it can be argued that when or if the affective or the 'human face' of education was considered in that sector prior to the 1970s, it was presumed that the 'good teacher' or the 'small school' or the 'religious sisters and brothers' were addressing it. Formerly the pursuit of affective education was regarded as subsumed within the overall goals of Irish education as expressed in the main official state documents. Certainly, many teachers in many schools were catering for those in need. It could also be argued that teachers of history, of literature, and, indeed, of any subject, were educating through the medium of love for, and appreciation of the subject, and thus communicating at the affective as well as at the academic or cerebral levels. Some teachers could also argue that they spent many after-school hours helping young people with difficulties which could be labelled 'affective'. Significant systemic change came with societal change and legislative response. With free education for secondary students and the development of large comprehensive/community schools in the late 1960s and early '70s it was evident that changes were needed to meet the new school populations. The numbers were larger, and the sociological needs were many. School had been structured to meet academic needs rather than personal/social needs, and it became obvious that both had to be addressed.

The first of these changes was the training of guidance counsellors, and the state's provision, at national level, for a guidance counsellor in each of our secondary/post primary schools. Even with this generous provision it was soon evident that one guidance counsellor per school could not answer the affective/pastoral needs of the students, and there began what has been a twenty-year search for the systemic approach to pastoral care/affective education. From 1974 to 1980 a number of Irish teachers studied, each summer, with Douglas Hamblin and with Leslie Button at Swansea University, where they learned about the British school approach called 'Pastoral Care'. Gradually, this model was copied, questioned, challenged, and certainly became widely known. There was, however, no formal training, and no official resources. There were no formal personal and social education programmes. It was at this time that a number of Irish Health Boards (regionalized, unlike the National Education Department) began to provide health education modules and training. There was no official central recognition in

Department of Education literature of the need for such programmes in the curriculum or school timetable. Recognizing the needs of students, many schools began to restructure their staffs to provide a pastoral dimension. Many gave a class period each week, and timetable for personal social health education (PSHE), programmes. From 1980 to 1981 one of the major teacher unions, the Association of Secondary Teachers of Ireland (ASTI), 'banned' pastoral care in schools. The union's concern, one may argue, was justified in the sense that teachers were being given pastoral roles and responsibilities without negotiation or training. In 1981, the central executive committee of this union negotiated with school management, and subsequently an agreement was reached about pastoral roles being negotiated before their introduction into the secondary/post-primary school system.

The 1980s witnessed an ongoing awareness that care provided by the 'good teacher' and 'good school' was still central, but that society and family change, and the development of larger comprehensive and co-educational schools, necessitated clearer structures, definite programmes, and suitable teacher in-service training.

This decade also saw the development of significant work with post-primary schools by the Psychological Service of the Department of Education.

THE MARINO INSTITUTE OF EDUCATION

In 1991 the Marino Institute of Education (MIE), a voluntary third level education centre, began providing teacher in-service in the area of pastoral care. Between 1991 and 1995 over four hundred post-primary schools have had staff members attend courses, or have had school-based in-service provided by the Institute. Currently, MIE offers the following service in this whole area of pastoral care/affective education.

Higher Diploma in Pastoral Care (HDPC)
This course, offered in partnership with St Patrick's College, Maynooth, can lead to a Master's Degree accredited by the National University. The partnership with Maynooth and the leadership of Professor John Coolahan in recognition of and support for pastoral care/effective education have been key factors in the support available for schools.

The Diploma course is a whole-school systemic approach to affective education.

> Pastoral care is a systemic approach by the school, to valuing the young adult in each student, and to providing a formal affective education within the school curriculum. It implies the engagement of all the school's policies, processes and programmes in the development of appropriate systemic structures, roles and resources to support these core values.
>
> (Úna M. Collins, 1995)

The course enables teachers to study the school as a system, pastoral values, the family, society today, with its impact in the school. There is an in-depth study of the adolescent, of appropriate school structures, students at risk, counselling theories, counselling skills, roles in the pastoral school, personal/social education within the curriculum, and classroom management. Each of the higher diploma class members is required to engage in an action research study on some aspect of pastoral care in her/his own school practice. The HDPC is in its second year, and there is already an interesting bank of action research studies in this area of affective education now available in MIE. 'I learned always to go back to the classroom, hear the voices there' (McNiff and Collins, 1994).

Pastoral care courses
MIE provides, on an ongoing basis, specific pastoral care courses for school staffs. Heads of schools, deputy heads, and middle management teams attend the planning and evaluation sections of these courses, and school staff teams attend the personal and social education, and relationship sexuality education modules.

Counselling Skills for Teachers
This course has provided appropriate in-service training for over three hundred teachers between 1993 and 1995.

In-service days for whole staff
The MIE staff is constantly involved in enabling whole staffs to evaluate and plan the school's development of pastoral care.

Development of resources
The development of resources for staffs, in relation to the school's systemic approach, and in the area of personal and social education within the Irish context, is central to the MIE commitment to pastoral care/affective education. The National Association of Pastoral Care in Education (NAPCE) has offered invaluable help in this development.

THE NEED FOR A SYSTEMIC APPROACH TO SCHOOL PASTORAL CARE

A needs analysis conducted by MIE in 1994 confirms the belief that teachers and schools need pastoral care courses, and that they are asking for more help in a whole-school approach.

1994 was a significant year in Irish education, and is entitled 'Fiche Bliain as Fás' or 'Twenty Years a-Growing'. 1994 was particularly significant for pastoral care/affective education in Ireland because one can trace the development of awareness about the need for whole-school and systemic approaches to pastoral care over a twenty-year period culminating in 1994 at the national Education Convention. Reading the relevant educational literature, and the official documents up to the late 1980s, one searches in vain for any clear reference to pastoral care/affective education or to personal/social education. Certainly one can argue that these concepts are presumed, or otherwise included, both in the system and in the documentation, but the search does not provide evidence.

The general aims of secondary education seem to be so taken for granted, or its values so deeply institutionalised, as not to require articulation or justification.

(Hannon and Shortall, 1991)

Evidence that there is a lack of a formal approach to the affective in the educational system is within the finding of the research carried out in 1991 by the Economic and Social Research Institute (ESRI) *School-leavers' views of educational objectives and outcomes.*

There is a general consensus on the importance of personal and social development goals in education by almost all involved; 90 per cent of the respondents consider it as a very important goal of education, only somewhat less important than basic education.

The respondents, while rating the 'affective' as very important, rate the school provision low:

... there is the need to considerably improve the content and quality of personal and social development education and pastoral care programmes in schools. These goals are given very high priority by school leavers, and rather low satisfaction marks result for their schools.

In a national research, conducted by MIE in 1992, on teachers' and school heads' assessment of the introduction of the New Junior Cycle Curriculum, we learn that:

A majority of respondents agreed that the New Junior Certificate Programme fulfilled the aims of personal and social development more completely than did previous programmes.

(MIE, 1992)

It is, however, that 'unprecedented democratic event in the history of Irish education', which took place in Dublin Castle in 1994, which is a significant landmark in this account of affective education/pastoral care in the Irish system. Prior to the National Education Convention, the Minister and the Department of Education had initiated, through a Green Paper, a national discussion around all aspects of education, and all interest groups in education were invited to participate. At the Convention all of these groups, who had been engaging at local level, and some at national level, in the ensuing debates, came together to make their positions public. The report of that Convention is very interesting from a number of aspects. It reflects a nation discussing what is probably one of its clearest core values, education. Most interestingly, it is in this report that pastoral care, personal and social education and a recommendation for their provision, come into the official literature.

This [re-organization of middle management structures] would free them [teachers] to concentrate their energies on academic and pastoral work ... Similar posts could also be created in other sections of the school, such as in curriculum development, pastoral care, and staff development.

(John Coolahan, 1994)

It is surely significant that in 1994 the new In-career Development Unit within the Department of Education (the unit providing funding for teacher in-service), first listed pastoral care as one of its priority areas.

CONCLUSION

As someone who has been involved with pastoral care/affective education whether in the classroom, the guidance counselling office, as a deputy head of a large comprehensive school, as head of a large all-girls secondary school, and now, as the head of a department offering in-service courses and university studies within this area of affective education, I would argue that within the twenty years 1974–94 we have taken the value of the young person who is learning (a value which already existed), developed it, seen its place within the context of formal education, appreciated that it is vitally important to formalize it, recognized that it needs formal structures within school to support it, recognized that teachers need support in order to commit themselves to this, recognized, from research, that students believe it isn't really yet in place as they would like it to be, and recognized that help generally is needed so that the system can address this most important value of the human face in education. In 1994 the support came in various ways, significantly, from official literature. Official literature, however, is only reflecting what has been happening at the grass roots. It is in the schools, in the classrooms, that significant change is being experienced. Teachers are realizing that this is not a lesson to be postponed until students leave school, but is a lesson which is being learned within the school experience. The adults who are the formal educators within the school are themselves modelling a learning lesson for the young people, and all of this new development is challenging us to continue our learning because we are in touch with that mystery which is another human being.

This brings the 'fiche bliain' (twenty-year) story up to date. What has grown is not only a spirit of caring and a realization of the importance of affective education, but also the actualization of a more systemic and formal approach to it by the school. This has led to an evaluation of the school's effectiveness, and the implications for on-going professional training for teachers.

We are, to use Christa McAuliffe's words, 'anonn ins na todhchaí' (touching the future).

POSTSCRIPT (1997)

The 'fiche bliain' (twenty-year) story of the development of Affective Education/Pastoral Care in Ireland has an interesting postscript (1994–7):

IAPCE
In October 1995 we hosted a National Symposium for teachers and school principals on the theme of Pastoral Care and School Discipline. At the close of the symposium we devoted time to the introduction of an Irish

Association of Pastoral Care, an Association 'to support and resource those concerned with any aspect of Pastoral Care (Affective Education)'. The Marino Institute of Education supported the development and the interim committee's work for 1995–6. During that year five regions were inaugurated in different parts of the country, evening lectures were given, and we began our search for funding. It is pertinent to this development that the founding committee and the regional committees were largely members of the Higher Diploma in Pastoral Care classes 1993–6.

In May 1996 the official launching of IAPCE (the Irish Association of Pastoral Care in Education) took place in Dublin. The first General Meeting was held, the Constitution adopted, and the first official committee elected, with regional committees approved. Funding has been granted for this first official year by the Gulbenkian Foundation in London. IAPCE's office is in the Marino Institute, and the Association's membership is growing daily. In-service courses for teachers are currently being given by IAPCE members in regions throughout the country.

REFERENCES

An Roinn Oideachais (1971), *Curaclam Na Bunscoile*, Dublin: Department of Education.

Andrews, J. H., 'A Geographer's View of Irish History', in *The Course of Irish History*, Cork: Mercier Press.

Coolahan, J. (1994), *Report on the National Education Convention*, Dublin: Department of Education.

Drudy, S. and Lynch, K. (1993), *Schools and Society in Ireland*. Dublin: Gill and Macmillan.

Hannon, D. F. and Shortall, S. (1991), *The Quality of Their Education*, Dublin: ESRA.

Husen, T. and Postlethwaite, T. N. (1985), 'Ireland, Republic of: System of Education', in *The International Encyclopaedia of Education*, Great Britain: Pergamon.

Hyland, A. and Milne, K. (1992), *Irish Educational Documents*, Dublin: Church of Ireland College.

McNiff, J. and Collins, Ú. (1994), *A New Approach to In-Career Development for Teachers in Ireland*, Dublin: Hyde Publications.

Ryan, L. (1993), Paper given to AMCSS, Galway.

CHAPTER 5

Affective education: a Russian perspective

Yuri Zabrodin, Margarita Popova and Alex Minaev

INTRODUCTION

Until recently affective education was not an identifiable aspect of the Russian education system. However, long-standing ideas relating to the humanizing and psychological role of the school relate closely to the ideas underlying affective education. In the writers' view the psychological approach that has characterized the development of aspects of education in Russia has a close connection with a number of the concerns of affective education. Therefore, in this chapter a key focus will be on the development and influence of psychological approaches.

This emphasis on the school's humanizing and psychological role is rooted in ideas that can be found as far back as the time of Peter the Great, i.e. since the 18th century, where they can be traced through literary sources. These perspectives had their origin in Russian philosophical thought and Russian education.

Russian philosophers envisaged a human being and his mental and emotional life as connected with the physical world and looked at the soul itself as a unified whole that could not be represented as a sum of separate elements. In Russian pedagogy the idea of affective education has developed in both explicit and implicit forms. On the one hand psychology was the basis of the pedagogical systems of many Russian thinkers and thus the educational process itself was seen as a psychological one. On the other hand psychology was introduced into the school programmes as an independent subject. Thus, since the first half of the 19th century humanistic ideas have been developed by leading Russian pedagogues.

HISTORICAL BACKGROUND

Ideas of the development of a whole personality were a particular feature of progressive Russian educational trends. The idea of self-development as a goal of education was explicitly formulated by Kapterev (1982). He suggested that the most important acquisition for pupils was the ability to reason, speak and learn, i.e. psychological skills and aptitudes. The idea of acknowledging the unique individuality of each child was developed by Vakhterov (1986). The idea of development was the foundation of his educational theory. The idea of the 'value' of the personal life experience of a child and the centrality of this to education has been elaborated by Shatsky (1980). Leo Tolstoy (1989) considered 'the basis of education of a pupil to be the comprehension of the purpose and meaning of human life, the question that every reasonable human being asks regardless of type of society.'

The perception of Russian education in essentially psychological terms involved an approach to psychology based on a holistic view of personality which did not assume a mechanistic division of a whole into parts. Its emergence was promoted by the development of a psychological perspective peculiar to Russian thought and to philosophy manifesting itself in literature, educational and philosophical works. That is why frequently the ability to empathize with the other person, to look at him in the system of his relations to others, the world and himself was considered an important human quality.

Another area that started to be elaborated by Ushinsky (1990), Blonsky (1910), Nethchaev (1911), Tchelpanov (1912) and Kornilov (1916) was personality research in a natural philosophical variant. In that variant cognitive processes and affective phenomena were studied separately from the concept of the human being as a whole. The tendency to research 'a dismembered human being' was reflected in all taught courses of psychology at the time.

Since 1906, when psychology was introduced as a separate subject in a comprehensive school curriculum plan, serious attention was paid by psychological research circles to the following task: 'to teach psychology so as to make its educational importance absolutely evident and to make the reverse movement impossible' (Tchelpanov, 1912). The nature of lessons in psychology were said to have the following requirements by the then popular professor of psychology, A. P. Nethchaev (1911):

- Teaching of this subject should be based strictly on facts.
- It must be empirical.
- It must bring forth pupils' experience.
- There should be relevant practical exercises.
- The course should not be too extensive.

The influence of psychology on pupils was identified as highly significant by a famous Russian pedagogue and psychologist, Professor P. P. Blonsky (1910). In spite of the fact that psychology as a curriculum subject was popular with teachers and pupils, four years later it was excluded from school as such. Among many reasons three were singled out by Professor G. I. Tchelpanov as decisive:

- absence of special qualifications of teachers (psychology was taught by teachers of history)
- methodological vagueness of courses (also lack of textbooks, study time etc.)

- the weak position in the curriculum of the subject as an experimental and a secondary one.

As a result, from 1910 to 1954 psychology was not taught in schools as a curriculum subject, though even under these circumstances the schools were still of interest to psychologists who elaborated research programmes, in particular observing the development of children in educational conditions. Intensive co-operation between schools and psychologists lasted till a notorious resolution of 1936: 'On pedagogical mistakes in the system of Narcompros' (the term then used for the Ministry of Education). As a result of this resolution, the involvement of psychologists in the educational process was prohibited.

Explicit concern with affective education therefore ceased at an institutional level but its ideas continued their expansion beyond the framework of a curriculum subject. The psychological conceptions of Russian pedagogy have been developed by psychologists. For example Professor L. S. Vygotsky (1982) stated the necessity of basing the education of the child on experience; Professor S. L. Rubinstein had already noted that pedagogics had to be built on the basis of a creative child self-activity because 'the creator himself is being created in this process'.

In the history of the Soviet State there was a period when psychology was moved back to school for four years (1954–8). No substantial changes were introduced to the conception or to the methods of teaching of psychology as a curriculum subject. The subject contents and its structure were retained intact as they had been proposed by Professor A. P. Nethchaev (1911). New scholars (Fortunatov and Petrovsky, 1954) enriched and enlarged the contents considerably. At that time there was a rather peculiar situation in that the psychological courses for school students were borrowed from higher education courses and were neither adapted nor modified but only simplified.

In 1958 psychology as a curriculum subject was removed from a list of compulsory subjects. But psychologists went on working within schools within the framework of science research programmes, elaborating ideas of developmental education (Davydov, 1986; Amonashvily, 1987) and relating them to education (Makhmutov, 1975; Matyushkin, 1985). The more psychologists were involved the more schools appreciated the contribution that psychological knowledge could make to the secondary education system.

THE CURRENT SITUATION

Now that the whole of Russian society is experiencing fundamental change, even the most conservative institutions cannot remain unaffected by the process. It manifests itself through changing attitudes to the affective part of education both at national level and at the level of individual schools. Affective education is starting to gain a new and visible identity.

> The vacuum created by social upheaval has encouraged a move towards greater attention to the development of emotions as opposed to solely cognition on the one hand and on the other the study of man

as a whole existential being. At the moment only one per cent of curriculum time is devoted to studying man from an holistic perspective.
(Mesheryakov and Mesheryakova, 1991)

Thus, along with the curriculum subjects such as 'Ethics and psychology of family life', 'world art', etc., elaborated by the Ministry of Education together with the Science-Research Institute of Schools, new courses are being produced by individual schools and authors. For example in some schools of the former Soviet Union, courses like 'Ethics and behaviour', 'Study of human nature' and 'Psychology of learning' are being taught. It is clear that schools have significant expectations of psychology if they are prepared to take responsibility for introducing it into the system of secondary education.

At the moment Russian secondary education can be seen as being in the process of searching for a place, content and form for introducing psychological knowledge. Mutually beneficial and enriching relationships between schools and the social sciences are starting to appear. The relationships are something new, a kind of integration initiated at practical institutional levels, as opposed to being imposed by authorities. Centres are being set up dealing with different sorts of personal development, psycho-diagnostics and correction, personal creativity etc.

A negative aspect of the emergence of affective education as a socio-educational phenomenon is, we believe, a necessary and inevitable phase peculiar to any growth and development. This is that affective education is at present developing in a chaotic situation where what happens in one place is unknown in another. This results in a low level of generalization, and lack or even absence of concepts and theory at socio-educational levels. This hampers educational researchers, teachers, and all those interested in joint research, teaching and educational activity. It hampers the integration of efforts to develop a coherent policy in this extensive domain, to transform psychology into a real social force. A further inhibiting factor is the material, economic and financial situation that currently exists in Russia.

Nevertheless, we consider the overall atmosphere in Russia and the spirit of experimentation as favourable to the emergence of affective education, as articulated through the psychologically orientated developments described above. We are optimistic that the current stage will be followed by a stage of interpreting accumulated experience and integrating it. Out of currently incoherent experience a stable building of affective education will emerge. There are prerequisites and conditions but now time is necessary. In fact it is a decisive factor.

So far as we consider affective education to be 'a response to a number of key social problems in relation to which it can be seen as offering something positive' (Lang, 1995), this aspect of its current relevance is of particular importance and significance.

If in the USA aspects of affective education appeared in response to the vocational problems, or from a broader perspective to problems of industrialization; and in Great Britain partly in response to the emergence of comprehensive schools; in Spain as 'an antidote to the legacy of years of dictatorship' (Lang, *ibid.*) then in Russia it is emerging in response to the collapse of a unified secondary school system, more broadly to radical changes of society, the hallmark of which is the stress now being placed on individualism and the value of the individual.

A SPECIFIC APPROACH

The first articulation in the full sense of the word in a Russian school of the type of development being discussed, is one developed by Zabrodin and Popova (1994), the authors of the course *Psychology for Adolescents*.

The course was designed for adolescents aged 13–15, taking into account the psychological peculiarities of that age. It is based on the idea that it is adolescents particularly who need an enrichment through psychological insights which are not traditionally academic, but personally oriented and which encourage them to address the problems of personal growth and development. The overall principle underlying the teaching programme is the fact that it would be the basic one in the system of secondary education regardless of the future of a growing person in terms of choice of vocational or social activity.

The programme is conceived within the context of philosophical conceptions of Russian humanism. The basic idea underpinning it is that psychology is a science dealing with a world outlook, and thus related to approaches to the understanding of human beings, existing in philosophy. It was also very important to examine the problems of a human being as expressed in the Russian philosophy, described as 'Cosmism'. This trend in philosophy was represented by such great thinkers as P. A. Florensky (1992), Y. L. and N. K. Rerikh (1982), V. S. Solovyov (1990), F. Dostoyevsky (1986), N. A. Berdyaev (1991) and V. L. Vernadsky (1991).

The theoretical basis of the course involves the idea that every human being lives in nature and society and cannot exist outside them. This idea is expressed through four separate strands. The first strand is the idea that human beings are not the only creatures possessing consciousness, that there is a consciousness which exists beyond that of the individual. The second stresses the uniqueness of human beings and consequently underlines a diversity of people in nature. The third is connected with the idea of the development and self-development of personality. The fourth is the idea that human beings cannot live outside human culture (the latter may be understood as the experience of previous generations), or without understanding the way in which culture develops.

Within this conceptual approach, three levels of issue are considered:

- human beings and nature (the development of essential human potentialities)
- human beings and society (the development of human relationships and the formation of conventional norms, namely morality, values and law)
- human beings and culture (transmission of human experience as a value for the future)

The contents of the teaching course is being developed in relation to these issues.

THE COURSE CONTENTS

The contents of the course *Psychology for Adolescents* includes knowledge about the nature and structure of human culture, about the place of a human being in this culture, about their role in the world that surrounds them, about their relationship with this world and about their interrelations with other people. The guiding principles for the selection of content embody a holistic approach to psychological phenomena research and the principle of age-needs in relation to theories of adolescent development (L. S. Vygotsky, 1982).

Five basic psychological categories are involved: relationships, emotional experience, behaviour regulation, development and creativity. All psychological knowledge and experience are organized in accordance with and within this framework of the five categories. In the relationships area, students explore the problems and laws of communication and interaction, mechanisms of perceiving others, means of solving conflict and the varying nature of individuals and their relationships with the world, others and themselves. Emotional experience concerns themes that illustrate the nature and value of emotional life for human beings, methods of psychological defence, the role of emotions in art, science and communication and the nature of emotional experience and the possibilities of emotional control. Behaviour regulation examines the interconnection of human behaviour with psychological aspects of personality, value-orientation, role prescriptions, emotional states, motives, will and consciousness. In development, the following questions are examined: holistic approaches to development, the place of a human being in nature, the development of aptitudes and personality resources of a human being in the course of a whole life and the possibility of developing a productive life plan. Finally, in creativity, ideas are presented about creativity as a general and a specific human aptitude and about the nature of the creative process. The influence of environment, communication and activity on the formation of a subjective creativity is shown. Different kinds of creative activity are examined.

The ideal model of personality is not designed to foster particular skills. Key structures of consciousness and personality need to be fostered and made explicit, keeping in mind that the aim is to promote changes not in relation to separate social and personal skills but to personality as a whole. In this sense personality change is encouraged through the psychological support of development and through developing a humanistic orientation in pupils and the development of their creative aptitudes. This model of humanistic development involves the development in adolescents of an interest in themselves, a willingness to accept the standpoint of others, the ability to analyse psychologically their own psychological reality, the skill to control emotional states, and the ability to build a perspective on their own future. The framework of creative aptitudes development involves the development of reflection, sensitivity to the problem, intellectual flexibility, aptitude for self-analysis, constructive decision-making and the generation of ideas.

The writers of this chapter believe that the above-mentioned aspects will enable us to teach the rising generation to solve the problems (individual and those of the generation) better than the other generation does theirs. We would like to see adolescents more powerful, more stable and socially adaptive in life, feeling comfortable and safe, being naturally integrated into the world. The basic rationale of the course is that if psychological knowledge is appropriated by an adolescent, it results in changes in personality as a whole. That is why there is a fundamental difference between the notions of 'appropriation' and 'mastering' of psychological knowledge. Mastering is understood as the use of knowledge by a pupil as a response to a specific demand, while appropriation implies a personality transformation in activity, transformation in determining and making personality perspectives, in actions and behaviour.

The psychological basis of the course is the assumption of the unity of Man and the World, about relationships that tie people together and in which they manifest their intrinsic qualities. That is why the formation of basic relationships is one of the central features of the course. Apart from real relationships, simulated relationships are used. Work with these helps young people to solve problem situations and the problems of disharmonized relationships without detrimental consequences. A more positive self-concept is encouraged by the course through the humanistic supportive atmosphere, balanced by attention to experimental and experiential methods.

The course not only engenders self-concept through the experience of specific situations and the promotion of its structural and functional growth but also involves addressing some significant adolescent life tasks. Thus adolescents create a psychological approach for themselves, the basis of which is an understanding of self-concept. This is an effective psychological means to achieve significant adolescent life tasks and solve problems in the critical period of their transition to an adult world. The educational rationale of the course consists in teaching the child common ways of dealing with reality. The main thing in education is assumed to be the mastering of a scientific, objective method for cognition of subjective phenomena by an adolescent, while instrumentalism and functionalism are consciously avoided.

Working with psychological phenomena, adolescents are taught to discern this phenomenon in themselves and later work with it as with a reality.

How do pupils master a method of working with a psychological reality? How do they acquire psychological knowledge? This involves three basic stages. The first stage is identifying a specific phenomenon from a wide range, which is then described and explained by the teacher. At the second stage, an adolescent seeks this phenomenon in himself or herself, in others and in relationships. At the third stage, the teacher demonstrates the evolution of the self in different aspects of the self through the prism of a given phenomenon.

In relation to this some special teaching methods have been developed – reading aloud, reflective training, introspective analysis. Also, some well-known methods of psycho-correction and personal growth have been adapted for the course and for the specific age range. These include methods of creative self-expression (on the basis of methods of therapy devised by Burno through creative self-expression), methods of expression (on the basis of methods of C. Rogers and art therapy), psychodrama, and methods of psychic self-regulation (auto-training, psycho-physics, social training). In addition, there are methods of knowledge transmission, project-work, experimental and differential psychology, problem-solving, observation studies and the 'plunge method' (when a group of students and their teacher totally immerse themselves in a topic over a period of time). The essence and the task of these methods, their description and procedures how to use them, the appropriate role and functions of the teacher of psychology in each method, and what each method gives in the sense of personal growth, are set out in writing in a Teacher's Manual.

HOW IS IT BEING DONE IN PRACTICE?

Let us take as an example the topic 'How can I learn what the other person feels?' This has been worked through with different teaching methods and appears periodically over two years. It also is included in an examination. Having acquired understanding, pupils are able to build constructive relationships with people by themselves. There are given modes of effective communication and interaction, but concrete situations are not described. Knowledge is given but it is neither instrumental nor functional: it is not tied to concrete situations. Situations are of a generalized character (tales, parables, fiction are used). Simulations are also used. The contents of these situations are filled with a personally important effectively charged experience.

The lessons last for three hours altogether (3 x 45 minutes with two breaks in between) once a week. Each lesson is planned individually by a teacher who draws on the programme of the course and on the Teacher's Manual. During the psychology lesson the teachers use a lot of psycho-technical games and creative exercises, although the main focus is on formulation and performance of psychological tasks. In this respect the use of encouragement and feedback in the process of teaching is thought to be important in the teaching of psychology.

The course *Psychology for Adolescents* is elaborated as a teaching and methodical set that includes the Programme of the course, a Reading Book, Collected Diagnosis Methods and a Teacher's Manual. One of the most important things from the point of view of the course methodology is working with psycho-diagnostic methods. The introduction of diagnostic procedures into the teaching process enables learning the subject through its own logic and also the gaining of psychological knowledge by psychological means themselves. The psycho-diagnostic methods that are applied may be divided into three groups:

- psycho-diagnostics as part of the subject of psychology (as a didactic method)
- diagnostics of mastering psychological knowledge
- psycho-diagnostics of development

The diagnostics as part of the subject are used to present an abstract psychological knowledge from the context 'anywhere' to pass on to the conscious context 'meaning for me' for the examined psychological phenomenon to acquire a personal meaning. The diagnostics of mastering psychological knowledge enable the teacher and learner successfully to control the educational process.

The psycho-diagnostics of development enable the teacher to recognize the emergence of new psychological structural phenomena in the personality of each pupil and consequently more effectively to manage the formation of personality traits.

EVALUATION

The analysis of results of psycho-diagnostic research shows that on all dimensions there are statistically significant differences between experimental and control groups. Thus experimental group adolescents showed a considerable decrease in their level of aggressiveness and conflict compared with the peers from control groups (49 : 7 per cent), an increase of constructive behaviour reaction (24 : 2 per cent) and increase of level of understanding of the others (49 : 7 per cent). The adolescents in the experimental group showed a developed sense of self-worth and dignity. In the course of the research, considerable changes were found in the following parameters: re-structuring of interests of experimental group adolescents towards socialization, higher level of achievement motivation, a higher level and broader scope of cognitive activity and an ability to forecast and plan life long in advance.

The experimental group adolescents showed a rather higher level of introspective analysis, reflection of psychological reality (72 : 30 per cent) and perception of the psychological life of human beings as a reality with philosophical dimensions. Expert assessment of pupils by subject teachers (literature, history, biology) who worked with experimental adolescent groups identified the emergence of a deeper interest and claims to a higher level of knowledge in other subject areas. This bears witness to the ability to transfer the effect of psychological knowledge to other subjects of secondary education.

Very often in adolescent self-reports one comes across such phrases as: 'Thanks to the course I became a different person'. The research is focused on the phenomenology of the adolescent in conditions of appropriation of psychological knowledge by him or her. Here a substantial difference in personality orientation was found between experimental and control groups. In defining their future perspective the experimental group used the expressions 'I should become' and 'I want to be able' while their peers from control groups expressed their life perspective in notions like 'I must be given' and 'I want to have'. The interpretation of this data leads us to conclude that psychology as a subject at school for adolescents in the framework of the proposed conception should be part and parcel of the system of secondary education. It stimulates the cognitive activity of pupils, promotes their development and opens a broad perspective on the humanization of secondary education.

The data of psycho-diagnostic research confirms the hypothesis about the specificity of appropriation of psychological knowledge by an adolescent. Its essence consists in a development of humanistic orientations of an adolescent relationship system and brings forth his or her creative resources. Thus the children were not taught to solve concrete problems. Rather the goal was to teach them to see the whole richness (multitude) of psychological phenomena, to recognize them and to form adequate means of interaction with them, thus bringing them into the culture of personality. Using the classification proposed by Lang (1995) one could say that the programme stresses the importance of the third (developmental) stage of affective education that brings the personality to such a level of development that the students are able to find solutions to their problems themselves, bringing the problems to a conscious level and in forms that are most amenable to solution.

CONCLUSION

We support the overwhelming majority of the ideas put forward by our foreign colleagues concerning the goals and means of affective education (personal growth, responsible autonomy, awareness of one's assets and weaknesses, problem-solving, decision-making, striking a balance between cognitive and emotional development, etc.). However, proceeding from our experience in a certain situation peculiar to Russia, we would like to emphasize particular priorities.

We think that affective education in Russia should now concentrate its efforts on the problem of self-awareness and on what and how it should be brought to consciousness, since the essence of our position is that full and adequate self-awareness is an important prerequisite for overcoming alienation. It is an implanted mechanism of sensitivity to meaning that enables one to solve the problem of fundamental discrepancy (Rogers, 1983). Although the problem of self-awareness was envisaged as a cornerstone by almost all known Russian philosophers and was experienced and thought over by Russian intelligentsia, this idea did not touch the population at large. In Berdyaev's opinion, the people and the intelligentsia in Russia are two different nations with a huge abyss between them.

Now that the whole of Russian society is in flux, when the very foundations of personality are being influenced by it, when the system of values is being fundamentally revised to find and create new ties with the rest of the world, with other people and with ourselves on a stable basis, the problem of self-awareness acquires new meaning, not merely in psychological terms but also in terms of social colouring. Without it, many fundamental problems of personal and social being, such as the meaning of life, the value of human activity, and human self-worth cannot be adequately and effectively addressed. The introduction of psychology in the above-mentioned form, contents and means might well promote the solution to the problems which radical social change generates.

In the situation in Russia we see the following perspectives for growth and development of affective education:

- the accumulation of phenomenological experience emerging from school activity
- the elaboration of the theoretical and methodological basis of affective education with a close practical co-operation that would serve as a means of mutual understanding, thus promoting an organizational unity
- the creation of a social institution that would have integrative functions both on scientific and organizational levels.

REFERENCES

Amonashvily, S. A. (1987), *The Unity of Goals: Teacher Manual*, Moscow: Pedagogics.

Berdyaev, N. A. (1991), *Self-cognition*, Moscow: Mysl.

Blonsky, P. P. (1910), *The Results of a Questionnaire on Teaching Psychology at Secondary School*, Moscow: Kushneryov.

Burno, N. (1989), Therapy through Creative Self-expression, Moscow: Medicine.

Davydov, V. V. (1986), *The Problem of Developing Teaching*, Moscow: Pedagogics.

Dostoyevsky, F. M. (1986–95), *Collected Works*, 15 vols, Leningrad: Nauka.

Fortunatov, G. A. and Petrovsky, A. V. (1954), *Psychology: The School Text Book*, Moscow: Posvesheniy.

Fyodorov, N. F. (1989), *The Philosophy of Common Work*, 3 vols, Moscow: Kharbin.

Kapterev, P. F. (1982), *Selected Educational Works*, Moscow: Pedagogics.

Kornilov, K. N. (1916), *The Simplest School Psychological Experiences. For Secondary Schools*, Moscow: Dumnov.

Lang, P. (1995), 'International Perspectives on Pastoral Care (Affective Education)', in Best, R., Lang, P., Lodge, P. and Watkins, C. (eds), *Pastoral Care and Personal and Social Education: Entitlement and Provision*, London: Cassell, pp. 268–84.

Makhmutov, M. I. (1975), *The Problem of Teaching*, Moscow: Pedagogics.

Matyushkin, A. (1985), *The Problems of Psychodiagnostics, Teaching and Development of School Students: Collected Scientific Works of Academy of Education*, Moscow: Academy of Education.

Nethchaev, A. P. (1911), *How to Teach Psychology*, St Petersburg: Dumnov.

Popova, M. V. (1993), *The Basics of Psychological Knowledge as a Factor of Humanisation of Secondary Education*, unpublished doctoral thesis: Moscow, State Educational University.

Rogers, C. (1984), *Freedom to Learn in the 1980s*, Chicago: Merrill, Bell and Howell.

Semyonova, S. G., and Gatcheva, A. G. (eds) (1993), *Russian Cosmism: Anthology of Philosophical Thought*, Moscow: Pedagogics.

Shatsky, S. G. (1980), *Selected Educational Works*, 2 vols, Moscow: Pedagogics.

Skovorada, G. S. (1973), *Works*, 2 vols, Moscow: Mysl.

Solovyov, V. S. (1990), *Works*, 2 vols, Moscow: Mysl.

Tchelpanov, G. I. (1912), *The Psychology and the School: Collected Articles*, Moscow: Dumnov.

Tolstoy, L. (1989), *Educational Works*, Moscow: Pedagogics.

Ushinsky, J. D. (1990), *Educational Works*, 6 vols, Moscow: Pedagogics.

Vakhterov, V. P. (1986), *Selected Educational Works*, Moscow: Pedagogics.

Vvevdensky, A. I., Losev, A. F., Radlov, E. L., Shpet, G. G. (1991), *Review of the History of Russian Philosophy*, Sverdlovs: Sverdlovsky University Press.

Vygotsky, L. S. (1968), *The Psychology of Art*, Moscow: Nauka.

Vygotsky, L. S. (1982), *Collected Works*, 6 vols, Moscow: Pedagogics.

Zabrodin, Y. M. and Popova, M. V. (1990), *Psychology, the Course Programme*, Moscow: State Educational University.

Zabrodin, Y. M. and Popova, M. V. (1994), *Psychology at School: Experimental Course for Adolescents, Manual*, Moscow: VNPT.

CHAPTER 6

Affective education and the Greek school curriculum

Alkistis Kondoyianni, Rea Karageorgiou-Short and Athena Sideri

In the Greek language, the term 'affective' signifies all that pertains to or is influenced by the emotions. The term 'affective education' can be rendered into Greek in a number of ways, each of which places the emphasis on a different aspect of the notions embodied by this term. In one of these renderings, the emphasis is put on the emotions of the student and his or her overall personality; more particularly, the student's relation to his or her own emotions and self image. In another, the emphasis is on the feelings the student experiences in dealings with the environment and in particular relationships with other people, the communication and mutual influence that ensue and the emotions that are thus created in the student.

Our analysis focuses on the official curriculum of the Greek school in order to determine the presence of this conception of affective education; this analysis is particularly relevant, due to the fact that research in this domain is scarce. Therefore, this chapter will cover the official curriculum for the kindergarten and the primary and secondary school, to identify affective education themes.

THE EDUCATION SYSTEM IN GREECE

Education in Greece can be offered either by state-run institutions or by private ones, but they are all controlled by the Ministry of Education, which in collaboration with the Institute of Education is responsible for designing and overseeing the implementation of the curriculum framework.

Every year, all teachers, at all levels of education (kindergarten, primary and secondary) receive the official curriculum for their subject for that academic year. The curriculum states, in some detail, those areas of their subject they are expected to cover within the academic year and the particular aims for teaching that subject. In recent years, the curriculum for primary schools has been accompanied by a teacher's guide book that explains in greater detail how the teacher should go about implementing it. The responsibility for the implementation of the curriculum rests with individual teachers, but they are closely supervised in this by the school's head. Furthermore, schools are grouped together according to their location and catchment area and for every area there are school counsellors, separate ones for kindergartens, primary and secondary schools, whose job, among others, is to monitor the implementation of the curriculum.

The curriculum itself is quite binding, in that it represents the state's views on what is necessary for Greek school children to learn during the academic year, and it is illegal for any teacher to ignore or by-pass it. As it is also quite extensive, it is quite unusual, though not impossible, to teach a subject in excess of what has been specified in the curriculum.

The school system encompasses the kindergarten, the primary school, and the secondary school, with nine years of compulsory education. The kindergarten includes pupils between the ages of four and six; the primary school, from grades 1 to 6, for pupils usually between the ages of six and twelve; the secondary school, including the high school (grades 7 to 9) and the lyceum (grades 10 to 12). The lyceum is divided into three distinct types: the general, the multi-directional and the technical. These three types share a number of subjects that are considered to be core ones, as well as teaching those specific to each type of school.

KINDERGARTEN

The curriculum framework for the kindergarten states that the aim of this type of institution is the support of the balanced and well-rounded development of children in a free, safe and open-minded environment. More specifically, it mentions the psycho-motor, social, emotive, moral and religious, aesthetic and mental development, as well as the cultivation of motor and mental skills (Michalopoulou Dimaki, 1988; Chrysafides, 1994). Thus the kindergarten aims to help the child:

- gain a better knowledge and understanding of him/herself
- communicate with other persons
- influence and be influenced by the environment in which he or she lives.

In particular, in the areas of social, emotional and moral development the curriculum specifies that the child is to be assisted in:

- establishing healthy personal relationships with the other children, the teacher and other adults
- integrating smoothly in his or her peer group as an active, equal and creative member
- discovering the joy and empowerment inherent in collective work
- developing the social values of responsibility, honesty, co-operation and love for his or her country, thus aiming ultimately to assist the development of the child's independence and moral growth.

The specific aims of the various areas also include objectives in the domain of affective education. In the area of psycho-motor development, the curriculum states that the child is to be assisted in discovering and organizing a cognitive framework for his or her body (an aspect of this being the encouragement of personal exploration and of creativity) and developing his or her creative psycho-motor expressiveness (including the exploration of spatial relationships). In the area of aesthetic development the child is to be assisted in developing ways of creative expression using various forms of art, and in the area of mental development the child is to be assisted in developing an active and inquisitive way of relating to his or her environment, the world and reality.

Looking critically at the aims of the Greek kindergarten, as stated in the curriculum and the accompanying activity guidebook, we can see that whereas the curriculum claims that social education must proceed in conjunction with the emotive, moral and religious education, as all these areas are complementary and mutually influenced, in effect the emphasis is placed more on the purely social elements of the educational process. Therefore, while stating the need for a balanced and rounded development, the child's relationship to himself or herself is somehow neglected in favour of the child's relationships to other people. Related research (Petroulaki, 1992; Nova Kaltsouni, 1995; Gotovos, 1985) supports this observation, namely that social education is the dominant aim of the curriculum for pre-school education in Greece, when compared with emotional and moral education.

PRIMARY SCHOOL

To examine the provisions made as far as affective education is concerned in primary schools, we shall be looking at the curriculum framework and a number of presidential decrees concerning primary education. Our main focus is on the various subjects taught: environmental studies, Greek language, social and political education, aesthetic education, religious studies, history, geography, natural sciences and physical education.

The subject of environmental studies (Presidential Decree 399/1-8-85 FEK 140A)[1] covers a wide range of topics and is taught during the first four grades of primary school. Its purpose is to teach the pupils about their environment and the relationships they can form with it as well as with the people that constitute the pupil's community, both their immediate and the wider one. Through this subject the pupil is also encouraged to explore his or her own self, his or her needs and strengths and the ways in which he or she influences and is influenced by this environment. According to the official documents (Presidential Decree 528/26-11-84 FEK 185A) the aim of this subject is the study and understanding of human beings, their social and natural environments and their culture as well as the interplay of the above.

The subject of environmental studies is also concerned with various activities undertaken by the pupils, as parts of their learning process, that contribute to a creative approach to learning and thus to a more balanced and well-rounded development of the pupils (Georgopoulos and Tsaliki, 1993). The aim of environmental studies is to facilitate the active learning of the pupils in ways that could ensure:

the progressive acquisition and clarification of fundamental experiences, concepts and knowledge as well as the development of those necessary skills that will enable the pupils to learn, understand and appreciate to the best of their abilities the world that surrounds them, both human and natural, and the dynamic interplay between these two.

(Presidential Decree 528/26-11-84 FEK 185A)

The subject is divided into seven main units that are returned to frequently, in an ever deeper way, in the course of the first four grades. These seven units are the following: human beings among themselves; human beings in their geographical environment; how human beings communicate; human beings and plants; human beings and animals; how human beings satisfy their needs; human beings and machines. Apart from these main units, there are also various seasonal ones related to current events and celebrations, etc. Each unit, whether main or seasonal, is subdivided into smaller areas, offering opportunities for learning that are different from one grade to the next, reflecting the changing needs and capacities of the pupils. As an example of how all the above is translated in the classroom, we describe at greater length in an appendix some of the aims of environmental studies for the first grade of primary school.

The subject of environmental studies is possibly the most important one in satisfying some of the objectives of affective education in the Greek primary school. In the process of environmental studies pupils acquire fundamental experiences and knowledge pertaining both to their human and natural environment. They also develop such values and attitudes as will enable them to integrate in a positive way in their natural, cultural and social environment. On the whole, pupils are encouraged to approach the subject in an active and creative way with the emphasis put on collective work and group projects, thus developing their skills at cooperation.

Greek language is taught in all six grades of primary school and is the only subject explicitly trying to develop the pupils' capacity to become aware of their feelings, attitudes and choices, their sense of self and their part in the world. This subject also focuses on the development of the pupils' social skills and their capacities for forming relationships. Among the various aims of the subject and the various units in which it is subdivided, we shall concentrate here on those relating to affective education.

During the first and second grade, the pupils should learn relevant communication skills. For instance, in the role of speaker to express their impressions, thoughts, wishes and emotions in a clear, natural and polite way, and in the role of listener to follow the speaker's words silently and attentively and to make pertinent comments. Additionally, they learn both to ask for information and give answers to questions in a correct way, in a variety of circumstances and to converse in a polite way that contributes to the enjoyment of communication. The topic of conversation aims to make the pupils capable of following the speakers as they alternate, waiting for their own turn, and keeping track of the more important points raised in the conversation without losing sight of the topic. Not least, they are encouraged to tolerate the criticism of others and maintain throughout a constructive and positive atmosphere. A specific unit is on dramatization, so that through role-playing pupils become acquainted with a variety of ways of speaking and specific vocabularies used in different settings and circumstances. The relevance of self-expression through writing is also emphasized, and pupils are encouraged to make their writings as personal as possible by expressing their feelings about the things described or by commenting on them.

In grades 3 and 4, the curriculum aims to promote the development of listening skills (e.g. to recognize and interpret the emotional tone of speech) and of speaking skills (e.g. the capacity to express thoughts, wishes and emotions in a clear, natural and polite way and to take part in a discussion constructively), among others. Dramatization is also used as an important means to promote awareness of feelings and emotions.

In grades 5 and 6, the emphasis is, supposedly, placed on expression and communication through the use of texts. Somehow, though, the specific aims seem to indicate that the emphasis is put more on the development of mental skills than on expression and communication. Thus the text used comes from literature and pupils are encouraged to delve both into the text's meaning and its historical context as well as its aesthetic characteristics and literary style.

Social and political education (Presidential Decree 168/3-5-84 FEK 56A) is taught at grade 5 of primary school and shares in part the content and objectives of affective education, as it concentrates on topics such as groups and how they function, social structure and development of attitudes and value systems. The aims of this subject are to enable the pupils:

- to learn about the structure and the working of Greek society and become acquainted with its dominant value systems
- to understand the importance of social and political institutions both for the individual and the group
- to develop a capacity to think critically about contemporary social issues
- to develop a social conscience that will enable them to participate in the life of a democratic society in a responsible and creative way
- to become aware of being ultimately part of a global community.

The subject is divided into the following units: human beings living together, social life, duties and rights of citizens, work as a social function and as a means of earning a living, and state and society. The first unit, human beings living together, is particularly relevant when it comes to affective education concerns, since it aims to help pupils learn about the ways in which human beings create various kinds of groups, the interdependent relationships that develop in the groups and the principle of mutual support, and to develop criteria and think critically about the rules and values governing an established society. The other units also include relevant aims. For instance, in social life they analyse the structure and function of the family in communities in general and the Greek community in particular, in order to develop the kind of attitudes that will enable them to participate creatively in the community, while the fostering of positive attitudes towards the principles and values of a democratic state is addressed in state and society.

Aesthetic education (Presidential Decree 53/10-4-90 FEK) is taught in all six grades of primary school. It is subdivided into three main areas of creative activities in the classroom, namely art, music and drama. The aim of aesthetic education is to enable the pupils to express their feelings and creativity and communicate with each other through the medium of expressive arts. Therefore, aesthetic education is another subject in the Greek curriculum that seems to share in part the aims and contents of affective education. Its objectives, as specified in the curriculum, are among others the following:

- to enable the pupils to give full expression to their personal experiences, thoughts and feelings
- to enable the pupils to develop progressively the capacity to appreciate and enjoy beauty in art as well as in nature
- to activate the pupils' creativity at all ages and encourage each one to express it in ways that mirror his or her particular talents and interests
- to acquaint the pupils with artistic treasures from Greece and from all other cultures, in order to develop their aesthetic appreciation and recognize artistic creations to be our common human heritage.

Looking at the three areas of creative activities separately, we also notice among the objectives a number which are relevant to the affective. In art the pupils should learn to appreciate their own capabilities as well as those of their peers, and are encouraged to create art works that satisfy their personal expressive needs; in music the pupils should learn and recognize music as a means for self-expression; and in drama the pupils express their creativity and acquire a clearer sense of self, discover new and more varied ways of communicating, get a better understanding of human interactions and relations and can connect their classroom experiences with the wider social and cultural environment.

The subject of religious studies (Presidential Decree 133/4-9-91 FEK) is taught in the last four grades of primary school. It aims to introduce the pupils to some basic beliefs of the Christian faith and help them to connect these beliefs to their everyday life experience. The subject's primary aim is to acquaint the pupils with the life and teachings of Jesus Christ and the Church. Nevertheless, considerable emphasis is placed on human life, its course and its meaning, making choices and facing their consequences. This aspect of religious studies is relevant for affective education, as it encourages the pupils to take a closer look at themselves as well as their peers. Among the subject's various aims the pupils are encouraged to understand, appreciate and cultivate feelings of love, true friendship, understanding and empathy towards their peers, so that they can encounter each other in openness and truth.

The subject of history (Presidential Decrees 186/19-10-87 FEK, 203/23-11-87 FEK, 226/6-10-89 FEK) is taught in the last four grades of primary school. Many of the units of this subject are partly related to the contents and aims of affective education, as they are concerned with the study of human beings in specific spatial and time contexts and their ways of forming social groups. Specifically, the pupils are encouraged

- to appraise critically both the positive and the negative acts of their ancestors, in order to develop the ability to participate in the life of their community, their country and the wider community of all nations in a free and responsible way
- to develop a feeling of love and respect towards democratic ideals and their country
- to identify the underlying causes and effects behind the various events that occurred in the histories of the Greek and other nations, learning about the traditions and values of these nations, throughout the centuries, and thus becoming better able to clarify and contextualize their own, in the present time.

The subject of geography (Presidential Decree 7/9-1-89 FEK) is taught in the last two grades of primary school. Its aim is to enable pupils to learn about the interrelations that exist between human beings and their spatial environment, within a global as well as a local perspective. Among the objectives that geography shares with affective education are: to help the pupils become aware of global problems that are faced by humans everywhere and of the importance of international co-operation in solving them, and to develop a love and respect not only for their own country but for the entire planet and the various nations that inhabit it.

The subject of natural sciences (Presidential Decree 140/1-8-85 FEK) is taught in the fifth and sixth grades of primary school. It is interesting to note the following aims: to develop the pupils' interest and inquisitiveness about the natural world in conjunction with the development of their capacity for creative thinking; to help the pupils become aware of the necessity of maintaining a balance between humans and the natural environment that is ultimately essential for the survival of human beings, and to foster in them certain attitudes, such as co-operative spirit, responsibility, perseverance, self confidence, etc. that would be helpful in the pursuit of knowledge in research. Thus it can be claimed that natural sciences shares some common aims with affective education in that it partly focuses on life, human or otherwise, and is concerned with interrelations and achieving a balance that may encompass divergent elements.

Lastly, the subject of physical education is taught in all six grades of primary school, and it may be considered as having very close links with affective education, as it focuses on the pupils' acquisition of a better sense of themselves and a more positive attitude. The clearer sense of self may result in better self-esteem and will consequently influence the pupils' social competence. Physical education aims to assist in the pupils' psychomotor development and ultimately enable them to integrate better in their peer group and the wider community. Among its various objectives, some also have relevance for affective education, such as helping the development of such qualities and attitudes as strength of will, perseverance, self-confidence, initiative, discipline, altruism and co-operation in the pursuit of various goals.

Looking critically at the aims of the Greek primary school, as stated in the curriculum, we can consider that the issues that concern affective education seem to have a dominant role both in the structure and the content of Greek primary education that appears to be essentially person-centred. By placing great importance in the development of the pupils' understanding of human beings in their natural and social environment, of social institutions (i.e. family, schools, state, etc.) and of cultural heritage, it enables them to appreciate the significance of human inter-dependence and to expand their communicative and relational capacities by encouraging their interaction within the learning process (Matsagouras, 1994; Vrettou and Kapsali, 1990; Gotovos, 1985).

SECONDARY EDUCATION

As mentioned earlier, secondary education in Greece is divided into the high school and the lyceum. High school consists of three grades and is part of compulsory education, involving children between the ages of 12 and 15; the lyceum also consists of three grades and is for young people between the ages of 15 and 18.

In secondary school, different subjects are taught by teachers whose studies have been in those specific fields. It is worth noting that, depending on their special field of expertise, secondary education teachers have received different amounts of pedagogic training. This is dependent on the university department they have graduated from. For example, those teaching science subjects and who have graduated from the science departments of Greek universities may not have had any pedagogic training at all, as this is not a compulsory unit of their courses. Of course, if they choose to have some pedagogic training they may do so, by taking an optional unit. On the other hand, those who teach the humanities will have had extensive pedagogic training, as at least one unit per academic year will have been compulsory in their courses.

Focusing on the curriculum frameworks of both high school and lyceum, we can see that some objectives of affective education are included in most lessons, but a number of these are stated in such a vague and general way that their implementation ultimately depends on the individual teacher, and his or her personality and proclivities. Of the various subjects taught in secondary education, we will concentrate here on those from the area of humanities and try to establish their connection with the aims of affective education. Our data are collected from a book issued by the Greek Institute of Pedagogics, under the auspices of the Greek Ministry of Education, where guidelines are set out concerning every individual lesson for the use of the teachers of secondary education (Greek Ministry of Education, Institute of Pedagogics, Department of Secondary Education, 1995–96, *Guidelines for the Teaching of Lessons in High School and Lyceum*, Athens, OEDV).

We will first examine the aims set out for the language and humanity subjects for the three grades of high school, namely ancient Greek literature, modern Greek language and literature, and history.

The subject of ancient Greek literature brings the students into contact with a number of very important human values, such as freedom in the context of a democratic society, the desire for self-knowledge and self-respect, respect for truth, love of beauty, the quest for knowledge and ultimately the value of human life. The main aim of this subject is to instruct students in the humanistic principles of understanding and experiencing the aforementioned values that have been passed on to us from our ancient ancestors (Kakridis, 1995; KEME, 1976, 1977).

More specifically, the subject aims to:

- develop the students' personalities in a well-rounded way, mentally, emotionally and morally
- bring the students in contact with, and instil in them admiration and respect for, the timeless creations of the ancient Greek civilization, so that the students may be moved and inspired by them
- teach the students the ideals and principles of democracy in order to prepare them for their future role as active members of a democratic society
- cultivate their aesthetic criteria and sensitize them to all expressions and manifestations of beauty.

The subject of modern Greek language and literature has the following aims among others:

- to instruct the students in the content, values and peculiarities of modern Greek culture in their positive as well as negative manifestations
- to enable them to encounter, and develop trust in, the creativity and vitality of contemporary Greek civilization, in order to become able to contribute towards its progress
- to acquire enough knowledge about contemporary Greek culture and civilization so as to be able to encounter other cultures and civilizations, whether the ancient Greek one or those of other nations, with a sense of confidence and equality
- to develop their appreciation of literature so as to be able to find pleasure in the beauty of language in its spoken and written forms
- to learn more about the psychological profile of the Greek people and thus to be better able to develop and understand their own selves
- to develop their own expressive capabilities and be able to express themselves fully, accurately, clearly and elegantly both in the written and the spoken form.

The subject of history has the following aims among others:

- to help students understand that the Greek as well as all other civilizations are the products of collective human endeavour, efforts and sacrifices
- to make them become aware of the fact that human beings live in historical time, and are indebted for much to the past and responsible for the shape of the future
- to make them realize that understanding the motivations behind the actions of individuals, groups and societies in the past helps us find better solutions to the problems and questions that face us today (Haritou, 1988; Prevelakis, 1982, 1983; Vorou, 1991; Leontsini, 1991).

Besides more specific objectives, the subject of philosophy also aims to develop the students' logical and creative thinking, their capacity to question and to form personal opinions and their ability to support these opinions in a debate.

During the last stage of secondary education, the three grades of the lyceum, we once more encounter the aims of affective education as being part of the aims of language and humanities subjects, this time in an even more expanded form. In the lyceum, the emphasis is placed on students' gaining personal experience of human values in the course of their school life, developing their personalities in a well-rounded way and acquiring a strong sense of responsibility towards their role as citizens of a free and democratic society.

More specifically, in the subject of modern Greek language and literature the aims that are shared with affective education are the same as in high school. Part of this subject is an element called free composition and essay writing. This is already practised in the three grades of high school, but even greater emphasis is placed on it during the lyceum years. Some of the objectives of free composition and essay writing are:

- to enable the students to acquire a wider knowledge of the flexibility and the nuances of the Greek language, so as to respond in any communicative context in an appropriate way
- to help them communicate their thoughts and opinions in a convincing way and examine all kinds of issues, particularly social ones, in a fearless and critical way while being able to propose constructive solutions
- to offer opportunities to the students to work on collaborative projects, in order to increase their capacity for collective work.

In the subject of history the aims are also similar to those in high school, with an even greater emphasis placed on the following:

- to teach the students to seek the reasons and the motives behind actions, to evaluate the results, to observe the contradictions and inconsistencies in the accounts of the various historians and their different viewpoints
- to encourage them to think critically and form their own opinions, which they should be able to express freely while respecting the differing opinions of others.

In the subject of philosophy the aims are similar to those in high school but extended and enlarged to encompass the students' greater maturity and capacities.

In the three grades of lyceum the students are taught the subject of psychology. In common with affective education, this subject aims to help the students gain a better understanding of themselves as individuals and as social beings and in particular help them realize the importance of interpersonal contacts and relationships in the formation of personality. The objective of the lesson is the study and understanding of human behaviour at an individual as well as a collective level. Among the aims of this subject are the following:

- to teach students about human beings and enable them to gain self knowledge
- to enable them better to understand their own behaviour and the behaviour of others
- to enable them better to appreciate the ways in which human beings are mutually influenced in a social context.

CONCLUSION

The official curriculum for the various subjects of primary and secondary education in Greece encompassses among its aims and contents some of the aims of affective education. The guidelines for the teachers urge them to approach their work by applying the knowledge and information to the needs of the individual student and his or her peer group, as well as the wider social group. Therefore the curriculum seems to be making provisions for affective education and the whole body of scholastic knowledge seems to be connected to the personalities of the students and their development.

Nevertheless, due to the comparatively open structure of the curriculum, the successful implementation and achievement of these aims depend to a great degree on the personality of the teachers and their capacity to handle the group dynamics in the classroom. This fact may work to the students' great benefit, as well as enabling teachers to experience themselves as active and creative members of the social group of their class, but it may also, on occasion, yield less than satisfactory results.

Additionally, it must be noted that this affinity for the aims of affective education and the comparative openness of the curriculum applies mostly to kindergarten, primary and high school, as for most types of lyceum the emphasis seems to shift towards academic achievement and the students' preparation for the very demanding examinations for admission to university.

Thus Greek education seems to be encompassing, to a significant degree, the aims of affective education and making appropriate allowances for their achievement, at least at the level of the official curriculum. However, self-understanding and one's relation to oneself is one aspect of affective education that does not seem to feature very prominently in the Greek curriculum, but as it is a core value of the ancient Greek culture that through the centuries has been transmitted to the modern Greek society, it can be expected that both students and teachers would show a considerable aptitude for including it in their approach to education. Additionally, due to the geographical location, the climate of the country and the cultural traditions, self-expression, communication and social skills are particularly developed in Greece.

The combination of all the above factors with the economic conditions and the need to survive contribute to the development of creativity and ingenuity that eventually offer the pupils and students the benefits of affective education of some intensity and quality. But more in-depth research as well as an effort in the area of teacher training is undoubtedly necessary to understand how intentions are turned into practice, to reinforce effective educational strategies, and to realize how students themselves experience the affective dimensions of education.

APPENDIX

Unit 1. Aims of environmental studies for the first grade of primary school

In the classroom
The process of adaptation by the pupils to their new environment is facilitated. They get to know their peers and are helped to achieve a greater understanding of their common elements, beyond apparent differences, and to develop among them co-operation, mutual support and love.

Classroom life
Pupils become familiar with the ways and means of working in the classroom, of learning and of enjoying themselves. They progressively develop their role within their peer group and learn their rights and obligations. They develop an interest and an emotional investment in the process of learning, in school life and in being part of a group.

Family life
The pupils explore the concept of family and its function as a social group. They progressively become more conscious of their own role within the family group and their potential and scope for contributing towards their family's well-being. They acquire a growing understanding of the need and value of family unity and familial love, while becoming aware of various kinds of problems and difficulties that can exist in a family.

Neighbourhood life
They learn about the persons, locations, buildings, etc. in their neighbourhood and develop a community spirit based on mutual respect, appreciation and the willingness to help their community.

Unit 2. Human beings in their geographical environment

Life in our city/town/village
The pupils are helped to identify specific life-styles and related problems in their local area, i.e. style of clothing, and its relation to both the landscape and the climate of the area, etc. They learn about the ways in which the people of the area are trying to improve their lives.

Unit 3. How human beings communicate

Transport
The pupils learn about the various means and ways of transport. They learn about basic traffic rules and signs and meet people who work in transport and learn to appreciate their contribution.

Communication

The pupils learn about the various means and ways of communication and acquire a hands-on experience of some them. By reference to specific instances they learn to appreciate the value of those means as well as the contribution made by people working in communications.

Unit 4. Human beings and plants

Why do we need plants?

The pupils learn about the value of plants for humans and are helped to develop a positive and respectful attitude towards the world of plants.

Unit 5. Human beings and animals

Why do we need animals?

The pupils learn about the value of animals for humans and are helped to develop a positive and respectful attitude towards the world of animals.

Unit 6. How do human beings satisfy their needs?

Needs of the growing child

The pupils are helped to become conscious of their basic needs and also of the fact that these are the same for all children in the world. They are assisted in developing mutual understanding and support.

Needs of the family

The pupils are helped to see the needs of a family as an extension of individual needs. They learn to appreciate the role of the family in meeting the child's needs.

Where do we get the things we need?

They are encouraged to develop a caring and protective attitude towards the natural resources and wealth of their area.

Unit 7. Human beings and machines

How do machines help us?

The pupils learn about the role machines play in the work field and in the production of various goods. They learn about the inventiveness of humans and the ways in which machines have been harnessed to the common good.

Seasonal units

The seasons

The pupils are helped to realize the ways in which their life is interconnected to the different seasons of the year. They are encouraged to explore their related experiences and feelings in a number of creative and expressive activities. They learn about the ways in which the various seasons affect the life work of the people in their community, as well as their effect on plant and animal life.

National events
The pupils are assisted in progressively developing a sense of social and national identity.

International events
The pupils become acquainted with international events and concerns. They are assisted in developing a spirit of community towards the other nations on the planet.

NOTE

1. A presidential decree is when the president of the republic gives the official seal of approval to a decision concerning any matter that has been proposed by a ministry, in this case the Ministry of Education, regardless of whether or not this decision has been previously discussed and endorsed by parliament.

REFERENCES

Chrysafides, K. (1994), *Experiential-Communicatory Teaching*, Athens: Gutenberg.
Georgopoulos, A. and Tsaliki, E. (1993), *Environmental Studies: Principles, Philosophy, Methodology*, Athens: Gutenberg.
Gotovos, A. (1985), *Educational Interaction*, Athens: Contemporary Education.
Haritou, H. (1988), 'From local history to self knowledge', *Ekpedeutica*, Vol. 12, 223–7.
Kakridis, E. (1995), *The Teaching of Homeric Poems*, Athens: OEDV.
KEME Proposals (1976), 2nd edn, Athens: OEDV.
KEME Proposals B (1977), Athens: OEDV.
Leontsini, G. (1991), *Local History and Environment*, Athens.
Matsagouras, E. (1994), *Teaching Strategies*, Athens.
Michalopoulou Dimaki, E. (1988), *Activities for the Kindergarten*, Athens.
Ministry of Education, Institute of Pedagogics, Department of Secondary Education (1995–6), *Guidelines for the Teaching of Lessons in High School and Lyceum*, Vol. A, Athens: OEDV.
Nova Kaltsouni, C. (1995), *Socialisation: The Genesis of the Social Subject*, Athens: Gutenberg.
Petroulakis, N. (1992), *Curriculum, Aims and Methodology*, Athens: Grigoris.
Prevelakis, E. (1982), 'Generalisation in History', *Mnemon*, Vol. 8, 107–16.
Prevelakis, E. (1983), 'The teaching of language through various lessons. The case of History', *Ekpedeutica*, Vol. 14, 192–203.
Vorou, F. (1991), 'Local history', *Ekpedeutica*, Vol. 20, 98–105.
Vrettou, G. and Kapsali, A. (1990), *The Know-how of Designing and Reforming the Analytical Curriculum*, Thessaloniki.

CHAPTER 7

The development of affective education in England

Ron Best

TOWARDS A DEFINITION

> **affect** *n.* (*Psych.*) feeling, emotion, desire, esp. as leading to action. [f. G *affekt* f. L *affectus* disposition ...]
>
> (*The Concise Oxford Dictionary*)

The use of the word 'affect' in the course of general conversation is rare, although the use of its derivatives (such as 'affectionate': a disposition to act from a kindly feeling or love towards one another) are more common. In psychology, the term is commonly used in conjunction with cognition (e.g. Clark and Fisk, 1982; Tomkins and Izard, 1966), but not so in educational discourse, where references to 'affective education' or 'affective learning' are infrequent.

For those of us who trained to be teachers during the 1960s, our main – or only – contact with this word was probably through the influential *Taxonomy of Educational Objectives* associated with the American psychologist and pedagogue, Benjamin Bloom (Krathwohl *et al.*, 1964). In this analysis of the aims and objectives identified by American teachers, the *affective domain* was one of three domains of human experience and development, the other two being the cognitive and the psycho-motor.

Teacher objectives falling within the affective domain were

> those which emphasize a feeling tone, an emotion, or a degree of acceptance or rejection. Affective objectives vary from simple attention to selected phenomena to complex but internally consistent qualities of character and conscience. [The authors] found a large number of such objectives in the literature expressed as interests, attitudes, appreciations, values and emotional sets or biases.
>
> (Krathwohl *et al.*, 1964, pp. 6–7)

Within this taxonomy, the concept of 'affect' has been elaborated to relate feeling-based dispositions to action to a range of human characteristics, expressed in concepts which bear a 'family resemblance' to feelings – emotions, appreciation and so on – and to values, beliefs, etc. which seem to underpin them.

The concept of affective education needs to be seen in this broad way. Thus the entry for 'Affective Learning of Adults' in the *International Encyclopedia of Education* defines affective learning as

> learning which allows the individual to understand and cope with his/her emotions in order to get more satisfaction from life ... Learning which reduces anxiety associated with phobias such as fear of animals and insects or fear of heights, is affective in nature. As an adult strives to manage his/her behaviour under stressful working conditions or learns to love more openly and be more loveable, affective learning is ... taking place.

(Simpson, 1985, p. 224)

All learning which is concerned with the emotions, feelings or passions that motivate, constrain or shape human action would qualify as 'affective learning', whether this concern is to develop, comprehend, constrain or come to terms with such dispositions.

Following the conceptual analysis of Peters (1964) and other philosophers of education in the 1960s, we may see affective education as the intentional and structured bringing about of affective learning, undertaken in ways which recognize the intellectual and moral autonomy of the learner.

THE SIGNIFICANCE OF AFFECTIVE LEARNING IN SCHOOLS

The concern of British educators for the development of the whole child has a long history. It is to be found in the commitments of the educational reformers of the late 18th and 19th centuries (Lang, 1982; Ribbins and Best, 1985), in the progressive educators of the present century (e.g in A. S. Neill's Summerhill School), in the advocates of comprehensive secondary schools in the 1950s and 1960s (e.g. Pedley, 1969; Miles, 1968) and in the thrust of the broadly child-centred approach to primary education, influenced by the great European educators (Froebel, Montessori), and legitimated in the Plowden Report (DES, 1967). Within such perspectives, the place of the emotions, often as part of a 'seamless robe' of learning experiences within integrated studies or topic work, was clearly of some importance.

The concept of the teacher in loco parentis is also testimony to the concern of educators for children as 'more than empty buckets to be filled with knowledge' (Haigh, 1975). In having both rights and obligations to respond to children's needs in the place of the parent, the teacher must necessarily be concerned with the affective domain.

The significance of the affective for education is threefold. First, it is arguable that a concern to educate the whole child necessarily means a concern to educate the emotions (or 'affects') themselves. However, within the UK, the teacher's role is most often associated with instruction in subject knowledge and the maintenance of discipline (Hargreaves, 1972, pp. 154–61)[1]. Second, emotional states (and the values, attitudes, sensitivities, etc. which underpin or express them) may promote or impede the child's learning in other domains. It is necessary to address emotional matters in order to promote learning within the curriculum. Children are ill-disposed to learn (say) geography if they are afraid, unhappy, anxious or depressed. Where emotional states lead to anti-social or disruptive behaviour, the learning of peers may also be hindered. In the UK it seems that rather less attention is given to the development of the emotions as an aspect of educating the whole person than is given to the effects of disaffection on pupil behaviour and achievement (Booth and Coulby, 1987). A central concept here is that of self-esteem, which seems to be linked directly to academic performance (Lawrence, 1988; Charlton, 1988).

Third, schools are institutions for socialization. The relationship between affects and moral values, successful social integration and effective interpersonal relations is powerful. In order to achieve the dual aims of social integration and personal development, schools must necessarily address the affective dimension of personal and social adaptation. In England and Wales, these concerns seem to be expressed in three dimensions of schools as institutions, and in three of the major roles which teachers play. These may be identified as the academic or curricular dimension, the pastoral or supportive dimension and the behavioural or disciplinary dimension.[2]

SOME INFLUENTIAL PERSPECTIVES

To understand the shape which affective education has taken in UK schools, one must appreciate that this is the outcome of an evolutionary process in which a number of separate traditions have been influential (Ribbins and Best, 1985). Some of these – those which reflect a holistic model of education as 'all-round development' through a curriculum broadly conceived as 'everything the child does in school' – have been noted above. There are other traditions which, I suggest, are in part shaped by professional roles and informed in varying degrees by different disciplines.

I conjecture that these traditions include those of counselling, curriculum innovation and pastoral care, and that although some writers and practitioners straddle the boundaries, these traditions may be related to three reasonably distinct groups.

Counsellors
Simpson (1985, p. 225) notes that

> of the three major families of learning theory, behaviourism, cognitivism, and humanism ... affective learning is most commonly associated with the last. Humanistic theory explains learning in terms of the total person and emphasizes perceived needs and the affective domain as essential elements in understanding the act of learning ...

He attributes this view to Carl Rogers (1961). For most people, I suspect, Rogers will be thought of more for his contribution to the model of client-centred, non-directive counselling than to his educational theory, but the connection between counselling and education is an important one. Informed principally by psychology, counselling emphasizes the emotional and psychological state of the learner as significant both for successful performance within the curriculum and satisfactory social integration.

During the 1960s and early 1970s, a considerable number of teachers and others underwent counsellor-training (Daws, 1967), and a good many of them found their way into schools where they worked more or less independently from the teachers. Not all were Rogerian by any means, and some were more fully integrated than others into the curricular work of the school (Hamblin, 1974; Milner, 1980; Best *et al.*, 1983, pp. 174–85).

The influence of the counselling perspective is also to be seen in the work of the careers and child guidance services provided by local education authorities. These agencies serve as part of a 'welfare network' with which schools interface (Johnson *et al.*, 1980).

The political and economic climate of the 1970s and 1980s checked and reversed the trend towards schools having resident counsellors, but the influence of the counsellor perspective has been considerable, not least through in-service courses in counselling skills for teachers. This has made an impact on teachers' performance as form tutors, heads of year, etc. in what is sometimes known as pastoral casework (Watkins, 1985).

Curriculum innovators

The 1960s and 1970s witnessed a number of significant curriculum reforms. Very often initiated and supported by independent bodies such as the Schools Council, a government-supported body upon which teachers comprised the majority, these typically involved the analysis and redefining of specific subjects, the advocacy of new or additional subjects, or the integration and restructuring of old ones (Hargreaves *et al.*, 1988, p. 32).

Perhaps the best-known of these was the Humanities Curriculum Project (Schools Council/Nuffield Foundation, 1970). This set out to devise an integrated scheme for teaching about issues of social, political and moral concern, in a value-neutral way, to secondary pupils of average and below average ability. The topics considered were personally significant, politically sensitive and potentially controversial. The affective domain was well-represented in the consideration of emotive issues such as war, education, poverty and race. Other projects in careers education and guidance, Health Education 13–18 (Williams and Williams, 1980), and personal and social education (David, 1982) were similarly concerned with the values and attitudes to self, others and society which are part and parcel of the child's affective dispositions.

Those involved in careers guidance and counselling advocated the development of careers education as a broader, more developmental experience than the more instrumental vocational guidance which was common in earlier times (e.g. Law and Watts, 1977). They also promoted what might be generally labelled as 'life and social skills' (e.g. Hopson and Scally, 1981; Hopson and Hough, 1979), where the emphasis is placed on self-determination through rational and informed choice in social contexts.

Although some of these initiatives have foundered, lapsed, or been revised beyond recognition, as in some cases have their originating institutions (e.g. the Schools Council), their influence on today's curriculum has been considerable. This is especially so in regard to the tutorial programmes and courses in personal and social education (PSE) which make up what is sometimes known as the 'pastoral curriculum' in secondary schools (Marland, 1980).

If psychology is the educational discipline which chiefly informs the counselling perspective, I suggest that philosophy and curriculum studies jointly inform the work of the curriculum innovators. Thus the work of people like Stenhouse and Pring is grounded in rigorous philosophical analysis of, for example, education as emancipation (Stenhouse, 1983), and/or takes the conceptual analysis of the 'self' or 'person' (Pring, 1984, 1989) as their starting point for considering the shape which the curriculum ought to take. Their work also appears to reflect the influence of such curriculum theorists as Lawton (1978, 1983) in making their selection from the culture for inclusion within it. More recently, White and others at the University of London Institute of Education have begun to examine the underlying assumptions about the nature and aims of personal and social education (White, 1989).

Pastoral carers

The origins of the pastoral perspective seem to lie more in the professional teacher than in any of the foundations disciplines *per se*. Among the most influential contributors to this field in the early days were prestigious practioners – headteachers and their deputies – rather than academics or specialists in related fields (such as counselling). In particular, we may note the seminal books of Marland (1974), Blackburn (1975) and Haigh (1975), which articulated the caring roles which teachers play typically as form tutors or heads of year/house/division in secondary schools. The thrust of their work was to advocate good practice based on their own experience in schools, and informed in a fairly eclectic way by a mixture of psychology, sociology and common-sense. The same appears true of those who came later and whose concern was more critical and theoretical (e.g. Best *et al.*, 1977; Lang, 1977). Typically, their origins were in secondary teaching and, later, teacher training.

The history of pastoral care in the 1970s and 1980s charts the transition from professionally informed but largely unresearched prescription to a literature of technique and critique (Lang, 1983; Ribbins and Best, 1985), and from a concern with discipline and casework towards a more developmental and pro-active stance on the desirability of a pastoral curriculum (Marland, 1980). Throughout this period, the understanding and practice of form-tutors and their pastoral 'middle-managers' became more sophisticated and, through the creation of the National Association for Pastoral Care, more professionalized.

However, the pastoral role of the teacher remains to some extent a divided one, for the casework dimension (influenced by the perspective of counselling) and the curriculum dimension (influenced by the perspective of the curriculum innovators) remain to some degree separate within many school structures. Thus form-tutors, identified as the first line of support for children with problems of a personal, social or emotional kind, may or may not be involved in the delivery of curricula in personal and social education. They are, however, typically required to teach tutorial programmes of more or less formality.

A significant factor in the development of affective education among the 'pastoral carers' has been the more or less commercial production of tutorial programmes. The influence of the Lancashire County Council/Blackwell *Active Tutorial Work* (Baldwin, Wells and Smith, 1979–83) deserves special note. As the first of a new kind of comprehensive and staged programme of exercises designed specifically for the 15- to 30-minute daily form period which characterized most secondary schools at the time, its title soon became synonymous with tutorial work generally. Rightly or wrongly, all subsequent series (e.g. *Group Tutoring for the Form Teacher*, Button, 1982; *Longman Tutorial Resources*, Watkins, Marsh, Dolezal, Leake and Leake, 1989) tend to be seen as a development or up-dating of this concept.

AFFECTIVE EDUCATION IN SCHOOLS

One might expect the interplay of these various perspectives, against a background of a holistic view of the teacher's role *in loco parentis*, and of the intellectual and moral appeal of the idea of educating the whole child, to have produced a coherent, unified and comprehensive educational experience for our children. Moreover, within such enlightened traditions, one might expect affective education to receive its proper due. In fact, the situation is a great deal less tidy than this.

For one thing, there are significant differences between private and public (i.e. state) education. The former, being subject to less rigorous scrutiny and less state control, is very variable indeed.[3] No doubt many independent schools offer a curriculum and pastoral care which are comparable to those of the state sector; however, there are in all likelihood others where standards of both learning and support are less satisfactory. Second, there is a significant discontinuity between primary and secondary schooling (Curran, 1993) and, where they exist, between first, middle and upper schools. In secondary schools there is a degree of specialization of function and division of labour between staff according to the extent to which they carry responsibilities for an aspect of the curriculum (the 'academic' dimension) and personal and social support (the 'pastoral' dimension). To some extent this is reflected in alternative career ladders for secondary teachers. At its worst, this may comprise a 'pastoral–academic split' (Best and Ribbins, 1983), which is counterproductive in a number of ways.

No such split seems evident in primary schools. This may be because primary schools are sufficiently small not to require a structural division of the pastoral and the academic; because no differentiation of the primary career ladder in these terms exists; or because the relative immaturity of primary children makes the distinction between 'academic' or subject-based learning and social/personal/moral development inappropriate (Best and Curran, 1995). The Plowden Report's concept of the primary school as a supportive and facilitative environment aiming to develop the 'whole child' through experiential learning took its contribution to personal and social development for granted. A powerful influence on the Committee's deliberations was the Froebelian tradition of early childhood education (Liebschner, 1991, pp. 153–5). The emphasis given by Froebel and Froebelians both to play as 'a child's work' (Liebschner, 1992) and to the integrity of all human experience in unity with Nature is clearly in tension with such distinctions as those between curriculum subjects and 'extra-curricular activities', and between teaching subjects and caring for children, which typify the secondary tradition.

In any event, the vocabulary of pastoral care which is generally shared by those who teach in secondary schools has limited currency in the primary sector, although some recent publications suggest that this situation may be changing (David and Charlton, 1987; NICC, 1989).

Casework, in both primary and secondary schools, is a significant occasion for affective learning. In making the valid point that 'prevention is better than cure', or, as Hamblin (1978) has argued, that 'emotional first-aid' is no substitute for well-timed courses in making friends, study skills or decision-making, it is easy to underestimate the amount of learning which goes on when an individual is being counselled or morally supported in other ways. Whether the 'case' is presented as an emotional, interpersonal or behavioural problem, the child may learn a great deal about her or his feelings, values and attitudes while being 'treated' by the teacher or the specialist to whom referred.

Within both primary and secondary schools, some affective education is achieved through the curriculum conventionally conceived as the subjects teachers teach. One might speak sensibly of 'affective education across the curriculum' when one considers that the following are to some extent taken for granted:

- the development of aesthetic appreciation through art, music and literature
- the promotion of empathy through literature and history, and the accompanying development of moral concepts and dispositions
- the development, appreciation, expression and control of the emotions through educational drama
- the mastery of such emotions and dispositions as timidity and the fear of physical intimidation through games and physical education
- opportunities to reflect upon more or less deeply felt feelings of spirituality and religious belief in Religious Education
- growing self-confidence and self-understanding achieved through any subject where the pedagogy is appropriate.

In primary schools, learning activities which enhance self-esteem and develop social skills may be invisibly interwoven with the teaching of the formal curriculum. Sometimes, they are also addressed quite consciously to overcome affective states which are antagonistic to learning and symptomatic of deficiencies in social skills (for example, see chapters by Charlton, Wooster, Rushton, Braddy and others in Lang, 1988).

The affective is more visibly and more directly addressed in secondary schools in those subjects which have a 'pastoral flavour': personal and social education, careers education, health education, moral education, etc. (nowadays most usually encapsulated in the umbrella concept of 'PSE').[4] Here, the exploration of one's own feelings, values, attitudes, beliefs, fears and hopes, often linked to rational and moral decision-making on the one hand, and the enhancement of self-esteem on the other, is central to the teacher's purpose.

Here we must note that the last eight years have seen significant changes in the statutory obligations of schools where the affective domain is concerned. Under the requirements of the National Curriculum, the opportunities for some affective learning may be being restricted through an emphasis on a more formal and traditional approach to subject teaching. Cases in point are English literature in secondary school and History across all ages. In the former, the prescription of a set of 'approved' novels, plays and poetry from which the teacher must select may impede the study of other literary works preferred by teachers precisely because they bring about particular affective states, or raise particular values and attitudes on which they would like children to reflect. In the latter, the teaching of history by getting children to identify and empathize with (for example) children in Victorian London may be squeezed out by a return to the more factual and sequential pattern commonly known as 'Kings and Queens'.

However, the architects of the National Curriculum designed a number of 'cross-curricular elements' – dimensions, skills and themes – which schools were required to address in their curriculum planning (NCC, 1990). Affective learning was implicit or explicit within a number of these. They included:

> *dimensions* such as a commitment to providing equal opportunities for all pupils, and a recognition that preparation for life in a multicultural society is relevant to all pupils, should permeate every aspect of the curriculum.
>
> (NCC, 1990, p. 3, my italics)

This was explicitly related to affective states in the following example:

> … introducing multicultural perspectives into a curriculum is a way of enriching the education of all our pupils. It gives pupils the opportunity to view the world from different standpoints, helping them to question prejudice and develop open-mindedness.
>
> (NCC, 1990, p. 3)

Personal and social skills received specific mention under cross-curricular skills, and four of the five cross-curricular themes appear to have been derived from the curriculum innovations of the 1960s and 1970s noted above: careers education and guidance, health education, education for citizenship and environmental education. These emphasized the encouragement of self-knowledge and the promotion of 'positive and responsible attitudes' (NCC, 1990, p. 6), and of a concern for the well-being of self and others.

Whether or not the requirement that schools address such themes would significantly have improved the quality of affective education may never be known,[5] not least because the subsequent revision of the National Curriculum under Sir Ron Dearing reduced their status to that of options (SCAA, 1995, p. 8). However, in a general switch of emphasis from curriculum planning towards curriculum accountability, schools now find the provision they make for spiritual, moral, social and cultural development subjected to particular scrutiny by the Office for Standards in Education (OFSTED, 1994). In a move which seeks to put the planning 'horse' back before the accountability 'cart', the body which replaced the NCC (the Schools Curriculum and Assessment Authority or SCAA) has responded with a discussion paper of its own (SCAA, 1996). The future of what we have termed 'affective education' within this volatile context remains to be seen.

IN CONCLUSION

There is, I think, a relative neglect of the emotions in the mainstream of UK schooling. Given that our motivations to act are so often (always?) in the realm of feelings, sentiments or passions, rather than in the cold, clinical exercise of the intellect, this deserves explanation.

Historically, it may be accounted for in terms of the pervasive influence of the Enlightenment in European culture, and of those traditions of thought which Raymond Williams charts through the Industrial Revolution and beyond (Williams, 1961). In more recent times, a preoccupation with national economic competitiveness has led to a greater emphasis on science and technology in the curriculum, with rational efficiency prized above the more 'feminine' qualities of the arts and humanities. It may not be too fanciful even to invoke the supposed national trait of British reserve – the 'stiff upper lip' – as part explanation for this neglect. Be that as it may, the Romantic challenge to intellectualism seems something of a rear-guard action; certainly it appears less powerful today than it did even thirty years ago.

The core of the curriculum remains a mixture of factual knowledge, cognitive operations and technological competences. The consideration of values, beliefs, emotions and sentiments is almost always subordinate. Affective states may be exploited as a means of cognitive development, as in the use of empathy as a method of teaching history rather than as an end in itself; or they may be addressed in individual casework as non-rational impediments to cognitive development; or they may be accorded a place in the curriculum but as after-thoughts in the cross-curricular periphery of the core and foundation subjects. I consider this to be a less than satisfactory state of affairs.

The counselling tradition alone has provided educators with more than sufficient grounds for placing the affective domain more centrally in teachers' work, and the best practice in pastoral care and PSE does this. Such a view is out of tune with the times, and for the foreseeable future the prognosis is not good. True, there is a new-found interest – not least on the part of SCAA, OFSTED and successive Secretaries of State for Education (e.g. Patten, 1992) – in developing morality and spirituality through the curriculum. However, there are indications that this is to be achieved less through courses in personal, social and moral education than through pressure for a more structured and more absolutist curriculum in religious education, together with a restatement of the requirement for daily collective acts of worship. In these contexts, I suspect more weight will be given to promoting conformity and obedience to moral rules than to the exploration of the emotional states with which spiritual conviction and moral passion are associated.

Schools may frequently claim to be committed to 'the education of the whole child'. If such claims are to be more than mere rhetoric, the architects of the school curriculum need to take much greater account of the affective domain than they currently do.

NOTES

1. It is indicative of a certain neglect of affective education in regard to the school curriculum, that the *International Encyclopedia of Education* has entries for affective education of adults, and of student-teachers, but not of children.
2. In a model which has been much revised over the years (see, for example, Best, R. *et al.*, 1983; Best and Ribbins, 1983; Lang and Ribbins, 1985; Best, 1989; Best, 1990), these are presented as three dimensions of the school's pastoral work. There is a fourth: management, which may be thought of as the organization and administration of the infrastructure within which the curricular, pastoral and disciplinary functions are performed.
3. My comments are limited to the state sector as I have experienced it. For reports of fairly recent evaluations of pastoral care and PSE in state secondary schools, see HMI, 1988; 1989.
4. The precise titles of such courses vary from school to school. PSHE (to include Health) and PSME (to include Moral) are common, as are the titles of commercially available programmes (for example Skills for Adolescence).
5. For two recent and critical analyses of cross-curricular elements in the National Curriculum, see Dufor (1990) and Buck and Inman (1992).

REFERENCES

Baldwin, J., Wells, H. and Smith, A. (1979–83), *Active Tutorial Work* (6 vols), Lancashire County Council/Basil Blackwell.

Best, R. (1989), 'Pastoral care: some reflections and a restatement', *Pastoral Care in Education*, Vol. 7, No. 4.

Best, R. (1990), 'Pastoral care in schools: some implications for teacher training', *Australian Journal of Teacher Education*, Vol. 15, No. 1.

Best, R. and Curran, C. (1995), *The Caring Teacher in the Junior School*, London: Roehampton Institute. CEDARR Occasional Paper No. 1.

Best, R. and Ribbins, P. (1983), 'Rethinking the pastoral–academic split', *Pastoral Care in Education*, Vol. 1, No. 1.

Best, R., Jarvis, C. and Ribbins, P. (1977), 'Pastoral care: concept and process', *British Journal of Educational Studies*, XXV, No. 2.

Best, R., Ribbins, P., Jarvis, C. with Oddy, D. (1983), *Education and Care*, London: Heinemann.

Blackburn, K. (1975), *The Tutor*, London: Heinemann.

Booth, T. and Coulby, D. (eds) (1987), *Producing and Reducing Dissaffection*, Milton Keynes: Open University Press.

Buck, M. and Inman, S. (1992), *Whole School Provision for Personal and Social Development: The Role of the Cross-curricular Elements*, London: Goldsmiths' College.

Button, L. (1982), *Group Tutoring for the Form Teacher*, London: Hodder and Stoughton.

Charlton, T. (1988), 'Using counselling skills to enhance children's personal, social and academic functioning', in P. Lang (ed.), *Thinking About ... Personal and Social Education in the Primary School*, Oxford: Basil Blackwell.

Clark, M. S. and Fisk, S. T. (eds) (1982), *Affect and Cognition*, Hillsdale, New Jersey: Erlbaum Associates.

Curran, C. (1993), The Management of Induction: *Caring for Children at the Point of Transfer from Primary to Secondary Schooling*, Paper presented to the annual conference of the British Educational Research Association, University of Liverpool, September, 1993.

David, K. (1982), *Personal and Social Education in Secondary Schools*, London: Longman/Schools Council.

David, K. and Charlton, C. (1987), *The Caring Role of the Primary School*, London: Macmillan Education.

Daws, P. P. (1967), 'What will the school counsellor do?', *Educational Research*, Vol. 9, No. 2.

DES (1967), *Children and their Primary Schools*, London: HMSO [The Plowden Report].

Haigh, G. (1975), *Pastoral Care*, London: Pitman Publishing.

Hamblin, D. (1974), *The Teacher and Counselling*, Oxford: Blackwell.

Hargreaves, A., Baglin, E., Henderson, P., Leeson, P. and Tossell, T. (1988), *Personal and Social Education: Choices and Challenges*, Oxford: Basil Blackwell.

Hargreaves, D.H. (1972), *Interpersonal Relations and Education*, London: Routledge.

HMI (1988), *A Survey of Personal and Social Education Courses in Some Secondary Schools*, report by HM Inspectors, Stanmore, Middlesex: DES.

HMI (1989), *Pastoral Care in Secondary Schools: An Inspection of Some Aspects of Pastoral Care in 1987–88*, report by HM Inspectors, Stanmore, Middlesex: DES.

Hopson, B. and Hough, P. (1979), *Exercises in Personal and Career Development*, 3rd edn, Cambridge: Careers Research and Advisory Centre.

Hopson, B. and Scally, M. (1981), *Life Skills Teaching*, London: McGraw Hill.

Johnson, D., Ransome, E., Packwood, T., Bowden, K. and Kogan, M. (1980), *Secondary Schools and the Welfare Network*, Hemel Hempstead: Unwin Educational.

Krathwohl, D. R., Bloom, B. S. and Masia, B. B. (1964), *Taxonomy of Educational Objectives*, London: Longman.

Lang, P. (1977), 'It's easier to punish us in small groups', *Times Educational Supplement*, June.

Lang, P. (1982), 'Pastoral Care: some reflections on possible influences', *Pastoral Care in Education*, Vol. 2, No. 2.

Lang, P. (1983), 'Perspectives on Pastoral Care', *Pastoral Care in Education*, Vol. 1, No. 1. Review of R. Best *et al.* (ed.) (1980), *Perspectives on Pastoral Care*, London: Routledge.

Lang, P. (1988), *Thinking about PSE in the Primary School*, Oxford: Blackwell.

Lang, P. and Ribbins, P. (1985), 'Pastoral care in education', *International Encyclopedia of Education*, Oxford: Pergamon.

Law, B. and Watts, A. G. (1977), *Schools, Career and Community: A Study of Some Approaches to Careers Education in Schools*, London: CIO Publishing.

Lawrence, D. (1988), *Enhancing Self-esteem in the Classroom*, London: Paul Chapman.

Lawton, D. (1978), *Theory and Practice of Curriculum Studies*, London: RKP Longman/SCDC Publications.

Lawton, D. (1983), *Curriculum Studies and Educational Planning*, London: Hodder and Stoughton.

Liebschner, J. (1991), *The Foundations of Progressive Education*, Cambridge: Lutterworth.

Liebschner, J. (1992), *A Child's Work*, Cambridge: Lutterworth.

Marland, M. (1974), *Pastoral Care*, London: Heinemann.

Marland, M. (1980), 'The pastoral curriculum', in R. Best *et al.* (ed.), *Perspectives on Pastoral Care*, London: Heinemann.

Miles, M. (1968), *Comprehensive Schooling: Problems and Perspectives*, London: Longmans Green and Company.

Milner, P. (1980), 'Changing patterns of care in schools', in R. Best *et al.* (ed.), *Perspectives on Pastoral Care*, London: Heinemann.

NCC (1990), *Curriculum Guidance 3: The Whole Curriculum*, York: National Curriculum Council.

NICC (1989), *The Pastoral Dimension of the Primary School*, Belfast: Northern Ireland Curriculum Council.

OFSTED (1994), *Spiritual, Moral, Social and Cultural Development*, London: Office for Standards in Education. OFSTED discussion paper.

Patten, J. (1992), 'Don't sell pupils short', *The Tablet*, 10 October.

Pedley, R. (1969), *The Comprehensive School*, Harmondsworth: Penguin.

Peters, R. S. (1964), *Ethics and Education*, London: Allen and Unwin.

Pring, R. (1984), *Personal and Social Education in the Curriculum*, Sevenoaks: Hodder and Stoughton Educational.

Pring, R. (1989), 'Developing personal and social education in schools', in R. Best, P. Maher, G. Baderman, K. Kirby, A. Osbourne and P. Rabbett (eds) *Whole Person: Whole School*, London/York: Longman/SCDC Publications.

Ribbins, P. and Best, R. (1985), 'Pastoral care: theory, practice and the growth of research', in P. Lang and M. Marland (eds), *New Directions in Pastoral Care*, Oxford: Basil Blackwell/NAPCE.

Rogers, C. (1961), *On Becoming a Person: A Therapist's View of Psychotherapy*, Boston, Mass: Houghton Mifflin.

SCAA (1995), *Planning the Curriculum at Key Stages 1 and 2*, London: Schools Curriculum and Assessment Authority.

SCAA (1996), *Education for Adult Life: The Spiritual and Moral Development of Young People*, London: Schools Curriculum and Assessment Authority Discussion Paper No. 6.

Schools Council/Nuffield Foundation (1970), *The Humanities Project: An Introduction*, London: Schools Council.

Simpson, E. L. (1985), 'Affective Learning in Adults', *International Encyclopedia of Education*, Oxford: Pergamon.

Stenhouse, L. (1983), *Authority, Education and Emancipation: A Collection of Papers*, London: Heinemann.

Tomkins, S. T. and Izard, C. E. (eds) (1966), *Affect, Cognition and Personality*, London: Tavistock.

Watkins, C. (1985), 'Does pastoral care = personal and social education?', *Pastoral Care in Education*, Vol. 3, No. 3.

Watkins, C., Marsh, L., Dolezal, A. and Leake, A. (1989), *Longman Tutorial Resources* (6 vols), Harlow: Longman.

White, P. (ed.) (1989), *Personal and Social Education: Philosophical Perspectives*, London: Kogan Page/The Institute of Education, University of London.

Williams, T. and Williams, N. (1980), *Personal and Social Development in the School Curriculum*, London: Longman/Schools Council.

CHAPTER 8

Affective education and the new Spanish educational reforms

Ana Martínez Pampliega and
Manuel Marroquín

INTRODUCTION

The legacy of the last fifty years of Spanish history presents a significant challenge to Spanish educationalists. This challenge involves trying to develop education that integrates ethics, morality and values in the process of overall personal development of pupils, and which does not just focus on the intellectual aspects, in a situation where for many years work of the former kind was neglected.

Current educational reforms in Spain are very significant in relation to this. These reforms have as their overall objectives the improvement of the quality of teaching. They are clearly concerned with promoting the personal development of pupils in relation to information, abilities and moral values in their personal, family, social and professional life. This is one of the key aims expressed in the General Ordination Law of the Educative System (LOGSE, 1990).

This aim can be seen as having three aspects:

- to awake in pupils the joy of living.
- to promote attitudes that encourage the development of individuals who can live in harmony with themselves and with others.
- the creation of a homogeneous society in which social relationships are more harmonious and a greater humanity exists.

To this end, Spain is embarking on reforms that include the development of moral values and moral education. There are two main lines of intervention through which these reforms seek to achieve these objectives, tutorial and guidance work, and the development of cross-curricular themes.

Tutorial and guidance work

Every teacher is seen not only as an instructor and transmitter of information, but as a true educator with a concept of education for personal development that embraces the physical, affective, social and intellectual dimensions of the person.

Cross-curricular themes
The cross-curricular themes are specific curricular proposals. In the new curriculum not only concepts, but also methods, values, attitudes and rules are included. Cross-curricular themes are intended to operate as continuous strands of experience which serve to heighten awareness. They involve areas of social and personal experience and the basic development of the ethical dimension of the person.

In this paper we will consider each of these initiatives and then briefly illustrate the way they are taking place using work that is being carried out at Deusto University as an example. First, however, it is important to understand the history of affective education in Spain if we are to understand the role that it plays today.

THE PRESENT SITUATION OF AFFECTIVE EDUCATION IN SPAIN

The significance attached to affective education in Spain today is the result of a long process which at times has been very active and at others more or less inactive.

Martín suggests that in Spain we have moved from an authoritarian state to a democratic one. The transition to democracy and its subsequent consolidation and development have taken place in an atmosphere of political tension and economic and social problems. Today, Spain is a modern democratic state, fully accepted and integrated in Europe (San Martín and Paniagua, 1989).

During this period, education has been one of the key elements in the process and has made a significant contribution to the development of a democratic society, not only because it encourages knowledge and adoption of the values that ensure freedom, participation and co-existence, but also because it provides 'a laboratory in which to practise and design ways to initiate children, young people and even adults into the social and democratic life of their country' (Ballesteros, 1989, p. 9). This has meant a great change from the approaches prevailing only twenty years ago.

Until quite recently, education was the privilege of the few, a situation which in 1970, when Spain was still under Franco's dictatorship, was amended by long-awaited educational reform, introduced through the General Education Law (Ley General de Educación) also called the Villar Law (Ley Villar). This arose from the urgent need to improve the population's low educational level in order to produce skilled people for the roles demanded by an industrial society.

The establishment of compulsory free unified basic education was among the main features of the law. It also enabled private schools to offer free tuition within the compulsory levels with economic support from the government. In this way, the support with public funds of compulsory education began, and it was developed till it reached all types of education, despite the relative stagnation of the public sector. On the other hand, this law involved a technocratic conception of the curriculum, and during this period education was restricted to a mainly instructional mode.

The political, social and economic changes which began from 1975 onwards forced the newly formed political parties to discuss alternatives to the Villar Act (Ley Villar). The new Spanish constitution of 1978 provided the normative context that integrated the different educational options, and set out the rights and liberties that should be innate to education. Hereafter, the following was assured: the right to education, free education, the parent's right to choose the pertinent religious and moral education, freedom of conscience, the participation of teachers, parents and students in the control of schools and the right to found new schools.

In short, this constitution was intended to democratize the education system, introducing fundamental rights and liberties (Ballesteros, 1989). And, of course, it also implied the responsibility of the public sector to create an overall programme for education which would guarantee every single person a place in school.

There are some points of particular significance about the aims that underpin the constitution. After a partial development of these provisions by the Ley Orgánica del Estatuto de Centros Escolares (LOECE) in 1980 (Ley Orgánica are basic laws and statutes affecting individual rights and duties, approved by parliament and giving legal effect to the constitution), the Ley Orgánica del Derecho a la Educación (LODE) drawn up by the socialist government sought to establish once and for all the rights and liberties that should underpin education supported by the constitution. This law was passed by parliament in 1984 and came into force in 1985. In accordance with it, education should be based on the principles of freedom, tolerance, pluralism, participation and equality. This demonstrated a progressive interpretation of the constitutional mandate.

However, there are still substantial problems such as those highlighted by Santa-Cruz and Bejarano (1989, p. 252):

- A lack of humanistic projects in actual practice can be detected. The type of person which education should develop is still unclear.
- Education should be for everybody, but it is still enjoyed by very few.
- The educational system does not encourage a longing to learn.
- A critical approach is not favoured.
- Developing democracy in school cannot be achieved by 'law'.
- Changes are more apparent than real.

There was a need for more profound changes that would move education towards the aim of creating individuals through and capable of participating in the democratic process.

As Fernández and Mayordomo pointed out (1993), democratizing education means not only having classrooms full of children or young students, regardless of their social or economic status, in order to provide equality of opportunity, but also involves the necessary conditions for their human and personal development. In a democratic society, education should contribute to creating or consolidating a democratic culture. Therefore, if the school is to be democratized, critical reasoning, appreciation of other viewpoints, and group cohesion must be encouraged. And since it is both a 'community' and 'personal' democracy, education must be personalized. That is, a democratic school should aim to encourage the development of every individual and should educate the person as a whole, to facilitate a holistic education. In this type of school, moral education has great relevance but it must be developed in a way that promotes personal autonomy.

Only an education which is based on critical reasoning will succeed in being democratic in its broadest sense (Fernández and Mayordomo, 1993). This entails education that stimulates those values, knowledge and attitudes appropriate for democratic actions, 'a development of new educational ways which set goals such as that of educating for social responsibility, for a critical turn of mind, for peace and co-existence, for a disposition to dialogue, for deliberation and agreement, for the understanding of social and political issues, etc. It is also an education for other deeper values than those which are purely instrumental and that provide the opportunity for developing habits and attitudes, human resources, which are linked to a democratic society' (p. 158).

It is within this context that the educational reforms which have recently been put forward by the LOGSE (General Ordination Law of the Education System) should be understood and it is intended to make education the basic means to achieve a new, plural, free, participatory, more democratic society.

The nature of this reform will now be considered and the way in which it seeks to give greater significance to the affective dimension in Spanish education.

DEVELOPING AFFECTIVE EDUCATION IN SPANISH EDUCATION

As has been said, two main initiatives have been proposed to promote the development of affective education, each of which will now be considered in detail:

Tutorial and guidance work

The tutorial function and educational guidance refer to the personal dimension of education which involves two elements (Ministerio de Educación y Ciencia, 1992):

- *Individualization*: Education must be directed to the individual who has particular characteristics instead of generic collectives.
- *Integration*: the whole person is being educated and, therefore, the different aspects of development, personal, social, affective and cognitive, must be responded to in an integrated way.

Such an approach to education is contrasted with:

- The compartmentalization of knowledge, typical of traditional schooling.
- The lack of attention to the pupil's individual personality, treating them as just a number in the classroom.

So what we understand by the tutorial function means bringing to the fore those characteristics of education in which it is not reduced to mere instruction and, in fact, constitutes individualized education of the whole person. Thus every teacher should provide guidance and in particular the tutor.

The tutorial duty of every teacher is to integrate, balance, personalize and support education in general. This means that the teacher should offer:

- to be a guide to the pupil not only in his or her study, but also in his or her personal development and in the search for a fulfilling way of life
- a relationship which offers the potential of counselling support and the interpretation of experience.

It is not easy to make a distinction between the generic tutorial responsibilities of every teacher and the ones assigned to the teacher designated as a group tutor. There are wide shared areas regarding the tutorial responsibility of all teachers. However, the degree of systematization, globality, co-ordination and dedication required to the tutor includes specific functions.

Educational guidance partly overlaps with tutoring, although it covers a wider and more specialized field. 'Tutorial can be considered as a part of the guidance activity that underpins the whole educative process' (Ministerio de Educación y Ciencia, 1992, p. 15). As with tutorial work, the best educational guidance is part of personal and holistic education. Therefore, under the title 'Tutorial and Orientation' are included elements that are intentionally and systematically incorporated into teaching practice (Gobierno Vasco, 1992, p. 18), as it is expressed in the Order of 13 August 1992 (LOGSE).

The objectives are:

- To contribute to the personalization of education, which is to say, to its holistic aspect, favouring the development of all aspects of the person, and also contributing to an individualized education, directed to individuals with their different aptitudes and interests.
- To adjust the educational responses to the particular needs of the pupils, through the necessary curricular and pedagogical adaptations, accommodating the school to the students and not the students to the school.
- To highlight the guidance aspects of education – guidance in life and for life – paying attention to the real context in which the pupils live, to the future that awaits them and the ways that they can contribute to the project for themselves. In order to achieve this, the teachers have to favour the presentation of more appropriate topics, more related to the pupils' experience, so that the school provides a real 'education for life'.
- To encourage the personal process of maturation, development of self-identity and a value system, and the progressive decision-making that will prepare pupils to make decisions in life.
- To anticipate learning difficulties and act appropriately, and not just react when they arise, to take the same approach to issues such as isolation, failure and resistance to school.
- To contribute to the adequate relationship and interaction between

individuals, integrating the educational community: teachers, pupils and parents; and between the educational community and its social environment, assuming a mediating role and even a negotiating role, if needed, whenever faced with problems or conflicts between members of the school community' (Ministerio de Educación y Ciencia, 1992, pp. 25–6).

The range of responsibilities is so wide that sometimes the tutor can be overwhelmed by the responsibility. This is one of the reasons why specifically qualified professionals are needed for some of the guidance, intervention and support tasks. The tutor's responsibilities are related to three different groups, pupils, teachers and the parents (Ministerio de Educación y Ciencia, 1992).

The tutor's role in relation to other teachers
The tutor is responsible for the co-ordination of the design, implementation and evaluation of the tutorial programme in the classroom, seeking to establish coherence between the programme and general educational practice and the curriculum and the annual programme of the school. The tutor also participates in the creation of criteria that the educational guidance and the tutorial action have to meet in the school community.

The tutor and parents
The relationship with parents is an essential and basic aspect of the responsibility of teachers in general and one of the specific functions of tutors.

The objectives of tutorial work in relation to parents are:

- to collect information on the situation of the family, attitudes at home, relationship with siblings
- to inform parents of aspects related to the school's educational approach and curriculum
- to inform the parents periodically of the educational progress and personal development of their children
- to offer guidance concerning their relationship with their children so that they encourage their autonomy
- to help them to be objective in the evaluation of their children, to understand the things that influence their difficulties
- to ask for parental collaboration in order to create the proper conditions favouring their children's personal work: organization of study and free time, interest in homework
- to promote the parents' participation in the school's different activities: meetings, conferences, etc.
- to gather and pass on suggestions and ideas on the school
- to ask their collaboration in extra-curricular activities.

The tutorial and pupils
The goal is the development of two dimensions. From the individual pupil's point of view, the tutor is responsible for:

- the development of the pupil's personal identity, self-knowledge and self-acceptance
- the individualization of the teaching and learning processes
- the adaptation of the learning processes to suit the pupil's abilities
- the monitoring of the academic progress and personal development of each pupil through all cycles and stages.

From the tutorial group's point of view, the tutor is responsible for:

- the integration of the pupils in their group
- the development of participative attitudes in the group
- the participation of the pupils in the school's life.

Three main objectives which might encapsulate the tutor's responsibilities are:

- to teach how to be a person
- to teach how to live together
- to teach how to think.

Teaching how to be a person

The formation of a self-concept and identity, which will define the project of the pupil's life, is an essential element of education. Therefore, it is an element that has to permeate the different curricular areas as well as the work of the tutor. For this, the tutor must know the basic theories of personal development, its key stages, and the factors that enhance it, in order to develop a teaching and tutorial practice that contributes to this development.

The teacher must therefore encourage and nurture the children, set goals for them, offer them help and support, praise and reinforce their achievements, and help reframe their mistakes, in order to promote feelings of proficiency and security in them, making them feel cared for so that they develop a positive self-image. The educational environment should offer children and young people the best chance, after the family and together with it, to prove their abilities and to earn the respect of their peers.

The teachers' attitudes and behaviour, their expectations, their own value as individuals and teachers, the way they organize the classroom, their personal way of being in the classroom, are some of the aspects that most influence the development of a positive self-esteem in the pupils. In order to contribute to this, there are programmes directed towards the development of a positive self-esteem in the educational institution and in the classroom.

Teaching how to live together

The teacher has to address the extremes and limitations of pupils' behaviour. Not only has he or she to pay attention to the problems when they arise, but must also anticipate them with positive action that can be summed up as upbringing for living together and teaching to live together. Communicating, co-operating, creating solidarity and respecting the rules are things that, apart from being a teaching object, have to form the framework of school life.

The family and the school provide the immediate environment of the child and young person. Both parents and teachers provide the social interactions needed for the development of personality: the environment should offer models of behaviour that favour positive social relationships. Some of the adults' behaviour should offer proper models (solving conflicts through dialogue), to value the positive aspects (to value every achievement, however small, to produce situations that facilitate social skills and to teach problem solving skills).

In the educational environment, the teacher has to differentiate between the pupil's personal problems and social relationships problems, in order to be able to direct the intervention towards the individual or towards the group. As regards the individual, a teacher must know which skills children need to establish good social relationships with their peers and adults. Some of the basic communication skills are:

- to know how to listen (not interrupting, paying attention, expressing understanding, using open questions)
- to share things
- to participate and to collaborate in group activities
- to know how to give compliments and affirmation to others, and to know how to accept compliments
- to know how to participate in a conversation.

The educational intervention in the group-classroom will seek to create an enjoyable, active and joyful environment that makes schoolwork satisfying and helps solve the different conflicts arising in the group. The intervention can be directed towards:

- the improvement of group dynamics
- choosing the appropriate groups
- taking into consideration one's own attitudes
- initiating a methodological programme with the goal of developing the following aspects: social problem-solving, self-directed language, attributional style, self-control, establishment of goals, social relationships and communication skills, and body image.

Teaching how to think

Some pupils need educational intervention directed towards the development of learning and thinking abilities (pupils with significant handicaps in intellectual development, or with learning difficulties, pupils with special educational needs, pupils from disadvantaged socio-cultural backgrounds). Moreover, people with the same knowledge can be different in their ability to think and to apply their knowledge efficiently.

For this reason, and because the ability to think is not innate, programmes directed to enhancing cognitive performance are being developed by the Ministerio de Educación y Ciencia. Learning to think will contribute to the improvement of the intellectual achievement in abstract subjects and improve performance at school and skills in social situations.

Knowledge and the ability to think are the two sides of the same coin.

All areas have a cognitive dimension in order to plan, control and implement strategies in different learning situations. The programmes developed to teach how to think attempt to develop the four main aspects of thinking: problem solving, creativity, deductive and inductive reasoning, and metacognition, in relation to the strategies for the control of thought. The final aim is to learn how to learn.

Cross-curricular dimensions

According to LOGSE, the orders that have established the curricula of the different educational stages define some aspects of teaching that must be present through the different areas. These are the cross-curricular dimensions and involve the following: moral and civic education, education for peace, for health, for equal opportunities between sexes, environmental education, sex education, consumer education and traffic education. There are some themes that are cross-curricular in that they can be developed through all subjects of the curriculum.

The curricular contents relevant for cross-curricular education include conceptual knowledge and procedures, of course, but there are also attitudes and values linked to an ethical dimension that supports the development of moral autonomy in the pupils. To put it more clearly, cross-curricular topics make a direct reference to the education of attitudes and values, they make reference to areas of personal and social experience and to basic developments of the ethical dimension. The cross-curricular topics are important for:

* the personal and holistic development of the pupil
* the promotion of a freer and more peaceful society, with more respect for other people and for nature, which constitutes the environment of human society.

It is true that cross-curricular teaching is the responsibility of the whole educative community, but especially for the teaching staff. In particular, they must be present in the educational approach of the school, in the curriculum of each stage and in the programming that the teaching body makes. In order to promote understanding among teachers of the ways the cross-curricular topics might be developed and taught, the Ministry of Education has appointed specialists to provide guidance material for the development of cross-curricular topics in each subject. In relation to this, it is important to refer to the civic and moral dimension, because this 'constitutes an omnipresent cross-curricular dimension in all the areas, as well as in the rest of the cross-curricular themes', and, therefore, it should constitute the main idea from which the other dimensions could be made up.

Civic and moral education

If holistic education means to take care of all human abilities, it is logical to see education as more than just a quantity of intellectual acquisitions (Puig Rovira, 1992). Moreover, the need of principles, values and personal norms that give meaning and sense of direction is evident to prevent an important source of discontent developing. This is even clearer nowadays, when many problems (topics on relationships, economic and biological aspects) do not require a technical or scientific solution but an ethical reorientation.

A model of moral education, based on two principles, is suggested *(ibid)*:

- respect for the autonomy of each individual, as opposed to applying exterior pressure to conform
- the rational dialogue, as opposed to individual decisions.

It is evident that this model is a long way from those based on either absolute or relative values. It starts from principles of autonomy and rational dialogue, and uses them as tools that make possible informed criticism, openness to others and the respect of human rights. Therefore, moral education should involve the pupils in such a way as to facilitate the development and formation of all the abilities that are needed in moral judgement and action, together with the goal of making them able to act in a rational and autonomous way in those situations that produce a conflict of values. All this implies a moral profile characterized by the following traits:

- the development of universal structures of moral judgement that allow the adoption of general principles of value such as justice or solidarity
- the acquisition of discussion skills that lead to rational agreements and democratic participation
- building an image of oneself and of the way of life that one wants to lead with reference to one's personal values
- to develop the abilities and knowledge needed to participate in a critical and creative dialogue with reality, and on the basis of this to develop realistic and appropriate life-plans
- to acquire the skills needed to make coherent moral judgements and to assist them in developing the desired life-style
- to recognize and accept the universally desirable values stated in the Charter of Human Rights and the Spanish Constitution
- to understand, respect and build fair norms to regulate collective life (Puig Rovira, 1992, pp. 15–16).

It is about developing ways of thinking about moral and civic subjects and also about trying to learn to apply the ability to judge personal and collective history, with the purpose of improving it: what is valuable beyond everyday actions and should be applied to the development of a framework of fundamental rights for everybody. Currently, in this cross-curricular area, there is a need for planning. The central ideas have a great potential to humanize and personalize education. However, as these subjects are not clearly delineated and articulated in terms of specific approaches, they run the risk of being relegated, like some other elements of the curriculum, to a position of low priority. Therefore, it seems essential to reformulate the general objectives which appear in these cross-curricular elements into more specific and operational ones. The true integration of the cross-curricular themes in school life will be accomplished when they articulate its values and ethos.

Examples of work at the University of Deusto
There are a number of initiatives developed at the University of Deusto concerned with both the lines of intervention described above, which will now be described.

Tutorial work and guidance
Development in the field of educative guidance in infant and primary education. This initiative involves preparation for the role of infant and primary school adviser through the award-bearing 'Course of expert consultant-adviser of infant and primary education'. It is a 320-hour programme, to which all professionals in primary education currently working have access. Also available is the training of tutors of infant and primary schools through intensive courses, between 40 and 60 hours long.

Developments in the field of educational guidance in secondary education. In this area there are courses for tutor-teachers, and also for school advisers. An interesting project that is being worked on at present is the development of a Master's degree in Educational Guidance.

Participation in schools. For active participation in various educative centres of the Basque Autonomous Community, a Department of Guidance has been created for students on teaching practice in the fourth year of teacher training.

This activity features as an educational and psychological practical in the University course.

Evaluation and tutorial analysis in schools (secondary education). The aim is to evaluate the work and organization of orientation in the schools and assess the actual situation in schools. This is the first step in advising schools.

Work on self-awareness. Several methods of assessing self-awareness, for the age-range 5–14, have been developed and adapted (Valdivia, 1992; Villa and Auzmendi, 1992). Two intervention programmes have also been designed to enhance the self-awareness and motivation of pupils in the classroom (Elexpuru, 1992; Garma, 1992).

Cross-curricular elements
Work in the secondary school. This involves the preparation of a school-based project focusing on the values of the teachers. The cross-curricular subject of 'moral education', developed from the values of the staff, is used as the main idea for other cross-curricular elements: equality, co-education, etc. (Elexpuru and Medrano, 1993; Medrano and Elexpuru, 1993).

Analysis of the general ordination law of the educative system (LOGSE). The aim is to identify which values have motivated the government in this reform. On the other hand, in the second stage, the values of a representative sample of the teaching staff of the Autonomous Community have been collected with the purpose of comparison between what the government proposes and what actually happens in the schools (Buñes *et al.*, 1993).

Research areas

Apart from the above, there are many research projects carried out at the Institute of Educational Sciences of Deusto University connected with affective education. Research linked to the two previous areas:

- Project 14–16. A study on the needs and main problems of pupils who are underachieving in the secondary school.
- Disadvantaged youngsters towards the future (on the urgent development of article 23 of the LOGSE).
- Application of a programme of values in a context of rehabilitation.

Other areas of research

- Evaluation and self-evaluation of teachers
  – A self-evaluation system for secondary teachers
- Evaluation and management of schools
  – The first years of school management
  – Teacher evaluation by higher education students
  – Implementation of a programme for teachers' self-evaluation in schools
  – The managing team and the evaluation of pupils' performance
- Analysis of the needs and behavioural problems of pupils (social skills, handicaps, suicidal ideas, teachers' stress, quality of life, etc.)
  – Understanding of the process of adolescent suicidal thoughts and behaviour from a psychosocial perspective
  – Evaluation of the support services available to pupils with special needs in the Basque Autonomous Community
  – Quality of life of the mentally retarded in the Basque Autonomous Community

CONCLUSION

As a result of the reform of the Spanish educational system, the need to produce more fully developed individuals has been identified. The response focuses both on intellect and also on providing the opportunity for affective education. This need has been addressed through two lines of intervention. On the one hand tutoring and guidance, which emphasize the teacher's educational role, and on the other hand the cross-curricular elements, that is, focusing on relevant aspects related to attitude which permeate all the educational activity: moral and civic education, education for peace, education for health, education for equal opportunities for both sexes, environmental education, sex education, consumer education, and road safety education. All this is carried out by means of developing conceptual contents, contents of procedures, attitudes, values and rules, which relate to the main elements of affective education.

Not everyone is optimistic about the new reform. Echoing Beltrán's words (1991), it is a conservative reform that will not put an end to competitive individualism, academicism or to an emphasis on extreme efficiency and the other characteristics of techno-bureaucracy. Others, however, expect this reform to help students to become individuals, to co-exist and to think. It is intended that this will be achieved through the transmission not only of contents but also of attitudes and values which may contribute to their personal and comprehensive development, all within a larger project, already discussed, which is aimed at creating a freer, more peaceful society.

Achieving these goals is not an easy task. It requires much prior work aimed at the reformulation of general goals, that is to say, the first step is that of making operative the spirit of reform. This is precisely what is being carried out in Spain at present through numerous initiatives and projects, among which are those undertaken by Deusto university. We live in a competitive, scientific and technological society and the school system cannot afford to neglect its role in the task of 'educating individuals' in the broadest sense of the term.

REFERENCES

Ballesteros, R. (1989), 'Introducción: La educación tras la recuperación de la democracia en España: 1978–1988', in J. Paniagua and A. San Martín (eds), *Diez Años de Educación en España (1978–1988)*, Valencia: UNED.

Beltrán, F. (1991), *Política y Reformas Curriculares*, Valencia: University of Valencia.

Buñes, M. *et al*. (1993), *Los Valores en la LOGSE: Un Análisis de Documentos a través de la Investigación de Hall-Tonna*, Bilbao: Mensajero, ICE, University of Deusto.

Elexpuru, I. (1992), 'Un programa de intervención para la mejora del autoconcepto de alumnos entre 8 y 11 años', in A. Villa (ed.), *Autoconcepto y Educación: Teoría, Medida y Práctica Pedagógica*, Vitoria: Servicio de Publicaciones del Gobierno Vasco.

Elexpuru, I. and Medrano, C. (1993), 'El desarrollo de los valores desde la perspectiva de la interacción de los modelos de Kölbergh y Hall-Tonna', in *Valencia, Actas del II Congreso Internacional sobre Intervención y Desarrollo Humano: Intervención Educativa y Comunitaria*, p. 137.

Fernández, J. M. and Mayordomo, A. (1993), *Política Educativa y Sociedad*, Valencia: Universitat de Valencia, Departamento de Educación Comparada e Historia de la Educación.

Garma, A. (1992), 'Un programa de intervención en alumnos entre 11 y 14 años', in A. Villa (ed.), *Autoconcepto y Educación: Teoría, Medida y Práctica Pedagógica*, Vitoria: Servicio de Publicaciones del Gobierno Vasco.

Gobierno Vasco (1992), *Documentos: Modulo de Formación, Tutoría y Orientación*, Vitoria: Servicio Central de Publicaciones del Gobierno Vasco.

Ley 1/90 del 3 de Octubre, Orgánica de Ordenación General del Sistema Educativo (BOE del 4-10-90).

Medrano, C. and Elexpuru, I. (1993), 'Las ideas previas en torno al concepto de "Valor" y su relevancia para el trabajo institucional', in *Valencia, Actas del II Congreso Internacional sobre Intervención y Desarrollo Humano: Intervención Educativa y Comunitaria*, p. 136.

Ministerio de Educación y Ciencia (1992), *Primaria: Orientación y Tutoría*, Madrid: Ministerio de Educación y Ciencia.

Puig Rovira, J. (1992), *Transversales: Educación Moral y Cívica*, Ministerio de Educación y Ciencia.

San Martín, A. and Paniagua, J. (1989), 'Presentación', in J. Paniagua and A. San Martín (eds), *Diez Años de Educación en España (1978–1988)*, Valencia: UNED.

Santa-Cruz, C. and Bejerano, J. (1989), 'Repercusiones de la Constitución de 1978 en la educación preescolar y obligatoria', in J. Paniagua and A. San Martín (eds), *Diez Años de Educación en España (1978–1988)*, Valencia: UNED.

Valdivia, C. (1992), *La Orientación y la Tutoría en los Centros Educativos: Cuestionario de Evaluación y Análisis Tutorial*, Bilbao, Mensajero, ICE de la Universidad de Deusto.

Villa, A. (ed.) (1992), *Autoconcepto y Educación: Teoría, Medida y Práctica Pedagógica*, Victoria: Servicio de Publicaciones del Gobierno Vasco.

Villa, A. and Auzmendi, E. (1992), *Medición de Autoconcepto en la Edad Infantil (5–6 Años)*, Bilbao: Mensajero, ICE de la Universidad de Deusto.

CHAPTER 9

Affective education and the quality of life in Italian schools

Maria Teresa Crucillà

INTRODUCTION

This chapter outlines the educational policies and the specific initiatives recently introduced in Italy to improve the quality of school life and prevent or reduce the marginal status and resulting personal and social alienation of young people. Prevention is the key-word that may help clarify present Italian policy in the socio-health and educational areas. In fact, 'prevention' is a word frequently used in a number of ministerial documents concerned with school drop-outs, juvenile delinquency, drug abuse, AIDS, etc.

Another key-word, closely linked with the first, is 'promotion'. Recently, Italian politicians recognized that to prevent youth alienation it is necessary to promote their well-being. Unfortunately Italy, unlike many European countries, lacks a specific department for youth policy, as well as a minister responsible for this sector. This means that the different initiatives concerned with youth are carried out at national level by various ministries or at local level by different institutions, without any real co-ordination and, above all, without responding to the need to involve young people themselves in the development of these initiatives.

As a result, for the last few years a political-legislative approach has been implemented that is more reminiscent of social control, or repression, than the acceptance and guidance of the individual child–adolescent–youth or indeed of the notion of prevention in the broadest sense of the word.

On the other hand, a whole series of problems, such as school closure, de-motivation, aimlessness and confusion, along with school drop-out and school refusal, can be considered as 'indicators' of a situation of discomfort and trouble, which must be taken into account if we do not want to run the risk of seeing our children lose their way, or 'get lost in the woods': a very fitting metaphor used by Canevaro (1976) to talk about young people in trouble who risk losing the sense of their own existence.

In June 1988, the Italian Chamber of Deputies set up a specific Parliamentary Committee of Inquiry to 'assess the causes and nature of young people's social and cultural alienation'.

ASSESSING YOUNG PEOPLE'S ALIENATION

In March 1991, about two years after its constitution, the Parliamentary Committee concluded its work on the situation of young people and presented a detailed report to the Chamber of Deputies.[1] Through a number of visits to various areas of Italy, the Committee became a catalyst, providing young people with the opportunities to criticize and to make proposals. The picture that emerged is not a homogeneous one (the alienation of the young in many cities of southern Italy has a specific, dramatic force). However, the awareness of their 'marginal status' appears quite widespread among young people who, apart from their social-economic status, feel that society allows them only the expectation of becoming adults.

Hence the need felt by the Parliamentary Committee to set up a 'monitoring unit' to assess the level of youth alienation. This aimed to collect periodically relevant information about the attitudes of young people to health, sport, drug addiction, sex, culture, justice, social institutions and in particular data relating to the educational process in the family and the school.

In fact, the marginalization of the young may be aggravated into 'disruptive behaviour' by the school itself. Therefore, while a radical change of direction seems to be appropriate in relation to them, the policies carried out on all institutional levels highlight that one of the most urgent measures is to address the nature of the processes that go on in schools themselves. The latest circular of the Italian Ministry of Education (9–4–1994)[2], concerning initiatives for the prevention of the youth alienation in schools, stresses that 'active prevention must be on a cross-curricular basis' and that 'alienation cannot be prevented if one forgets to promote well-being in the school' and also that life-quality for young people is connected to school-quality.

PROPOSED STRATEGIES: THE ITALIAN HEALTH EDUCATION PROJECTS

The strategy proposed in the circular is 'a re-planning of the whole school system, in order to improve its efficacy and efficiency'. This re-designing should involve the 'entire educational community' in the broadest sense: teachers, families, all the human and structural resources existing in the community, should be mobilized to promote the well-being in the school of the child–adolescent–youth from the very first years of their life in school.

In fact, the circular underlines the importance of primary prevention 'seen as a timely identification of the risk situations, and as a result taking positive action aimed at the elimination of those forms of alienation which can lead to various forms of failure and delinquency'.

The aim is not to add a new subject of study (health education) to the syllabus, but rather to increase the scholastic quality of school and to raise the level of educational relationships, starting from primary classes. Therefore the nursery school system is included, for the first time, in a preventative initiative, with a specific project called *Rainbow* alongside the three existing ones: *Children 2000, Youth '93* and *CIC*.

The *Rainbow* project (*Progetto Arcobaleno*) involves the entire educational community (teachers, parents, experts in the socio-health services) in the early identification of those risk-situations in which different forms of school drop-out or delinquency can take root. The aim is to improve the quality of the environment, the relationships and the global life-quality of children as soon as they enter education.

Children 2000 (Progetto Ragazzi 2000) involves teachers and pupils of Primary Schools (age 10–14). Its main objective is to promote well-being among the children, as a consequence of a positive atmosphere of initiative and collaboration. A three-stage programme is carried out: *The others and I, I for the others, I with the others.* The idea is to reinforce individual and social growth as the essential basis for preventative action and health education.

Youth '93 (Progetto Giovani '93) involves teachers and pupils of Secondary Schools (age 14–19). Its objective is to develop aspects of positive action by young people, encouraging them to propose and develop ideas which might improve the quality of school life. The motto chosen by the students at the end of their first National Meeting (Rome, 22–25 February 1993) was 'To be the school, not to be only inside the school' (*'Essere scuola, non esserci solo dentro'*).

CIC (Counselling and Information Centres) can be seen as a help service for young people, a 'space of individual listening' inside secondary schools, but they are also a polyfunctional space where the young can meet with their teachers, talk, make plans and develop cultural activities and/or social solidarity, and feel real participants. The aim is to prevent or reduce situations of personal and social alienation among young people and to motivate them in relation to the school. The project will also create a greater collaboration between school and USL (local health unit).

Such projects, apart from the specific aims suitable for the various school levels and the different ages of the pupils, share the general aim of well-being (with oneself, with the others, in the institutions). In fact, they look after health training, understood in the broadest sense of the word by the World Health Organization, as physical, psychic, social and also moral well-being. The aim is to develop a harmonious condition of individual equilibrium, which might be seen as proaction, from the very first years of education.

A *Parents Project (Progetto Genitori)* is to be added to the above projects. Its general aim is to facilitate the involvement of the pupils' parents in school life. The project provides:

- meetings and exchanges of information between parents, teachers and social workers
- training courses to increase parents' knowledge with regard to the family 'developmental task' (Erikson, 1963)
- training courses to increase parents' competence and pedagogical sensitivity in relation to preventing youth alienation
- meetings between teachers and parents to compare their educational responses to young people's behaviour.

The general objectives of the *Parents Project* are:

- to create a more open school system

- to improve the relationship between school and family
- to make parents' involvement and participation in school life easier and more effective
- to start a dialogue between teachers and parents on the needs, expectations and problems of youth and ways of aiding their development.

All the projects mentioned are applications of a state law relating to the prevention, treatment and rehabilitation of conditions of drug addiction (Law n.162, 26/6/90). In order to enforce this law, the Ministry of Education, together with the Ministry of Health, has placed great importance on prevention and promotion, suggesting the following objectives of intervention, to apply to the various projects:

- to recognize the situations of risk
- to promote healthy behaviour and life-styles
- to create conditions that avoid problems of discontent, discomfort and trouble.

To this end, many schools or groups of schools at each level drafted various projects, for which they asked the central administration (Ministry of Education) or the local education offices for financial support. A special committee evaluated the projects, and many initiatives have been given financial support to develop traditional school aims into more proactive actions, that is:

- to create new competencies both in teachers and parents
- to facilitate new forms of collaboration between school and family and between schools and other institutions
- to reorganize curricular activity on every school level in order to improve the quality of educational relationships, providing more opportunities for young people to express their views and influence development.

In fact, all the Italian health-education projects, aimed at improving the quality of school life, and re-evaluating the 'affective dimension' of education, are intended to be a first, urgent response to the risk of youth alienation.

FROM THE TEACHING ROLE TO THE EDUCATIONAL ROLE

During the 1992 National Congress *Well-being in school: what are the institutional answers?* (Amantea, 24–28 February)[3], the results of the Parliamentary Inquiry Committee regarding the youth situation were confirmed. Moreover, as a result of statistical data on increases in juvenile delinquency, a worrying correlation between alienation, drop-outs and delinquency was underlined.

Sometimes, a troubled family background or difficult social situation is compounded by a frustrating school experience of anxiety and boredom, as well as ineffective interpersonal relationships. In such a case, the response is likely to be a rejection not only of school but also of life, which results in a progressive break-down: addiction to drugs, escape from home, deviance, delinquency, and violence towards others and towards oneself, even suicide (Laufer, 1984). If we recognize such risks, we cannot be solely 'information-transmitters'.

It is necessary, as Corradini says (1993), to have 'an extra soul'. But above all it is necessary for the teachers of junior and senior schools, who are in touch daily with adolescents, to develop new relationships and seek the opportunity for deeper communication, to rediscover the centrality of the educational relationship and the importance of empathy. It is necessary for us to consider carefully the tensions and needs of the young who, through the quality of the school, can be either helped or hindered in their growth process.

In fact, the words used, 'discomfort' and 'discontent', denote a lack, a deficiency or absence of something. This lack, leading to the discomfort and alienation of the young, can be seen as:

- a lack of dialogue and personal communication with the teachers, the parents, etc.
- a lack of ability to make plans, or as a lack of the possibility to plan their future
- a lack of meaning to life and/or as a lack of appropriate models.

For these reasons, teachers must review their teaching-role and assume the educational role, or rather the role of 'mentor' (*propositori di senso*) (Corradini, 1992).

None of this is easy, and moreover empathy cannot be imposed by law. At the moment, Italian teachers' initial training is more concerned with a general improvement of their teaching than with affective education.

There is no training for such important aspects of affective education as:

- the facilitation of positive interpersonal relationships
- providing for the well-being of the individual and the group
- promoting the participation and the acceptance of others
- improving students' self-knowledge and acceptance, self-esteem, and ability to question and listen.

In fact, at the Amantea Congress the following points were focused on and singled out as crucial problems:

- strong resistance from the teachers (mainly those of high schools) to reviewing their roles as 'culture transmitters'
- existence of didactic and assessment behaviour which humiliate students
- separation and impermeability of subjects which cause sectarianism and fragmentation.

EDUCATIONAL CONTINUITY AND THE NEW ROLE OF 'REFERRING TEACHER'

The fragmentation of the formative segments, their isolation within the curriculum (elementary, junior and senior high school) and the fragmentation within the same classroom (e.g. the various subjects) are, according to Bloom and Krathwohl (1956), the reasons for many school failures.

The same parliamentary committee, in facing the problems of the youth–school relationship, points out the great risk of fragmentation in the school system, and stresses that 'if each age (in its own specificity) is a separate moment, the total trend of society (and of school) should seek to encourage the harmonious growth of child–adolescent–youth, without any barriers and breaks that are not natural in terms of the passage from one age to another'.

The various projects mentioned, which have been conceived as mechanisms to improve the school service and to prevent alienation, should succeed, if carried through, in improving the quality of schools at the various levels. On the other hand, a real culture of change does not exist yet. The same ministerial circulars about the 'educational continuity', which aims at avoiding fractures both on the cognitive level and the rational one, are often disregarded and are not seen as concerning high schools.

Therefore, while we believe that development is taking place fragmentation, methodological and programmatic approaches are hard to challenge, particularly in senior schools. To address these problems, in every school (as part of the projects of prevention and health-education previously mentioned) a new professional figure, the 'referring teacher' (*docente referente*), has been created. Their roles include:

- diagnosing need and programming the relative interventions
- to propose and co-ordinate the health education projects inside the school
- to involve the students' families in proactive projects and activities
- to organize a mixed teacher/parent working-group for regular dialogue
- to take care of the circulation of information on the project in progress inside and outside the school
- to evaluate the results of the health-education projects in order to develop them
- to co-ordinate groups from different-level schools on common health-education projects, to realize a real 'vertical continuity'
- to promote the links between school, family and local institutions interested in the problem of prevention, to realize a 'horizontal continuity'.

CONCLUSION: AN 'ECOLOGICAL PERSPECTIVE'

The various Italian projects mentioned arise from the state laws pertinent to the prevention of drug abuse or youth delinquency. For this reason, Italian educational policy, compared to the European model of affective education (Lang, 1995), should be considered 'responsive', that is, a 'reaction' to the pressure of urgent problems.

But if we analyse the strategy proposed as 'an urgent measure', it is, in fact, 'a re-planning of the school system' that involves the entire educational community in the projects of prevention-development. Therefore, we can assert that the Italian educational policy, compared to the model proposed by Lang (*ibid.*), will be considered 'proactive' and 'developmental', rather than 'responsive'.

In fact, in Italy it is possible to find ample agreement of the educationalists on the following definition of the education process: 'The intentional organisation of all personal and environmental conditions that can promote the harmonious development of the person and the best social collaboration' (Laeng, 1990). The main point is that the alienation and the new social pathologies, involving the young people of today, create new tasks for teachers and parents and require a greater collaboration between school, family and institutions, in order to create an educational 'eco-system' (Lorenzetto, 1988) in a developmental 'ecological perspective'.

NOTES

1. *Atti della Commissione Parlamentare d'inchiesta sulla condizione giovanile. Ralazione conclusiva.* Doc XXII Anno 1991.
2. 9–4–94, n120, *Attività di prevenzione primaria e di educazione alla salute: Progetto Arcabaleno, Progetto Ragazzi 2000, Progtto Giovani '93, Progetto Genitori, CIC, Corsi di Formazione.*
3. *Progetto Adolescenza: Iniziative di intervento e di prevenzione sulle tossicodipendenze rivolte agli adolescenti di tre aree del Comune di Roma.* Relazione esplicativa, Anno 1992.

REFERENCES

Bloom, B. S. and Krathwohl, D. R. (1956), *Taxonomy of Educational Goals. Handbook II: Affective Domain*, New York: Mekay Comp.

Canevaro, A. (1976), 'I bambini che si perdono nel bosco: identità e linguaggi nell'infanzia', *La Nuova Italia*, 27–40.

Charmet, G. (1992), 'La rete integrata Scuola–Famiglia–Servizi per instaurare i valori che sostengono la crescita degli adolescenti', in Provv-Agli Studi Piacenza (ed.), *L'età dell'adolescenza e i nuova compiti educativi della scuola*, Piacenza: Ed. Vicolo de Pavone.

Corradini, L. (1990), 'Social and cultural values of young Italians', *Centrum fran Barn*, Report n. 29.

Corradini, L. (1991), 'Giovani e Ragazzi fra '93 e 2000', *Tuttoscuola*, October.

Corradini, L. (1992), 'Educazione e ricerca di senso nel Progetto Giovani '93', *Quaderni di Vita Italiana* 4/92.

Corradini, L. (1993), 'Incontrare l'adolescente a scuola', *Vita, Verità e Vita*, n. 144, October.

Erikson, E. H. (1963), *Childhood and Society*, New York: W. W. Norton; Italian edition A. Armando (1973) *Infanzia e Società*, Rome.

Laeng, M. (1990), 'La filosofia dell'educazione. Una pedagogia dello sviluppo personale e sociale', *Atlante della Pedagogia*, vol. I.

Lang, P. (1995), 'International perspectives on pastoral care', in R. Best, P. Lang, C. Lodge, and C. Watkins (eds), *Pastoral Care and Personal and Social Education: Entitlement and Provision*, London: Cassell.

Laufer, M. and Laufer, E. (1984), *Adolescence and Developmental Breakdown*, New Haven: Yale University Press.

Lorenzetto, A. (1988), 'Verso un ecosistema educativo', *Società, Ambiente, Progetto*.

Lumbelli, L. (1975), 'Comunicazione non autoritaria. Come rinunciare al "ruolo"', *Modo Costruttivo: Suggerimenti Rogersiani*.

Lumbelli, L. (1982), *Psicologia dell'educazione. Comunicare a scuola*, Bologna: Il Mulino.

Pontecorvo, C. and Pontecorvo, M. (1986), *Psicologia dell'educazione. Conoscere a scuola*, Bologna: Il Mulino.

Rogers, C. R. (1961), *On Becoming a Person*, Boston: Houghton Mifflin.

Rogers, C. R. (1962), 'The interpersonal relationship: the core of guidance', *Harvard Educational Review*.

Sgritta, G. B. (1988), 'Conoscenza e intervento: verso un approccio interattivo', in *Rassegna Italiana di Sociologia*, n. 4/88.

CHAPTER 10

Affective education in Portugal

Bártolo P. Campos and Isabel Menezes

The Portuguese experience of fascism and the transition to democracy, in the mid-1970s, are most significant in understanding the public, political and educational debate over the role of the school in preparing students for the opportunities and responsibilities of adult life. The educational system before 1974 was intentionally organized to inculcate Christian values and to preserve a bureaucratic and authoritarian model of society (Cortesão, 1982; Mónica, 1978; Stoer, 1986). Naturally, the implementation of democracy was accompanied by a stress on the role the school should play in preparing young people for active citizenship in the 'new' society (Grácio, 1981). However, with the exception of some episodic and discontinuous experiences that were abandoned almost immediately (Bettencourt, 1982; Bettencourt and Brederode Santos, 1983; Brederode Santos, 1984), a true debate over these issues was only systematically initiated in 1986 when the parliament discussed and revised the Education Act.

The Education Act (Law 46/86 of October 14) assumes as fundamental principles the democratization of education and that the state cannot determine or organize the educational system in accordance with any political, ideological, philosophical or religious orientations; even if paradoxically, this intentional stress on the so-called 'neutrality' of education clearly reveals that the memories of past experiences are still vividly present. The aims of school education reveal, however, that the legislators envisaged the profile of the ideal citizen: free, responsible, autonomous, and capable of commitment to social progress and transformation, with a sense of national identity that respects others and is open to dialogue in a democratic spirit that values universal humanism, solidarity and international co-operation. The attainment of these objectives involves changes in schools' organization towards democratic functioning and the creation of an area of personal and social education comprising ecological education, consumer education, family education, sex education, health education, accident prevention and civic education (Article 47).

According to this new Education Act, compulsory education comprises the first nine years of schooling and is divided into three cycles: the first cycle is composed of grades 1 to 4; the second, grades 5 to 6; and the third, grades 7 to 9. Apart from minor options in the third cycle, there is a common curriculum for all students. Secondary education, comprising grades

10 to 12, is organized into three types of course: general, technological and vocational. Although these courses differ both in the subject areas and in the relative importance of more academically-oriented or practically-oriented subjects, at the end of secondary education all students can have access to higher education.

The introduction of Personal and Social Education (PSE) was a complex process demonstrating that the practical translation of affective concerns in education is controversial. In 1989, the Ministry of Education stated that PSE should be the aim of (i) all subjects, thus constituting a cross-curricular theme; (ii) the specific subject of Personal and Social Development (PSD) as an alternative to Moral and Religious Education, of one hour per week; (iii) a project area called 'school area'[1], and involve (iv) extracurricular activities. In the third cycle, a specific national programme of Civic Education is to be implemented in the school area.

The curricular reform was only introduced at a national level in 1991 and the subject of PSD was only implemented experimentally in 19 schools; the programme of Civic Education was simultaneously tried out in those third-cycle schools that were involved in this experience. Therefore, the Portuguese praxis in explicit affective education is relatively recent and small. Nevertheless, there has been, since the mid-1980s, a quite intensive debate over the aims, contents and methods of PSE that may be useful in clarifying some relevant and controversial issues of affective education.

AIMS, CONTENTS AND METHODS OF PSE

The major theoretical proposals on the domain of affective education emerge from three perspectives on the role of school education:

- preparation for dealing with life problems
- emphasis on values
- promotion of students' development (Campos, 1991a).

The role of school education in preparing students for dealing with life problems and events is emphasized by the advocates of the first perspective. Since traditional school education is not capable of preparing youngsters for life and families are inhibited in their socializing role, the media has a powerful effect in shaping attitudes. Juvenile problems (e.g. drug abuse, delinquency, adolescent pregnancy, etc.) are increasing, and the school should adapt its curriculum by including up-to-date and relevant themes such as human rights, environment, national identity, national defence, AIDS, etc. Portuguese advocates of this approach are generally non-governmental organizations (for instance environmental and consumer associations), official groups (e.g. the commission for human rights education created by the Ministry of Education) or others that aim to draw teachers' attention to current affairs of great importance in the world that should be addressed by the school, such as environmental education, consumer education, multicultural education, peace studies, human rights education, media education, education for national defence, etc. Frequently, these groups elaborate specific programmes or activities to be implemented in the school context, either in the various disciplines or in PSD (e.g. Santos, Carvalho and Duarte, 1991). It is important to stress that these representatives of the life skills approach do not always have a common or consistent theoretical frame of reference; the common factor is their interest and expertise in one area of PSE that leads them to elaborate materials and make suggestions to schools and teachers.

Emphasis on values includes various approaches such as moral education (Kohlberg, 1985), character education (Ryan, 1989; Lickona, 1991) and values clarification (Raths, Harmin and Simon, 1978); in spite of major theoretical (and ideological) differences, all these approaches stress the ethical dimension of affective education. The emphasis on a content-oriented approach to moral education has been assumed by Cunha (1993, 1994) and Marques (1989, 1990, 1994). Cunha (1993) has stressed the value of character education while Marques (1994) seeks to synthesize the proposals of Kolhberg, Gilligan and advocates of character education, stating that schools should promote justice, caring and goodness. Both authors reject values clarification on the basis of value relativism. Oliveira-Formosinho (1986) and Lourenço (1991, 1992) advocate a strictly (early)-Kohlbergian approach, oriented to issues of justice (rather than 'sanctity'), in the subject of PSD. Valente (1989a, 1989b) defends values clarification as a means to promote opportunities for critical reflection within the school.

There has also been some debate on the role that PSE should play in the process of values construction. Authors such as Marques (1994) explicitly argue that PSE should inculcate certain values (such as courage and goodness) while Campos (1991a) considers that the school's role is problematic only when values are not commonly agreed: when there is consensus, it is probably not necessary that the school makes an explicit effort to transmit such values; when these values are still under discussion and far from reaching a social agreement maybe the school should not take sides; and maybe more important is the role that formal education can play in empowering youngsters to be active participants in the ongoing process of personal and social construction of values.

Finally, several Portuguese authors have stressed the psychological dimensions of PSE, stating that affective education must deal with the development of psychological processes if students are to acquire competencies to deal with the experiences, opportunities and responsibilities of adult life (Campos, 1980, 1985, 1988, 1990, 1991b; Brederode Santos, 1984, 1987; Oliveira-Formosinho, 1988, 1989); these include formal reasoning, social-perspective taking, empathy, principled moral reasoning, etc. (CRSE, 1988, p. 123).

The various perspectives discussed above have been shown to have differential effects in the quality of students' action-in-context – for example on the practical demonstration of social competencies in real-life situations (Barker, 1984; Coimbra, 1991; Higgins, 1980; Martin, 1990) – together with different justifications (Coimbra, 1991; Martin, 1990; Sultana, 1992); an important conclusion is that the development of psychological processes is instrumental to the acquisition of knowledge, attitudes, competencies and capacities: 'higher' developmental levels are 'better' because growing implies increases in the complexity, flexibility, self-regulation, creativity and self-organization of personal meaning systems (Campos, 1992; Coimbra, 1991; Guidano, 1991; Mahoney and Patterson, 1992; Sprinthall, 1991).

However, the ultimate goal of affective education also implies recognizing the impact of psychosocial climates, social resources and organizational features of the school, i.e. of the hidden curriculum (Campos, Costa and Menezes, 1994). Therefore, the need to intervene in the school's ecological system, deliberately transforming teaching practices, the school's regulations and climates has also been emphasized (Benavente, 1993; Campos, 1988, 1989a, 1989b, 1991a, 1991b, 1994; Campos, Costa and Menezes, 1994; Marques, 1989; Menezes, 1993; Roldão, 1993). The common claim is that to promote students' civic participation, democratic values or tolerance towards other people one should begin to consider the real-life opportunities students have to experience democratic action and respect for themselves and others within the school.

PSE IN PRACTICE: THE EXPERIMENTAL IMPLEMENTATION

In 1991, several basic education schools began to implement PSE, namely the specific subject of PSD (and the programme of civic education in those schools that were teaching the third cycle); the teachers involved in the experience attended in-service training courses and undertook supervised practical work. These teachers are not exclusively teaching PSD and ideally assume the role of class teacher. The class teacher acts as a co-ordinator of functions both bureaucratic (e.g. keeping records and controlling students' attendance) and academic (e.g. dealing with achievement and discipline problems across the various subjects) and as the main person responsible for communications with students' families.

The curriculum of PSD[2] emphasized the use of active methodologies, such as dilemmas discussions, debates, project and group work, classical group dynamics activities, etc., leaving teachers a wide range of autonomy and creativity in both selecting the issues to be addressed – even if recommending the active involvement of students in this process – and managing the class. In a general evaluation conducted after the first year, all teachers referred to had addressed almost all the issues in the Education Act, as well as co-ordinating the class projects of the school area and dealing with daily class problems (e.g. a conflict with another teacher, the rejection of a new colleague, etc.). In general, the opinion of teachers, parents and students was that PSD was very important and had beneficial effects on students' development and in the student–teacher and the school–community relationship.

The specific programme of Civic Education for the School Area includes three inter-related dimensions:

- the defence of fundamental rights, duties and liberties
- the organization of the democratic state as the basic support of these rights, duties and liberties
- participation in democratic life.

The strategies for the implementation of the citizenship programme include the development of various activities as a citizen in the school and the development of projects both within the school and the community. Naturally these activities and projects are defined locally by each school and by each class in that school. Citizenship activities enable the students to participate in the school as a democratic institution by discussing and defining class organization, by promoting and electing student representatives to the school's council, by discussing the school's rules and by taking responsibility for a students' area. An evaluation of citizenship programme with teachers and the senior management teams of the few schools where it was implemented (Cadima and Monteiro, 1993) reveals some unanimity on the importance of the programme – it allows the students 'an active and conscious participation in the society' (p. 11) – but also some inaccurate knowledge of civic education.

THEORY INTO PRACTICE: CAN PSE BE EFFECTIVE?

The introduction of PSE into the curriculum has been severely criticized for several reasons. A major criticism has been the alternative status of the subject of PSD to Moral and Religious Education, especially because this option may suggest that it is centred in an non-religious ethic. This is inappropriate, since it implies limiting the curriculum of PSD to a moral emphasis – an area which, as we have seen, is far from social, political or scholarly consensus, and, even more, is far from the reality within the schools (Campos, 1989c, 1991c; Oliveira-Formosinho, 1989). However, this debate can – and probably should – be ignored, since the current curricular organization of PSE has the potential for effectiveness which may be far more important from a practical point of view.

Research on the effectiveness of educational programmes has revealed some important criteria for the design and management of affective education in schools (Beane, 1990; Campos, Costa and Menezes, 1994; Coimbra, 1991; Sprinthall, 1991): giving students the opportunity for role-taking, that is for performing relevant activities in real-life contexts (preferably outside the school), balanced with the systematic reflection over the experience in a supporting environment that helps the student deal with the challenges of 'action-in-context'; moreover, programmes should be continuous and extensive if lasting results are to be expected.

Given the current organization of PSE in Portuguese schools, we propose the following scheme for actual practice: the school area, which is, by definition, a project area for the development and implementation of practical activities, can focus on real-life projects, giving students opportunities for relevant role-taking; various subjects can contribute to these projects through subject-matter emphasis on the various aspects involved; the specific subject has, obviously, the potential for providing a major and meaningful context for reflective inquiry over current experiences. The teacher's role is to facilitate students' interaction and to guarantee the complexity, creativity and responsibility of students' solutions for the various problems and challenges that real life presents.

This proposal rejects informative and exhortative types of pedagogy in the domain of affective education, that have proved both ineffective (Martin, 1990) and illegitimate (Campos, 1992; Coimbra, 1991; Sultana, 1992). The Portuguese experience prior to 1974 is clearly (and fortunately, we may add) the proof that an education that aims to inculcate some values and systematically exhorts specific virtues is condemned to failure. Studies in this domain have also shown that instructive approaches to civic education have negative effects (Torney-Purta and Schwille, 1986).

In democratic states the schools have the responsibility for giving future citizens all possible opportunities for maximum development and empowerment. However, we must be cautious with these attributions of responsibility in the process of social transformation (Campos, 1994): the school is a social institution within a larger macrosystem and therefore inevitably reflects the society's 'hidden curriculum'. This means that schools can certainly make a difference, but not all the difference, and, although they are involved in the defence of democracy, dignity and diversity (Beane, 1990), we cannot rely solely on them to create more democratic, respectful and pluralist societies.

NOTES

1. The school area has three basic aims: supporting personal and social education, strengthening the school–community relationship and favouring the practical application of knowledge.
2. A new curriculum of the subject of PSD for the third cycle was approved in 1994; the curriculum for secondary education is currently under analysis by the Ministry.

REFERENCES

Barker, J. R. (1984), 'Primary prevention and assessment', *The Personnel and Guidance Journal*, April, pp. 475–8.

Beane, J. A. (1990), *Affect in the Curriculum. Towards Democracy, Dignity and Diversity*, New York: Teachers College, Columbia University.

Benavente, A. (1993), 'Educação, participação e democracia: Valores e práticas na instituição escolar', *Análise psicológica*, XI, pp. 325–33.

Bento, P., Queiroz, A. and Valente, I. (1992), *Formação pessoal e social e democracia nas escolas*, Porto: Asa.

Bettencourt, A. M. (1982), *La Liaison école-milieu-production à l'école secondaire portugaise*, Paris: University of Paris V.

Bettencourt, A. M. and Brederode Santos, M. E. (1983), 'Papel da escola na formação democrática dos alunos', in *Política educacional num contexto de crise e transformação social*, Lisbon: Moraes Editores/IED.

Brederode Santos, M. E. (1984), *Education for Democracy: A Developmental Approach to Teacher Education*, Boston: Boston University.

Brederode Santos, M. E. (1987), 'Educar para a democracia', in A. M. Bettencourt and R. Marques (eds), *Percursos escolares, estratégias de vida, códigos de conduta*, Lisbon: GEP.

Cadima, A. and Monteiro, I. (1993), *Avaliação do programa experimental de educação cívica*, Lisbon: IIE.

Campos, B. P. (1980), 'A orientação vocacional numa perspectiva de intervenção no desenvolvimento psicológico', *Revista portuguesa de pedagogi*, XIVl, pp. 195–230.

Campos, B. P. (1985), 'Consulta psicológica e projectos de desenvolvimento humano', *Cadernos de consulta psicológica*, 1, pp. 5-9.

Campos, B. P. (1988), 'Consulta psicológica e desenvolvimento humano', *Cadernos de consulta psicológica*, 4, pp. 5–12.

Campos, B. P. (1989a), 'Elaboração de um projecto de formação/inovação', in *Questões de política educativa*, Oporto: Asa.

Campos, B. P. (1989b), 'Formação de professores centrada na escola e inovação pedagógica', in *Questões de política educativa*, Oporto: Asa.

Campos, B. P. (1989c), 'Mesa redonda: Caminhos para a formação pessoal e social dos alunos', *Inovação* 2, 4, pp. 483–513.

Campos, B. P. (1990), 'O psicólogo e o desenvolvimento pessoal e social dos alunos', *Cadernos de consulta psicológica*, 6, pp. 83–95.

Campos, B. P. (1991a) 'Educação escolar e desenvolvimento pessoal e social', in *Educação e desenvolvimento pessoal e social*, Oporto: Afrontamento.

Campos, B. P. (1991b), 'Formação pessoal e social e desenvolvimento psicológico dos alunos', in *Educação e desenvolvimento pessoal e social*, Oporto: Afrontamento.

Campos, B. P. (1991c), 'Psychological development and personal and social education in schools', in H. Starkey (ed.), *Socialisation of School Children and Their Education for Democratic Values and Human Rights*, Amsterdam: Swets and Zeitlinger.

Campos, B. P. (1992), 'A informação na orientação profissional', *Cadernos de consulta psicológica*, 8, pp. 5–16.

Campos, B. P. (1994), *Citizenship Education in Portugal*, In-Service Training Seminar on Human Rights Education, Council of Europe, Tyumen, Russian Federation.

Campos, B. P., Costa, M. E. and Menezes, I. (1994), 'The social dimension of deliberate psychological education', in G. Musitu *et al.* (eds), *Intervención comunitaria*, Valencia: Set i Set Edic.

Coimbra, J. L. (1991), *Estratégias cognitivo-desenvolvimentais em consulta psicológica interpessoal*, Oporto: ICPFD.

Cortesão, L. (1982), *Escola, sociedade. Que relação?*, Oporto: Afrontamento.

CRSE (Comissão da Reforma do Sistema Educativo) (1988), *Proposta global de reforma*, Lisbon: GEP.

Cunha, P. O. (1993), 'Objectivos, conteúdos e métodos da disciplina de desenvolvimento pessoal e social', *Inovação* 6, 3, pp. 287–308.

Cunha, P. O. (1994), 'A formação moral no ensino público (Evolução de uma ideia)', *Brotéria*, 130, pp. 59–80.

Grácio, R. (1981), *Educação e processo democrático em Portugal*, Lisbon: Livros Horizonte.

Guidano, V. F. (1991), *The Self in Process. Toward a Post-rationalist Cognitive Therapy*, Guilford Press, New York.

Higgins, A. (1980), 'Research and measurement issues in moral education interventions', in R. L. Mosher (ed.), *Moral Education: A First Generation of Research and Development*, New York: Praeger.

Kohlberg, L. (1985), 'The just community approach to moral education in theory and practice', in M. W. Berkowitz and F. Oser (eds), *Moral Education: Theory and Application*, Hillsdale, N.J.: Erlbaum.

Lickona, T. (1991), *Educating for Character: How our Schools Can Teach Respect and Responsibility*, New York: Bantam Books.

Lourenço, O. M. (1991), 'Educação para os valores morais na escola portuguesa: Considerações kohlbergianas', *Psychologica*, 5, pp. 1–11.

Lourenço, O. M. (1992), 'Desenvolvimento pessoal e social: Educação para a justiça ou educação para a "santidade"?', *Revista Portuguesa de educação*, 5 (2), pp. 129–36.

Mahoney, M. J. and Patterson, K. M. (1992), 'Changing theories of change: Recent developments in counseling', in S. D. Brown and R. W. Lent (eds), *Handbook of Counseling Psychology*, New York: Wiley.

Marques, R. (1989), 'Deve a escola ensinar a justiça? Algumas notas a propósito do altruísmo e da moral', *Aprender*, 9, pp. 10–12.

Marques, R. (1990), 'A educação para os valores no ensino básico: Resultados parciais de uma análise dos currículos', in J. Tavares and A. Moreira (eds), *Desenvolvimento, aprendizagem, currículo e supervisão*, Aveiro: University of Aveiro.

Marques, R. (1994), 'Modelos curriculares de educação pessoal e social', in J. Tavares (ed.), *Para intervir em educação. Contributos dos Colóquios CIDInE*, Aveiro: CIDInE.

Martin, J. (1990), 'Confusions in psychological skills training', *Journal of Counseling and Development*, 3, pp. 402–7.

Menezes, I. (1993), 'A formação pessoal e social numa perspectiva desenvolvimental–ecológica', *Inovação* 6, 3, pp. 309–36.

Mónica, M. F. (1978), *Educação e sociedade no Portugal de Salazar*, Lisbon: Presença.

Oliveira-Formosinho, J. (1986), 'A intervenção da escola no desenvolvimento sócio-moral', *Desenvolvimento*, 3, pp. 61–74.

Oliveira-Formosinho, J. (1988), in CRSE, *Proposta global de reforma*, Lisbon: GEP.

Oliveira-Formosinho, J. (1989), 'Mesa redonda: "Caminhos para a formação pessoal e social dos alunos"', *Inovação* 2, 4, pp. 483–513.

Raths, L., Harmin, M. and Simon, S. B. (1978), *Values and Teaching*, Columbus, Ohio: Merril.

Roldão, M. C. (1993), 'Desenvolvimento pessoal e social: contradições e limites de uma área curricular', *Inovação* 6, 3, pp. 337–43.

Ryan, K. (1989), 'In defense of character education', in L. P. Nucci (ed.), *Moral Development and Character Education: A Dialogue*, Berkeley, CA: McCutchan Publishing Corporation.

Santos, B., Carvalho, O. and Duarte, T. (1991), *A educação do consumidor. Um guia para professores, formadores e animadores*, Lisbon: Texto Editora.

Sprinthall, N. A. (1991), 'Role taking programs for high school students: New methods to promote psychological development', in B. P. Campos (ed.), *Psychological Intervention and Human Development*, Oporto:

Instituto de Consulta Psicológica, Formação e Desenvolvimento and Louvain-La-Neuve: Academia.

Stoer, S. (1986), *Educação e mudança em Portugal. 1970–1980, uma década de transição*, Oporto: Afrontamento.

Sultana, R. G. (1992), 'Personal and social education: Curriculum innovation and school bureaucracies in Malta', *British Journal of Guidance and Counselling*, 20, 2, pp. 164–85.

Torney-Purta, J. and Schwille, W. (1986), 'Civic values learned in school: Policy and practice in industrialized countries', *Comparative Education Review*, 30, pp. 30–49.

Valente, O. (1989a), 'A educação para os valores', in *O ensino básico em Portugal*, Oporto: Asa.

Valente, O. (1989b), 'Mesa redonda: "Caminhos para a formação pessoal e social dos alunos"', *Inovação* 2, 4, pp. 483–513.

CHAPTER 11

Affective education in the Netherlands

Ad Boes

THE DUTCH EDUCATION SYSTEM

One of the characteristics of Dutch schools is the fact that many are not state-controlled. Only one third of schools are public, one third are Protestant and another third Catholic. There are a few other types such as Muslim schools, so far only in the primary school system. A small percentage of the primary schools, about 5 per cent, could be described as traditional reform schools: Montessori, Vrije School, Dalton, Freinet and Jena-plan. They have had a significant influence on the new Primary Education Act of 1985. Both public and private schools are subsidized on an equal basis. This situation is the result of the so-called school struggle which took place in the 19th century. The issue was what education should be financed by the state, with full financial equality only being achieved at the beginning of this century. A legacy of this struggle has been that the government's attitude to involvement in the curriculum has been restrained. Thus it is only in relation to the primary curriculum that it has produced broad guidelines.

Since 1985, primary schoolchildren in the Dutch school system start at the age of four and continue until they are twelve. Following primary education, there are several types of secondary education, usually available within one school. During the first years of secondary school a general curriculum is followed, from two to four years, forming the so-called basic curriculum. Beyond this there is a range of five types of secondary education: Gymnasium, Athenaeum (both giving entrance to scientific education), Havo (access to higher vocational education), Mavo (access to middle vocational education and Vbo (access to lower vocational education). Those who have successfully finished the pre-university level of education are entitled to proceed to university, as are those who have passed the first-year examinations of any advanced education school.

The Netherlands has a large system of special educational schools, though a policy seeking to integrate pupils with learning and behavioural difficulties into mainstream schools is now being pursued.

AFFECTIVE EDUCATION

Every teacher in the Netherlands will tell you that affective education is a matter of great significance and that it plays an important part in the daily life of the school. But statements like this ignore a key problem, which is that in the Netherlands affective education as such is not clearly distinguished from other educational domains. The 1985 Primary Education Act states in article 8:

> Primary education aims to promote the development of the emotions, intellect and creativity as well as the acquisition of essential knowledge and development of social, cultural and physical skills. This can be realized through the subjects that are included in the curriculum.
>
> (*Wet op het basisonderwijs*, Leystad, 1985, p. 3)

In article 11, those subjects are listed without any details of content. Most of them are traditional, such as the Dutch language, arithmetic and mathematics, geography and history. Since 1985 new subjects have been introduced, including English, relations in society, religion, promotion of social abilities and health instruction.

The following creative activities must be included in the curriculum: use of language, art, music, handicrafts, play and movement. It is a great pity that drama is missing. Until some years ago the government was not very specific with regard to the contents of the primary school curriculum: schools were free to frame their own curricula. This lack of specific control can be explained by the nature of the history of Dutch education. Some discussion of this will lead to a better understanding of the situation.

PRIVATE AND PUBLIC EDUCATION

As has been said, it is significant that about two-thirds of the Dutch primary schools are private. These schools receive full financial support from the state, as do state-controlled schools. The history of this goes back to the 19th century when the so-called 'school struggle' took place. This involved a long-lasting debate as to whether the curriculum of the school was to be determined by the government or by parents. The essential question was whether private schools with their own special programmes should be eligible for full financial support from the state. The debate was fuelled by the fact that as time passed society required an increasingly extended curriculum and teachers became more professionalized and needed to be paid as such. As a result, many parents found it increasingly difficult to pay the total amount of school fees for their children's education. Finally, in 1920 the political struggle about the legitimization of private education, which had lasted for many years, ended in completely equal treatment for public and private education. Freedom of education was guaranteed, but this did not prevent political involvement in education. The Christian Democratic Party, which for many years had been a member of various coalition governments, dominated the political debate about education, in particular concerning the constitutionally founded freedom of education. As a result of the political domination by this party a fundamental national debate about the goals of education was blocked. This situation has now changed, but it is by no means certain that the predominance of the cognitive dimension in assessment will be replaced by a broader approach of education in favour of social, emotional and affective dimensions of curriculum development. In a government statement concerning article 8 of the 1985 Primary Education Act *Wet op het basisonderwijs*, Leystad 1985, p. 3, it is said that the development of attitudes in school are closely related to the religious standards and values of the parents on the one hand and the identity of school on the other. The government should remain detached. It is remarkable that this detachment, although not mandatory, is suggested in the instructions for state-controlled schools. Thus, so far as affective education is concerned, this is an issue for the individual school to decide. Some have cognitive objectives only, in others the development of the child's personality is also considered an important aspect. However, the freedom of schools in this respect is increasingly determined and restricted by national and supranational debates about the direction schools have to follow and choices they have to make. As in other countries, there has been intensive discussion about objectives and we have had variants of the 'back to basics' debate. The secretary of state recently sent a proposal to parliament by which primary and secondary schools would be compelled to produce an annual public report in which, among other data, school scores in relation to national results were to be published. There is no doubt that this is not an idea she thought of on her own! At the time of writing (early 1996) no decision has been taken about the way results will be calculated. According to article 23 of the Dutch constitution, the freedom to choose what is felt to be the appropriate evaluation system is acceptable. The Dutch government has some influence on the production of tests through the National Institute of Educational Measurement (CITO).

MAIN OBJECTIVES

In 1993 the government added the so-called *kerndoelen* (main objectives) to the Primary Education Act of 1985, which formulate the minimum teaching content of primary education. It is the responsibility of every school to translate the *kerndoelen* into their curriculum and to determine whether children have mastered the teaching content. Schools will have the opportunity to introduce these objectives into their curriculum between now and September 1998. As has been said, it is left to the school itself to determine whether children fulfil all the requirements. Secondary schools have to participate in a national evaluation system of the individual progress of their pupils.

If a primary school has serious objections to the *kerndoelen* and is a private school, it will be allowed to formulate its own. However, these must be of a similar level. Some Steiner schools raised objections: their view is that the *kerndoelen* are incompatible with the historically gained freedom of education, and they took the issue to court. Their case was not accepted and they have now gone to the higher court. Meanwhile, all

Steiner schools are working together to design their own *kerndoelen* according to the Steiner philosophy and Steiner curriculum.

The *kerndoelen* have a predominantly cognitive character. They leave enough space for sufficient attention to other aims. Having affective objectives does not necessarily imply that a child will have additional subjects. Affective education widens and intensifies the curriculum. Nevertheless, it is notable that the introduction of *kerndoelen*, instead of giving rise to a national debate, has caused so little discussion. The present broad general objectives can easily be replaced by much more specific, extended and detailed ones which will influence school life to a considerable degree. In the light of the above, it is clear that we cannot speak of affective education in the Netherlands in general, because schools differ in so many ways. Visitors from abroad easily get the wrong idea about Dutch education, because it is the progressive schools that are mainly selected for them to visit. In a critical report of the school inspectorate (Commisie Evaluatie Basisonderwijs, 1994) it is said that in about 75 per cent of primary schools the introduction of education according to the 1985 Education Act has still to begin. Many schools have a curriculum which is too narrow; repeating a school year still happens on a large scale, although contrary to the law. Inspectors lack the power to correct the schools which have not yet included the required developments in their curriculum. The government tries to promote suitable developments, but is not consistent in its opinions and advice. Sometimes members of the cabinet pass judgements in which they express their fear that a more extensive curriculum may lead to a decrease in the child's attention and the quality of the 'basics'. On the other hand, they promote innovation by means of which schools underline their own identity. In affective education, schools can develop their own unique approach. The cognitive dimension of the curricula tends to become increasingly uniform in all schools. This is the result of a trend to participate in a national testing programme. Many primary schools are under pressure from secondary schools to do so, although currently the law guarantees the teacher's freedom with regard to the method of evaluating the child's progress.

PEDAGOGICAL CLIMATE

In relation to affective education, considerable changes have taken place in the pedagogic climate of primary schools since the 1970s. This is a change for the better. The authoritarian teacher, who frequently punishes and tries to keep children in order with powerful language, is disappearing. Most teachers speak in a friendly way to their pupils, and shouting is now a rare phenomenon. There is no clear indication as to the cause of this change. During the 1970s, many key books were published about education and school; school and education became a matter of public debate. Much attention was paid to the effects of authoritarian education, both at home and in school. Parents became more aware of their own role in school education and began to participate in school policies. In the Netherlands, parents are free to choose a school for their children. In the past this choice was traditionally determined by their religion. Non-religious parents used to send their children to state-controlled schools. Nowadays parents decide on the school which they feel is best for their children, often irrespective of the school's particular belief system. In most schools nowadays teachers use the term social-emotional development and education, instead of affective education. This term is frequently used in special schools where the children's disabilities and limitations force the school to focus on the non-cognitive aspects of development. The child's well-being is a prerequisite. It soon became clear that this view would also include pupils in the mainstream schools, though in the first place specifically those children with learning and behavioural difficulties.

Influenced by the demand for increasing care for children with behavioural and learning problems, teachers in primary education have come to consider the optimal social-emotional development of their pupils as an essential part of their task. There is a growing awareness among teachers that a positive self-image, as well as being able to do schoolwork without supervision, is more important for successful secondary education than good results in, for instance, arithmetic and spelling. The same applies to the transition from secondary education to higher vocational training: the more rigid the school system in the secondary school, the greater the problems the students will face in higher education. J. R. M. Gerris (1980) was the first scientific investigator to initiate a curriculum which included social development. The approach was a traditional one, and it is presented as simply another new subject to be taught alongside the existing ones. Lessons (courses) in this particular field were proposed for three age groups in the current primary schools. The basic model is of American origin (Selman, 1976). The influence of Piaget is recognizable: social-emotional development is seen as a version of cognitive development. The programme aims at developing social skills as if the subject were arithmetic or language.

REFORM EDUCATION

A major contribution to the thinking underpinning our education has been made by M. J. Langeveld (1967), who is currently considered by many to be the most prominent professor of pedagogics in the Netherlands. *Schools Make People*, a study of the significance of the school in the life of a child, could well be called a school anthropology. This study provides a very broad perspective on education, seeing it not just as the transfer of knowledge and skills. Langeveld's work is inspired by the reform education theories, which have had a major influence on the development of views and opinions of the Dutch school system since the 1970s. The first Montessori and Steiner schools in the Netherlands, however, date from the 1920s. In Jan Ligthart (1859–1916), Cor Bruyn (1883–1956) and Kees Boeke (1884–1966) (Boeke, 1934) the Netherlands has had its own school reformers, who unlike Montessori, Steiner, Parkhurst, Freinet and Petersen have not had any direct followers.

The so-called traditional reform schools have played an important role in the change of the educational climate in our schools, a role which I consider essential for the development of affective education. Their influence can be found in the 1985 Act. There are five types of reform school in the Netherlands: the Steiner schools (Rudolf Steiner, 1861–1925), the Dalton schools (Helen Parkhurst, 1887–1973), the Freinet schools (Célestin Freinet, 1896–1966), the Jena-plan schools (Peter Petersen, 1884–1952) and the Montessori schools (Maria Montessori, 1870–1952). During the 1970s these schools all showed remarkable growth. Today about 5 per cent of the primary schools are reform schools. This number may not seem very significant, but many of their views and approaches have been adopted by other schools. Until recently it was relatively easy to found a school based on individual educational views, and the school would receive full financial support from the state. Recently the conditions for founding schools have been tightened up.

The five school types differ in many ways. Some may be called conventional, others are more flexible. The majority put emphasis on the educational task of the school. The Steiner and Montessori schools have developed their own curriculum, which is based on a unique philosophy and psychology. The Freinet and Jena-plan curriculum is more open. The Dalton school derives its organization from Montessori and includes certain forms of individualization.

AN EXAMPLE: JENA-PLAN

I would like to pay a little more attention to one of the so-called traditional reform schools, the Jena-plan school. The influence of Petersen's concept is one explanation for the changes in our educational climate, whereby more emphasis is put on the development of the pupil's individual personality. So far this trend has mainly been found in primary schools but now it also seems to be reaching the secondary schools.

Peter Petersen (1884–1952), the initiator of Jena-plan education, was professor of education in Jena from 1923 on. In his view school is a continuation and extension of education at home. Our society cannot function without an institution for the education of all its citizens in the broadest sense of the word. Petersen criticized the schools of his day and worked on an extensive alternative which was put into practice under his supervision.

Instead of the subject structure, school life is to be based on social activities: dialogue, play, work and celebrations. The four are derived from well-functioning human communities. Within a family parents and children communicate in a relaxed informal way, at home children have the opportunity to play. Useful work is an essential human occupation, during celebrations occasions are commemorated in a very special way. Together they form a framework in which various activities are geared to one another and are well-balanced in a so-called rhythmic week plan.

As in the Montessori schools, the Jena-plan school involves groups of children of different ages, around four to six years old, six to nine years and nine to twelve years old. In the English literature this is called family grouping: living together in a well-functioning family serves as an example for school education. Petersen was a strong advocate of the school where children integrate with other children of their own age from totally different backgrounds. School is a training ground for future life in a heterogeneous society.

Petersen's critical approach to school education in his day mainly concerned the one-sided curriculum, its strict character and rigid organization and the authoritarian educational approach through which it was taught. All children had to meet the same requirements, irrespective of their intelligence and abilities, which meant a heavy burden for the less gifted and a lesser challenge for the more intelligent ones. In such an educational system children become competitors, achievements are reduced to school marks and the school hardly succeeds in arousing the children's interest for whatever subject is actually presented. School life consists of a sequence of lessons of equal duration and structure.

In the Jena-plan school the obstacles for a more individual school education have been removed, and there are ample space and attention for social development in a wide context. A balance appears to be established between individual and collective education. The Jena-plan school involves activities which stimulate affective development. In this context the 'circle' should be mentioned first. During circle-time a lot of attention is paid to the free exchange of experience and thought. Within the circle the teacher has a different position which is not necessarily one for the purpose of transferring knowledge. During circle-time the children learn to listen to each other and to express their thoughts in words. In principle, they can bring up any topic they want. Various types of circles are distinguished.

In the meantime, the circle has been introduced in many non-Jena-plan schools, but not always with a similar central function. Sometimes circle-time is used solely as an outlet for those children who have something to say. They can express their ideas freely, without fear for any personal consequences. In a well-functioning Jena-plan the material presented during circle-time should contribute other activities during the week.

Circle-time is pre-eminently suitable for moments in which the child's affective development is stimulated. This happens not only when children themselves start to discuss matters, but also when the teachers themselves do so, whether or not according to a plan. For this purpose, books by Harold Bessell have been translated and revised as *Circletime*, in 4 volumes (1978).

RESEARCH

Research is being done at the University of Nijmegen in the field of social-emotional development. In projects by E. A. Gerris emphasis has been shifted from school to the child's family which is, after all, the most important institution for the child's personal development. School has a supplementary function and to a certain extent one of compensation.

In 1992, his colleague Van Lieshout (1992), working at the same university, stated that children should be happy during their school years and that they should have a sense of belonging to a group. He believes this to be, following Olweus' remarks in this respect, a fundamental democratic right of the child. National acceptance of these concepts would have considerable consequences for the character of our school life. One of the main aspects, in this respect, is first of all a certain continuity in school in terms of the allocation of teachers to class groups, and secondly close co-operation with the parents. These requirements can be interpreted as a realization of what is stipulated in the Primary Education Act: a guaranteed continuous development of every child. Until now this concept has received recognition only with regard to cognitive development. In this respect ordinary primary schools could learn from the special ones, where creating an optimal educational climate is a primary concern. Van Lieshout's concepts were further developed by de Boer (1994). The authors begin with the important observation that social-emotional development is significant and that problems of this kind should not be allowed to develop. The programme recognizes three basic aims:

- promotion of a positive self-image
- learning how to get along with others
- development of social skills.

The programme involves a curriculum of games and discussion. It has the character of an innovation for schools which would like or need to enrich their curriculum with greater attention to affective objectives. In the proposed curriculum games and moments of discussion play an important role.

SECONDARY EDUCATION

So far little has been said about our secondary schools. Generalization on this subject is even more difficult than on primary education. Contrary to, for instance, Great Britain and the Scandinavian countries, the Netherlands have several types of secondary school. During the 1970s the government tried to develop comprehensive schools, but this failed because of political disagreement. For some years now all secondary schools have in their lower years a government-prescribed programme in 15 subjects called *basisvorming* (basic education); pupils can take two or more years to master the programme according to their intellectual abilities. After *basisvorming* children start vocational training or continue with a general education. As a result of amalgamation many different types of secondary school operate in the same building. Recently a national debate has started on the advantages of large schools. The debate has been generated as a result of severe behaviour problems in many schools, such as aggression and a fundamental lack of motivation among pupils. For some years now many secondary schools have shown interest in reform education, especially Montessori, Jena-plan and Dalton. They hope to find ways of coping with these problems by broadening their curriculum. With the introduction of these ideas the importance of the whole of a school's life is being recognized in secondary education for the first time. Many schools have group tutors whereby each teacher has a group of pupils under their special care with which they work for an hour each week. Fortunately nowadays more attention is paid to this aspect of the teacher's task and this is absolutely essential: secondary school teachers are almost exclusively trained in the subject they teach and not for other educational tasks. Meanwhile, guidelines for teachers have been produced such as 'Life-style for the Young', a translation and revision of the training programme *Skills for Adolescence*, available for those who participated in a three days' training course on the subject.

There is much in secondary education that needs to be changed. We still cope with the rigid subject structure: high academic results and receiving one's diploma are the only matters that count. Many pupils struggle with problems of motivation and the number of drop-outs is considerable. Although elsewhere, as for instance in the USA, it has been suggested that the comprehensive system creates many problems, in the Netherlands it is still developing rapidly. It is becoming increasingly clear that a radical change in our secondary education is essential. As has been said, some of the schools focus on the reform theories. There are a limited number of Dalton, Steiner, Montessori and Jena-plan schools for children of twelve years and older. These schools may play a role in the spread of innovation in our secondary school system.

CONCLUSION

The future of our educational system, with emphasis on the affective development of the individual child, depends on a number of factors. I will mention a few.

The framing of suitable curricula with regard to affective development, as guideline material for primary and secondary school teachers, which are supportive and stimulating but not prescriptive, is not a matter of high priority at the moment. On the contrary, in the Netherlands a large gap still exists between school education in practice and research on the subject. In research people usually look for regular patterns. There is no tradition in the field of action research. Institutes which occupy themselves with the evaluation of school education usually have, for reasons of methodology, a strong bias towards evaluation studies of those aspects of children's school progress which are easy to measure.

This means that there is often no attention or hardly any given to affective development. However, under the supervision of the Department of Education, work is done in this field. An important paper about vital teaching skills has been published (Commissie Van Es., 1993). In our society we should all be aware of the fact that school is a vital institution for the transfer of essential human standards and values to the next generation, for the simple reason that there is no alternative. Under optimal conditions the school will play an invaluable role in the personality development of the individual child. Practically all recent publications on social-emotional development bear a direct relation to projects on care extension. This means that this development is mainly seen as the concern of preventive and curative care. This point of view does not do justice to the essential meaning of affective education.

REFERENCES

Bessell, H. (1978), *Het Kringgesprek, emotionele en sociale opvoeding op school*, Rotterdam: Lemniscaat.

Boeke, K. (1934), *Kindergemeenschap*, Utrecht.

De Boer, H. (1994), *Beter omgaan met jezelf en de ander*, Hoevelaken: C.P.S.

Commissie Evauatie Basisonderwijs (1994), *Zicht op kwaliteit*, Leiden: D.O.P.

Commissie Van Es. (1993), *Een beroep met perspectief*, Leiden.

Commissie Van Es. (1993), *Het gedroomde koninkrijk*, Culemborg: Educatieve Partners.

Gerris, J. R. M. (1980), *Denken over jezelf en de ander*, Den Bosch: Malmberg.

Langeveld, M. J. (1967), *Scholen maken mensen*, Purmerend: Muusses.

Lieshout, C. F. M. van (1992), *Basisschoolleerlingen met sociaal-emotionele problemen. Diagnostiek en begeleiding*, Nijmegen: Universiteit Nijmegen.

Selman, R. S. (1976), 'Social and cognitive understanding, a guide to educational and clinical practice' in Lickona, T. (ed.), *Moral Development and Behavioural Theory and Social Issues*, New York: Rinehart and Winston.

(1985) *Wet op het basisonderwijs*, Lelystad: Vermande.

CHAPTER 12

The Danish class teacher, a mediator between the pastoral and the academic

Niels Kryger and Kirsten Reisby

INTRODUCTION

In this chapter we focus on the Danish Folkeskole and especially on one of the central pillars in the Folkeskole: the class teacher tradition. In fact we see the class teacher tradition as an important part of a Danish educational tradition which counterbalances a tendency to see the affective and intellectual dimensions as two different aspects of school life when they ought to be considered as closely linked together.

THE FOLKESKOLE

The Folkeskole was founded in 1814, when all children were given the right to seven years of education. The subjects were religion, reading, writing and arithmetic. Since then, only five major changes have been made to the Education Act in 1903, 1937, 1958, 1975 and 1993. The most recent is intended to be of significance to Danish society as a whole, as its aim is to change and improve school instruction so as to give pupils the best possible foundation for living a full life in tomorrow's society.

In 1987, in preparing the present act (*Lov om Folkeskolen, Undervisningsministeriet, 1993*) the Folketing (Danish parliament) initiated a number of research projects in schools across the country. No less than 8296 projects were completed. Thus the new act has its roots in the everyday reality of school life.

Education is compulsory in Denmark for everyone between the ages of seven and sixteen. Whether education is received in publicly provided municipal schools, in a private school, or at home is a matter of choice, as long as certain standards are met and an adequate range of subjects is provided. It is education itself that is compulsory, not school.

89 per cent of children attend the public education system for their basic nine-year learning span, with an optional tenth year, referred to as the primary and lower secondary age range. This is called the *Folkeskole*,

with one year at each level, with an automatic progression from one year to the next irrespective of yearly attainment. Also, about 90 per cent attend a pre-school class, named kindergarten.

As defined in the Act of 1993, the aims of the Folkeskole are as follows:

- Section 1: The purpose of the Folkeskole is to work together with parents to advance the pupils' acquisition of knowledge, skills, study skills and forms of expression that will enhance the individual pupil's all-round personal development.
- Section 2: The Folkeskole must endeavour to create a framework for experience, activity and study from which the pupils will develop perception, imagination and love of learning so that they will acquire confidence in their own potential and the autonomy to form their own opinions and to take responsibility for their actions.
- Section 3: The Folkeskole must familiarize pupils with Danish culture and contribute to their understanding of other cultures and of man's interaction with nature. School prepares pupils for taking part in decision-making, for taking responsibility, for rights and duties in a society with freedom and democracy. The instruction and daily life in school must therefore build on intellectual liberty, equality and democracy.

Clearly, in many ways the affective dimension is central to the fulfilment of these aims. Thus all teachers have a common responsibility for the affective dimension in relation to their own teaching. However, one teacher has a special responsibility for the care of the individual pupil and the common social life of the class, namely the class teacher. Let us briefly introduce the Danish class teacher system.

THE DANISH CLASS TEACHER SYSTEM

The class group is the basic unit of the Danish Folkeskole. Usually this class group has its own room: the home room. At the start of every school year, new first grade classes are formed. Every class group consists of a maximum of 28 new starters (on average about 22 aged six to seven). In principle, this group of pupils (the class) will continue as an administrative and a social unit during the nine years of schooling.

A class teacher is allotted to each class (group) and has the possibility of having the same class group until the end of the ninth school year, and sometimes even including the voluntary tenth school year.

About a third of Danish class teachers seem to make use of the possibility of being allotted to the same class group for all nine years. Equally, it is frequently the case that the class group gets a new class teacher at the fifth, sixth or seventh grade.

In many ways, the task of the class teacher is comprehensive. It includes subject teaching, social and personal education and pastoral care. 95 per cent of class teachers are mother-tongue (Danish) teachers for their class group. In addition, they often teach their class groups one or two other subjects. The class teacher is also expected to be the co-ordinator of the teacher team allotted to the class group.

This model is unique to Denmark, facilitated by the pre-service teacher educational system. Teacher education is divided between a general compulsory course, which qualifies for teaching in a number of subjects at all levels in the Folkeskole, and a special course which gives a further qualification in two main subjects. Every teacher is qualified to teach Danish and mathematics, so in principle, a class teacher can teach his or her group Danish or mathematics from grade 1 to 9 even if they do not have main-subject qualifications. More and more, however, head teachers prefer teachers with main-subject competence for grades 8 to 10.

Before 1993, all classes were assigned a weekly timetabled period called 'home room time' (parallel to the subject lessons). According to the Education Act of 1993, the class group is now given an extra lesson in one of the subjects that the class teacher teaches, usually Danish. Even though the 'home room time' lesson is no longer timetabled as such, the intention is to maintain the spirit of this 'home room time' and to integrate its function into the daily life of the class group. During the week, this extra lesson can be used by the class teacher and her or his class group for planning, social problem-solving, social welfare, etc. It may seem strange that such issues are timetabled as part of subject teaching. It must, however, be seen as a result of the fact that different groups of planners and policy-makers wanted to remove timetabled home-room time for two very different reasons. One group hoped that this would mean that this kind of activities would decrease and that as a result subject teaching would increase. The other group hoped that it would result in a greater integration of 'home room activities' and subject teaching. Thus, there were two significantly different motivations for the removal of timetabled 'home room time'. It is up to the individual class teacher to respond to this new situation, but the writers believe that the majority of class teachers will retain a significant element of 'home room' type activity. In this they will be supported by the approach taken in the 1993 Act, which was drafted by those supporting the need for 'home room time' activities.

CLASS TEACHER TASKS

The class teacher is supposed to be the focal point of the whole of school life. The main tasks of the class teacher are described in a curriculum guide edited by the Ministry of Education following the 1993 Act (*Klasselæreren, Undervisningsministeriet, 1996*). The class teacher tasks include:

- co-ordinating the teacher-team allotted to the class group
- providing the back-up for linking subject-oriented and social activities
- providing a challenging learning environment in co-operation with head teacher and other teachers
- responsibility of the social life of the class group
- administration and discipline
- teaching certain non-scheduled themes such as road safety education, health and sex education, family education, etc.

- guidance and counselling concerning educational and vocational careers – in co-operation with the educational counsellor of the school, especially in the last period of the pupils' schooling (usually, a school has one educational counsellor)
- co-operating with parents
- pastoral care in relation to individual pupils
- co-operating with leisure time clubs (especially in pre-schooling), school psychologists, special education teachers, and the entire social system, etc., when needed, to support individual pupils or groups of pupils.

Of course, the class teacher is not the only person responsible for carrying out all these tasks. However, he or she is responsible for co-ordinating, co-operating and making sure that these tasks are fulfilled. The fundamental role of the class teacher is to ensure the most favourable environment for the class.

In our view the key educational aim is that the pupils on the one hand become democratic individuals with a feeling of solidarity and on the other hand become independent and self-motivated, i.e. that they themselves assume responsibility for their own learning process and in a wider context for their own lives. This is the teacher's long-term educational aim. Consequently, class teachers must work on two integrated levels in attempting to help the pupils become more self-motivated. They must make the teaching meaningful for the pupils and simultaneously work towards good pupil interpersonal relationships and relations with themselves.

Teachers must walk a narrow tightrope and use empathy and rapport with the pupils. However, these qualities are needed at the same time as they distance themselves from the situation in order to achieve long-term goals. This need for distancing means that class teachers must be able to take a serious look at the pupils, themselves, and the interplay involved. Only in this way can they perceive what is really happening. This perception is needed in order to evaluate whether the long-term aims as far as upbringing is concerned are being achieved.

It is often rather difficult to evaluate one's own practice. Decisions must be made all the time and appropriate action taken. Work with upbringing and caring assumes added importance when one considers the varying backgrounds of the pupils. One requirement is to create respect and understanding for the cultural differences and life-styles each student brings. Another requirement is to create common norms and values which can be developed in classroom time. The class teacher must often cross boundaries, and parents and the outside world must become more involved in classroom work. Awareness of the outside community is vital if it is desired to provide the pupils with wider experience than is usually available in schools.

When working on finding common norms, one must take account of different cultural elements and peculiarities and one must respect them. This aim stresses the need for every pupil to contribute to the social life of the class and the democratic processes in teaching and learning. This is also reflected in encouraging pupils to take responsibility for their own learning.

In the class and during home room time, in the student representative body, and through the teaching process, the influence of democratic approaches and developing responsibility in pupils takes place at a number of levels.

THE ROLE OF THE DANISH CLASS TEACHER

In Denmark, the class teacher system is often taken for granted. Since the 1870s, when the idea of class teacher was introduced, the class teacher has come to personify the task which schools carry out in areas of teaching, upbringing and caring. The system of today can be seen as a tool to ensure:

- a steady and continuous emotional relationship with one adult in children's school life. Not without reason, class teachers are often looked on as substitute mothers/fathers or extra mothers/fathers.
- co-operation between school and home.
- reinforcement of the connection between subject-oriented learning and social processes. There is a correlation between the subject studies and social sides of learning. The fact that the class teacher is a central person in both areas can ensure a closer connection between these two aspects of school life and a wider understanding of learning processes.
- progression in subject learning and co-ordination between different subjects (through co-ordination of the teacher team).

Of course, this system is not without problems. It has sometimes been accused of lowering the standard of subject teaching. Generally, the system depends on the single class teacher's professional and personal competence. For example: are they capable of dealing professionally with adolescent puberty problems which come into play in grade 6 to 8? Are they qualified to teach the mother tongue from grades 1 to 9? If not, are they prepared to deliver 'their' children to another class teacher, for example at grade 6?

Earlier, the tasks of class teachers were often seen as 'private affairs' between them and their class groups. Through current school improvement projects, however, there have been efforts to ensure a more collective school culture. By this, it is no longer seen only as the class teacher's private problem if they do not succeed in their class teacher role. It is a concern, too, for the head teacher and for the school as a whole. This school improvement perspective is emphasized in the Act of 1993 by underlining the importance of co-operation in teacher teams allotted to the class group. In this team-teacher work, the class teacher is not only responsible for the social life and subject teaching of the class but also to co-ordinate with other teachers and to ensure that the tasks are fulfilled.

REFERENCES

Andersen, K. H. (1994), *School Life in Denmark*, Vejle: Kroghs Forlag A/S.

Danish Ministry of Education (1996), *Klasselæreren – koordinering af arbejdet*, Temahæfte 14.

Harrit, O., Kryger, N., Moos, N., Reinsholm, N. and Reisby, K (1992), *Klasselærere: Tradition og fornyelse*, Copenhagen: Royal Danish School of Educational Studies. English summary as 'Form Teachers: tradition and renewal', in E. Noergaard (ed.) (1992), *School Improvement, Development and Innovation*, Copenhagen: Royal Danish School of Educational Studies.

Reinsholm, N., Kryger, N., Moos, N. and Reisby, K. (1994), 'Caring, upbringing and teaching', in P. Lang *et al.* (eds), *Caring for Children: International Perspectives on Pastoral Care and PSE*, London: Cassell.

Reisby, K., Kryger, N., Moos, L. and Reinsholm, N. (1994), 'The tasks of the class teacher: tradition and renewal – an evaluation of development projects carried out in the Danish Folkeskole', *Pastoral Care in Education*, vol. 12, no. 1, March.

CHAPTER 13

The strange concept of affective education: a French perspective

François Audiger and Daniel Motta

Anyone who mentions the subject of affective education to a French teacher, still more expresses an interest in it, is likely to meet with surprise, or even rejection. After all, to speak of the affective is to speak of feelings, of a private, hidden area of the individual, of something difficult to imagine and define, so that to make it one's concern is to commit a reprehensible intrusion into the most private area of the individual's personal life. School should surely confine itself to the spheres of knowledge and reason, to what is universal to us all, and not concern itself with this most intimate aspect of individual freedom. Certain present-day French authors are attempting to re-examine the history of French education in the light of this attitude, the history of an educational system which is thought to exclude from its area of interest, now as in the past, anything that might take emotions and feelings into consideration. School should be concerned only with instruction and reason.

This viewpoint is often shared by teachers, particularly secondary school teachers, who, grounded in their academic competence and mastery of their chosen subject, oppose any intrusion or initiative involving the affective. Of course, in the everyday life of the classroom some concessions must be made to this aspect of things, which is often present as a factor among pupils; it would be impossible for it to be totally absent from their relationships with the subject being taught, with the knowledge imparted and with the teacher. Often a pupil likes a subject because he likes the teacher. This is a common experience, one that has been familiar since education began. The youngest pupils are particularly susceptible to this; the older ones are still influenced by it, even though they are more reserved in their relationships with adults and more appreciative of the teacher's expertise. But once these general truths have been acknowledged, it is best to be cautious, to keep at a distance this uncontrollable world which could tip the world of knowledge over into that of the emotions, making relations in the classroom too difficult by far.

And yet, on closer inspection, there is something unrealistic – illusory or dishonest, even – in seeking to keep at a distance something which is so real a part of people's lives at school and of the knowledge being imparted there. School is not simply an institution where a body of knowledge is transmitted and constructed in an affective vacuum. There is an affective constituent in the relationships between the people in the school as well as in their relationship with knowledge. Some people – in French schools they are a minority, and often a marginalized minority – are calling for this constituent to be included in education, either in the form of an acknowledgement of its reality and the need to take account of it or, in the extreme case, by making it an actual part of the subject matter of education. In this chapter we shall leave aside these approaches, which already date back some time, and instead attempt to look at the affective element in various areas of knowledge.

However rigorous and objective they may claim to be, the various branches of knowledge are a product of our society, part of our discussions, our hopes, our divisions and our world view. They cannot, by their very nature, be kept totally separate from the sound and fury of the world, even though a great deal of energy is expended in attempting to do so. We must look more closely, therefore, and try to discover whether the affective life is as absent as some people would have us believe, and examine the various forms that its presence takes today.

To provide some answers to these questions, we shall develop our analysis in three directions:

- the past and, in particular, the French Republican school, basing our investigation on a work of reference which had a profound influence on generations of primary school teachers, the *Dictionnaire de pédagogie* compiled under the direction of Ferdinand Buisson at the end of the last century (Buisson, 1911). Here, far from being absent, the affective phenomena are constantly slipping out from beneath the outer layer of reason, but they are hinted at rather than manifestly present; although always present in the everyday practicalities which teachers are bound to meet in the course of their work, they could never be taught as a subject, but at most be used as a prop to make learning easier. A comparison with a more recent dictionary shows how slowly the situation is changing, even though new concerns mean that more attention must be paid to things connected with the affective life.
- the teaching of history and geography, with the questions raised by the introduction of social representation into educational thought. There is an affective dimension to the relationship of every pupil with the subject matter taught in these disciplines. But between noting this fact and acting on its implications, there is a gulf which is difficult to cross.
- a topic which, while not completely new, is becoming increasingly urgent – health education. This requires schools to be opened up and multidisciplinary collaboration allowed. Accepted with varying degrees of enthusiasm, the affective has an obvious place here, and is assuming it as new ways of working with pupils are explored.

Each of these three approaches illustrates in its way the 'French view', with its intellectual reserve, and the impossibility of ignoring this aspect of relationships and knowledge.

A CONCEPT OF EDUCATION WHICH KEEPS THE AFFECTIVE ON A TIGHT REIN

We stated above that the point of departure for this chapter would be the reluctance of French schools to take account of the affective dimension. The significance and force of this reluctance are bound up with the French concept of 'school', at least in its most common form, often known as the Republican school (*école républicaine*). In order to give a very brief description of this concept, we have consulted two dictionaries, the first of which has legendary status in the history of French education, the second of which is contemporary. The first was written between 1878 and 1887 and revised in 1911, under the supervision of Ferdinand Buisson, one of the leading thinkers behind the Republican schools, in collaboration with some of the great names of the day. A work both theoretical and practical, containing both philosophical reflections and practical information, for many decades it was the bible of the primary school teacher and of anyone else who worked in or studied primary schools. The modern dictionary is one among many, chosen for its variety, wide currency and recent date of publication; more general and containing no practical information, it reflects what is expected of educational science today.

So let us set out to discover what these publications tell us about the affective life in school. For this purpose we have adopted a rather broad definition of the word 'affective', which includes the characteristics set out in the introductory chapter of this book. A current dictionary of French, the *Petit Robert* defines 'affective' (or its French equivalent) as follows: 'relating to states of pleasure or pain (both simple – affects, sensations – and complex – emotions, passions, feelings)'; affectivity is defined as encompassing 'the phenomena of the affective life'. 'Affective' and 'affectivity' both relate to the emotions, passions, feelings, love, enjoyment, interest, etc. Thus equipped, let us set out on our journey into the *Dictionnaire de pédagogie*, which occupies such an important place in the French tradition. Let us look first at the list of contents: on 'affective' we find nothing; on 'love' (*amour*) only an entry concerning *amour-propre* (self-esteem). The latter is regarded as a means of helping the child to progress, but its many potential traps must be avoided: '... when he appeals to a pupil's self-esteem, the teacher must accept the obligation to watch even more vigilantly for the vanity and pride which could result'. The article refers the user to 'emulation, encouragement, reward'. These are all educational tools, not subjects for study. As we continue our reading, let us stop for a moment at 'civility': the word denotes '... the conventions which govern relationships between people'. So there is something relating to affectivity in our relationships with others. This needs to be taught, because children '... are only too inclined to do whatever they feel like, to say whatever comes into their head'. Here a particular view of the child is expressed: a half-formed individual in need of instruction, a delicate plant which could grow askew if it is not firmly staked and if the soil in which it grows is not constantly cleared of weeds. The entry on 'curiosity' is close in content to that on *amour-propre*: once again it is an educational tool. The author would like curiosity always to be lively, but notes that it declines rapidly '… as the child submits to the influence of discipline and organized study'. Further on, the long article on education is signed by Emile Durkheim, one of the great names in sociology at the turn of the century. In it Durkheim argues that man is a social being and that, in consequence, education is not a means of subjugating him to society, but of making him free. Through the acquisition of knowledge, the learning of languages, the development of physical activities, it is the means of '… making him grow and making him into a truly human being'. All of this is demonstrated, or rather argued, under the auspices of reason, reason working to justify the work of educating the reason. Moral awareness is at the heart of education, not as a result of being imposed, but as a result of freedom: 'For to be free is not to do what we please. It is to be master of oneself, it is being able to behave as reason dictates and to do one's duty'. Thus our attention is drawn to the strong link between education and reason, freedom and self-mastery. Going on through the alphabet, the next word to raise more personal questions is *'laïcité'* (secularity, non-religious nature (of education)). Education is not simply a matter of knowledge. The teacher is an educator; an educator must be '… a teacher of moral values as well as of languages or mathematics, if his work is to be complete … He must be entitled and morally bound to speak to the heart as well as the mind, to watch over the education of each child's conscience to at least the same degree as over any other aspect of his education'. We are moving here from knowledge to will. A new question arises: in the name of what are children's wills to be educated? In this move from knowledge to attitudes and behaviour, is the person not put so firmly in the foreground that the necessary prudence of the educator is forced aside? The author of the article returns to the subject and stresses that it is not the opinion of the individual that is required, or a comparison of different standards and values, but a raising of the status of moral awareness, of the conscience needed for life in a community even above and beyond dogmatic or partisan choices. The entry on ethics returns to and expands this concept. It includes an examination of the relationship between ethics and religion. While acknowledging the historical link between the two, the author tries to untie the knot, since if one continues to take religion as a point of reference, how is one to foster the sense of belonging to a community which embraces a number of faiths? As reason reigns supreme here, solutions are sought in science. But, while waiting for the sciences to be ready, if they are capable of it, to provide a rational basis for a new phase of moral thought, the author appeals to the most determined pragmatism: '… rudimentary decency, the decency that might be described as negative: thou shalt not kill, thou shalt not steal …'. This negative view is insufficient, it needs a positive complement centring around love of the good, voluntary support for what is good, with all that this contributes to personal, family and social life. Since religion cannot be used as a support, another must be chosen: it will be intuition, moral intuition, which has become natural after the 'long centuries of education which have shaped the man of today'. While the man, or the child, is not always inclined towards the good, he has its source within himself and his reason enables him to understand that complying with the rules of what is good is 'imperative in the conduct of life'. This is followed by an entry on 'Instruction, ethical and civic', which includes a school syllabus. The methodological advice talks about the 'heart', the 'feelings', 'good examples', 'sound ideas' and 'noble aspirations'. Here the affective aspect is used to raise the child above its everyday experience and attitudes. The syllabus comes to resemble a catalogue of principles and ways of behaving which seek to create a set of rules governing ideas of communal life and attitudes to oneself and others. Overarching principles are expressed in the form of small acts.

We will end this part of our survey here. The theory and concepts on which French schools are founded take a cautious, distant attitude towards anything relating to the affective life, with the exception of those aspects which can be explained by reason. The heart and the emotions are tools which can help to develop the child's moral conscience, but this development takes place in the name of reason. There is no place for the heart and the emotions as subjects for study or education. There is a great distrust of anything smacking of what we would now call manipulation. Such things are suspect and will remain so. And yet in the everyday life of the classroom, conscience does not simply meet with conscience, or intelligence with intelligence, but there are encounters between people in all their complexity, with their emotions, their attitudes, their affective life. Taking account of people is, of course, permitted, but this requires that everyone should be treated equally – with equal respect, equal consideration and equal interest. Once inside the school doors, there are no more class differences, no variations in wealth, opinion or belief. The person was, and always will be, at the heart of the educational relationship and the educational programme, but that person must, paradoxically, leave out of what is expressed publicly in the classroom anything deemed to be too far removed from reason or from the principle of equality. Described in this cursory way, this concept of education appears to give the affective life no place at all, but in fact it allows teachers great freedom of manoeuvre. There are countless reports bearing witness to the attention given to the personality of the pupil in the everyday life of the school and classroom.

However, school in France does not consist solely of the Republican primary school. Much though the latter dominates people's experience, and still more their imagination, we must make a brief reference to the fact that until the middle of this century there were three types of school in France: as well as the Republican primary school there were urban grammar schools, which children destined for the sixth form and university could attend from primary level onwards, and there were private schools, most of them Catholic. Here attitudes to the affective life and moral values, to education and socialization, were a little different: these were even less acceptable in the grammar schools than in the Republican schools, a little more so in the private schools when linked to religion. For the past thirty years state education has become steadily more unified, and private schools, while retaining their essentially religious roots, have increasingly come to function along the same lines as the state schools.

Since the time when these schools were founded, society has undergone considerable change: school subjects and populations have become more varied, there are new concerns related to cultural diversity, relations between school and home have changed, new areas of knowledge and competence have emerged and are considered a useful part of education, research on education and training has progressed, moral points of reference have become more individual, etc. Amid these developments, the structure we have briefly outlined is still present in minds and in discourse; it is still present because it is a convenient way of dealing with difficult problems, because we have no alternative structure which hangs together as well as this one, and because our minds are attracted by this organized structure, even though everyday life is less orderly.

Is there any sign of a possible rapprochement between this profound social change, changes in the nature of school and the relative permanence of an approach which mistrusts the affective aspect of life? In an attempt to answer this difficult question we shall now look at a present-day dictionary, the *Dictionnaire encyclopédique de l'éducation et de la formation*, published in 1994 (first edition) by Nathan, a publishing house which specializes in educational books. Let us look at the index, which is more than simply a list of entries. A brief glance comes up immediately with an entry entitled affective and sexual education. At last our subject is explicitly included, but surprise, surprise (or not?), the affective is linked with the sexual. Affectivity and sexuality go together. What does the entry say? 'By educating children and adolescents in affective and sexual matters we help them to understand that they have a personal responsibility – at least in part – for their sexual lives and relationships.' The traditional approach, as we have described it, would be inclined to keep such matters out of the classroom, but changing habits and new forms of family life exert pressure for things to be otherwise. In the 1970s sex education was put on the biology syllabus. Unless the teacher is exceptional, this usually goes no further than scientific information: sex is a matter of organs and reproduction. Anything sensitive or embarrassing is carefully ignored. Sometimes outside experts, such as doctors and psychologists, are invited into schools. But the subject is problematic. It raises questions about the division of responsibility between school and home, the line between private life and personal emotions and what can be said, talked about publicly in school. But despite the caution, the subject is constantly raising its head and pointing the way down new and unexplored paths, as the last part of this chapter says. The cross-references at the end of the entry are revealing: adolescence, training in parenting, parent-child relations, health (education). There is no sign of an explicit link with school subjects apart, as already mentioned, from health education and biology.

Let us go back to the index, then, and continue our exploration. The 'axiology' entry asks a direct question about moral values in education and consideration of these values; this, together with the cross-references, brings us back again to the concern of all education with morals and values and to everything which relates to the subject of the pupil. But there is no denying that affectivity and the affective life are not much talked about. French schools have difficulty in finding a place for emotion, passion and feeling, pleasure and pain, all of which form part of affectivity, as the general dictionary we consulted at the start of our voyage of exploration showed. The everyday lives of pupils and teachers are undoubtedly more open to these things than this apparent reserve would suggest, but the words, the analytical tools and the educational practice needed to give them their rightful place are lacking.

THE AFFECTIVE IS ALWAYS THERE, EVEN IN ACADEMIC SUBJECTS

This frequently noted reserve does not provide a full explanation. Are affective phenomena, emotions and feelings absent? They are certainly present in school life, when this is understood as meaning every aspect of life in school – the regulation of relations between people, between adult and adult, adult and pupil, pupil and pupil, conflicts and their resolution, co-operation, mutual assistance, etc. This whole vast area is viewed, essentially, as being irrelevant to what is taught in the classroom, but constitutes an area of social experience for the pupils, experience which relates to the personality of the pupil, including its affective dimension. We shall leave this aspect aside, and concentrate instead on two particular fields relating to academic knowledge, knowledge which is taught as part of school subjects: the first concerns the two subjects of history and geography and the necessarily affective relationship which pupils have to the subject matter taught; the second concerns the difficulties inherent in health education and considers new practices which endeavour to take the affective into account while respecting the private sphere.

The force of affective phenomena in history and geography

Returning one last time to the traditional concept of education which is paramount in French schools, we see in it three disciplines which are thought of as complementary: history–geography–civics. The first purpose of these subjects is to convey a shared representation of the nation's past, territory and power, in order to build a collective identity or, more precisely, to lead pupils into these three pillars of the collective identity so that they can recognize themselves in them and construct their own personal identity on this basis. Even though, here again, we find constant appeals in the texts to reason and intelligence, there is in the background an idea of belonging and, behind that, notions of the affective phenomena and of love. We must love our country, feel emotion towards the riches it contains and gratitude to those who built it, thus acquiring an emotional attachment to the narration of its history, the description of its geography and the explanation of its institutions, since they are ours. Although there are dark areas and tragedies in our history, there are even more moments of greatness and light, which, being greater than the pupils, inspire them to transcend themselves and put themselves, their intelligence and reason at the service of the country and its people. Collective identity and personal identity sail in convoy, and even though, once the link has been established, personal identity can move within the area of freedom allowed us by our democratic societies, it nevertheless maintains a strong link, of both the heart and the reason, with what goes to make up the collective identity.

This structure, which has been frequently analysed, reaffirmed and at times vigorously contested, is now a shaky one. We have already noted some of the contributory factors. Let us add, along lines more specific to the subjects we are discussing, the belief, widely held at the end of the last century, that the development of the historical, geographical and political sciences would lead ultimately to a unified discourse on the past, the present and the political organization of the present; since the sciences produce a unified discourse legitimized by reason, there could only be coherence and close interaction with the school subjects inspired by these sciences. What is taught at school thus produces a sense of belonging which is underpinned by both reason and affectivity. There is no need to point out the multiplicity of discourses which have arisen today from these sciences and the infinite variety of uses to which they are put. The sciences do not produce unity. They form part of the questions that are asked and the debates that go on in our society.

All of this obfuscates and complicates pupils' relationship with these three disciplines. Restricting ourselves to one aspect and to the subjects of geography and history, we shall examine more closely the relationships which pupils have with some areas dealt with in these disciplines. For the purposes of this examination, we shall base ourselves on the model of social representation as presented by social psychology. This model can be used to interpret the knowledge which a person or group has of the subject area under consideration. For the purposes of our own, inevitably brief, examination we shall take account of only three dimensions of social representation: on any given object, the subject (in this case the pupil) has a certain amount of information, develops a more or less broad concept of the object and has a certain attitude towards it. The last of these dimensions highlights the importance of the affective in the way in which any pupil approaches any subject taught. Attitude is particularly important in the disciplines we are concerned with here in so far as these deal with people's actions, their relationships and the ways in which they live together, shape their destiny, etc. There is no approach and no discourse on the social world which does not closely link knowledge and attitude, information and judgements or, in other words, without claiming any exact equivalence, the cognitive and the affective. The cognitive is present, and so is the affective. Traditionally, because they do not know how to accommodate it, teachers tend to neglect the affective, or at least not deal with it in the classroom.

There is research which highlights its importance at all stages of school life. This importance is of course linked in part to the human relationships which are formed between pupils and teachers. It is easier to like a subject and be interested in it if you like the teacher. We shall leave this aspect aside and concentrate on pupils' knowledge and perception of society, which underlie their learning. We will take some somewhat disparate examples, from geography and history, which illustrate the importance of the affective and its implications.

When asked about 'cities', pupils aged between 10 and 15 referred to the attraction of the city centre and their lack of interest in the outskirts, which were unlit and unwelcoming. The city centre is attractive because it has both shops and leisure facilities. The pleasure aroused by the city-centre makes it a more attractive subject for study, a more immediately interesting place. Conversely, this pleasure creates a kind of obstacle to understanding relations with the outskirts. Since the latter are unattractive, it is difficult to understand how they could be attracted by the centre and at the same time be supplied by it with goods and services, wages, decisions, etc. Judgement, being based partly on experience and thus even more forceful and unquestionable, takes the place of knowledge and ignores anything that might militate too strongly against it.

Schoolchildren aged between 10 and 17, when asked about the French Revolution some time (months or years) after they had covered it in history lessons, virtually all saw the same pattern in it. This pattern is based on an underlying concept of society which acts as both a criterion for the classification of knowledge and a basis for judgements. A society is divided, on the one hand, into rich and poor and, on the other, into those with power and those without power. The combination of the two means ultimately that the rich (kings and nobles) have power and the poor (the others, i.e. the third estate in a society divided along those lines) do not. It then becomes very difficult to place the middle classes, since they do not fit into the pattern, and to reach any judgement on the success of the Revolution, since in the final analysis it is still the rich who hold the power, even if the rich are no longer the exact same people.

Still on the subject of the French Revolution, we have observed that children have great difficulty in talking about the Reign of Terror, in situating this period somewhere in the revolutionary decade and making sense of it. The predominant idea which they use to make sense of the events of the latter period seems to be that of political progress centred on human rights and the Republic (the importance of the idea of progress in fact goes well beyond the history of the French Revolution; it is still the main, or even the sole, overarching principle used to give meaning to the history of mankind as a whole). In this scheme of things the Reign of Terror is absolutely 'unthinkable'. Either you are in favour of the revolutionary government and must therefore condone violence of a kind which is now considered criminal, or you are against the revolutionary government and thus hostile to progress and the Republic. The period of the Terror is a barrier that separates us from our history; it is best to banish it from our memory. Although it is taught, often in considerable detail, it is quickly filed away under 'problematical' and 'to be forgotten'.

The final example is taken from a study of the causes of World War I. Schoolchildren aged 14–15 were asked to write a one- to two-page homework essay, using textbooks, on the causes of the war (after a lesson by the teacher on the same subject). In some of the essays we observed the following two phenomena, both of which point to the marked presence of the affective dimension. Firstly, images of the war with its endless round of suffering and destruction thwarted every effort to give a reasoned, classified account of the causes. Everything written was coloured by this sense of suffering. Thought and intelligence did not come into play. The work was swamped by emotion and the pupils linked every action, decision and circumstance preceding August 1914 to the horrors of Verdun and the Somme. Secondly, the study of the causes merged into an attempt to apportion blame. Describing the causes of a morally reprehensible event became, instead of an attempt to find reasons, an exercise in attributing responsibility. Although this was not a reflection on the teacher's lessons or the content of the textbook, the culprit was spontaneously deemed to be the other side – in this case Germany. Alsace-Lorraine was a more powerful memory than any of our links with the more distant Austro-Hungarian empire.

So the study of geography, and still more history, is as much a matter of affective judgements and stances as of acquiring knowledge. Children who do best at school are those who keep the affective dimension at a distance; this distancing greatly complicates the relationship that pupils create between the history and geography they learn at school, their personal experience, the shaping of their own personalities and the huge number of messages they receive about the world.

Health education: an area where increasing account is taken of the affective dimension

The second example comes from an area which cannot be easily or seamlessly fitted into any particular school subject – health education. In our survey of the 1994 dictionary we noted the affective dimension of a subject such as this, and the accompanying risks. Health education is therefore a good example of current attempts to revise our approach. It appears that French society at large is more enthusiastic about health education in schools than educationalists are. Health education may be mentioned in official texts, but in practice it is rarely taught, particularly in the classroom itself. It is still usually taught by members of school health teams or by community workers as part of inadequately funded one-off local schemes. This can be seen as an effect of the allergic reaction of schools to subject matter thought of as being part of the personal sphere, to which we referred above, combined with its aversion to knowledge imparted by practitioners, even medical ones, and the reluctance of the medical world to share its knowledge with the general public. The existing teaching and instruction are largely based on the definition of health as the absence of organic disease.

The World Health Organization's definition of health (adopted more than fifty years ago) as physical, mental and social well-being gives rise to additional problems, mainly of a pedagogical nature. While the social sciences are accepted in schools, psychological knowledge forms no part of French education at any level below higher education. Syllabuses show that elementary psychological concepts such as the reflexes are taught in biology, up to quite a high level of complexity. And time is spent on complex functions – in animals. So animals have individual and social patterns of behaviour, a relational life, even a communicative life, but human beings only have apparatus. And yet research into human ethology has been going on for several decades, contributing to a body of knowledge which is recognized by the scientific community, taught in universities and used in the fields, *inter alia*, of perinatal medicine, pediatrics and mental health. School syllabuses tend to find room instead for the results of more recent work (on immunology, genetic engineering, etc.), probably regarded as more fundamental or likely to have more important social implications. And yet the social usefulness of knowledge about the biological foundations of affectivity, as manifested in early attachment and communication behaviour between the newborn and its parents, is indisputable, as is its importance in the personal education of pupils.

The methodological value of teaching human ethology cannot be doubted either, since it makes intensive use of observation, the reinforcement of which in science teaching in schools has long been called for. In fact it is widely referred to (or even practised) in the sections of the syllabus devoted to animal ethology. The veil which is drawn over the affective and the emotional dimension can be seen to start, incidentally, with their regulation by the central nervous system and hormonal systems, as if the subject became more and more doubtful about its own legitimacy as it moved upwards through the organizational levels of the human being. It is introducing into the behavioural level knowledge concerning specific biological systems that is a problem for school biology, as well as its interconnection within the psychic apparatus with the value systems operating at the social and cultural levels, systems which are taught as part of other school subjects (civics, philosophy, history, etc.). It is true that the tendency in the scientific disciplines on which school biology draws is towards compartmentalizing areas of knowledge rather than building bridges between them, and that these disciplines are happier to conduct a dialogue with the exact sciences than with psychology. They thus leave the field open for more random syntheses, academic in origin (sociobiology) or non-scientific (esoteric), in which children can seek answers, via the media, their families or their peers, to the questions life poses. It is precisely the behavioural level that is decisive in prevention, and the primary objective of health education in schools is to help pupils to adopt attitudes and ways of behaving which will promote their own health and that of others. Pupils must be in possession of an overall set of values consistent with attentiveness to their own and others' bodies, and be capable of finding a positive way of dealing with specific situations in which the contradiction between pleasure and health, freedom and health, the short term and the long term (for example in their eating habits, their sex life and their consumption of legal or illegal drugs) is crucial.

Basing themselves on preventive practices tried and tested by society, schools can enable pupils to acquire tools which will help them make sense of the circumstances of their everyday lives. They can also pass on skills of a more or less specific kind relevant to different areas of health. These skills can be based on precise scientific knowledge imparted at school, a role to which schools are happy to restrict themselves. But above all, they should be built on activities in the course of which pupils can prepare themselves for dangerous situations by experiencing them in advance, through writing, observation, discussion, drama and art, which can involve French, physical education and sport, social sciences and biology. The role of these activities is to give pupils, by means of their realistic effect, a wide variety of opportunities to experience the tension between emotional involvement and emotional distance, and to build up an 'affective frame of reference' which can be brought into play in real situations. These simulation and repetition activities, already widely used in training people for stressful or dangerous jobs, took on a significant role in health education campaigns outside schools at the time of the spread of the AIDS epidemic. They owe their success to their effectiveness in aiding comprehension of situations which have a strong emotional charge or where there is strong time pressure.

Introducing such techniques into the school situation and making them part of the curriculum would certainly raise some technical problems, but would require above all that the objectives of school subjects were no longer perceived as divorced from the objective of the pupils' personal development. A number of subjects can shed specific light, at every level of schooling, on the affective phenomena via which every human activity is brought within the norms of social life for each individual. This education on matters which are part of the private domain can take place without intrusion into the private sphere of each pupil, but in accordance with procedures which promote perception of the personal dimension of every item of knowledge acquired. This presupposes on the part of teachers not only the tact they habitually exercise when 'sensitive' questions come up in the classroom, but, above all, the professional skill to carry the handling of such questions right up to the threshold of the private sphere of each pupil. At the moment, where this private/intimate sphere is of concern to schools at all, it is through the school health system, the work and training of its nurses and doctors. And yet, and this is no small paradox, the growing involvement of the latter in health education campaigns assumes forms which tend to take them into the territory of teachers, blurring in the eyes of the pupils their status as members of the institution to whom they can go with their personal problems.

In addition, making health education and prevention school subjects means that forums for (theoretical and practical) dialogue between school disciplines must be created, with a view to the acquisition by each pupil of a physical and mental culture, and their introduction, like that of other areas of interest (such as the environment), runs into the limitations arising from the way in which schools usually function, the way in which subjects are divided up (into school and university subjects) and the still numerous reservations of many of those involved.

CONCLUSION

In the course of this very incomplete exploration we have deliberately focused on the widely held reservations regarding the treatment of the affective dimension in academic subjects and education in general. These reservations are linked to a concept of school at the forefront of which is the idea of passing on to future generations skills which have reason as their basis, that is to say which are acknowledged as universal, and which mistrusts anything that might impinge on private life, for example by bringing it into the classroom, into school, with the attendant risks of discriminating between pupils or manipulating them. We have not engaged in a theoretical or general critique of this approach; instead we have chosen to demonstrate, using two examples, how affective phenomena are inherent in subjects taught at school and constantly resurface if attempts are made to deny their existence. The repressed, in fact, always re-emerges. History and geography raise questions about the way in which individuals see their place in society and their relationships with others, how they fit into a community in both time and space. Current thinking on identity, citizenship, collective identity, the place of memory and relationships with geographical roots cannot ignore the ever-present affective dimension of these questions. In health education we have the example of the innumerable social concerns which society increasingly wishes its researchers and academics to investigate. and which more and more people think should be made part of school curricula without delay. There is rivalry among the subjects and skills which it is right and good and useful to teach in schools. Should society's imperatives dictate what is to be taught in our schools? Which of the many imperatives should take precedence? Subjects such as these place the relationships of individuals – in this case pupils – with the world and other people at centre stage. In history and geography there is the social dimension; in health education the affective is even more directly involved, since its subject matter is the body, with all the emotions, values and personal implications that entails. The affective dimension cannot fail to be present. Readers of this book probably need no convincing of this. Nevertheless, while our task is indeed to acknowledge this dimension of the person, including the person as learner, and of education, it is important that we should not cling blindly to it – and to be on our guard against any adverse effects. But that raises quite different questions about school, its purpose, its functioning and its place in society.

REFERENCES

Buisson, F. (1911), *Nouveau dictionnaire de pédagogie*, Paris: Hachette.
Champy, P. and Etevé, C. (1994), *Dictionnaire encyclopédique de l'éducation et de la formation*, Paris: Nathan.

CHAPTER 14

Affective education in Israeli elementary schools: principles and practice

Yaacov Katz

THE ISRAELI STATE EDUCATIONAL SYSTEM

Prior to the establishment of the State of Israel, the educational system was semi-private and partisan and catered to the different population groups on the basis of ideological affiliation. The Labour Party established and supported the 'General Educational Stream' and the 'Workers' Educational Stream', the religiously oriented Mizrahi Party established and nurtured the 'Religious Educational Stream', the Agudat Yisrael Party established and financed the 'Independent Educational Stream' and lesser known public organizations supported smaller and more limited educational streams (Bar-Lev and Katz, 1991). Immediately after the establishment of the State in 1948, the different educational streams functioned under the aegis of the Israel Ministry of Education and Culture, but the political parties served as 'supervising committees' of each of the streams. In the turbulent period 1948–53 which faced the state as a result of the mass influx of immigrants from Europe, North Africa and the Middle East, inter-stream competition led to much bitterness and a waste of precious resources. In addition, it was thought untenable by many that the state should shoulder the responsibility for the educational system without having any real say in the running of the different educational streams.

The first Prime Minister of Israel, David Ben-Gurion, led the struggle against the stream system, and after lengthy negotiations, in 1953, he succeeded in convincing the members of the Labour, Mizrahi and Agudat Yisrael Parties to support the call to do away with the stream system and to form a united state educational system. This system as set out in the 1953 Educational Act is based on state secular and state religious elementary and high schools which are subordinate to the Israeli Ministry of Education, Culture and Sport. School principals are subordinate to state inspectors of education who oversee the implementation of state educational policies and curricula throughout the system.

The Israeli elementary school, which offers a wide spectrum of basic education to pupils aged six to fourteen (first grade through to eighth grade), and the Israeli secondary school, which offers pupils a more specialized academic and technological education (ninth grade through to twelfth grade) have two major goals. The first goal is that which deals with scholastic achievement and the second focuses on affective aspects of education. Counselling, which is universally accepted as the vehicle for the advancement of affective and social goals, serves as an integral and central pivot of Israeli elementary and secondary schools, thereby providing the counsellor with the potential to influence significantly the affective and social development of the Israeli pupil during the years spent in the educational system and most especially during the formative years spent in the elementary school. Thus it is necessary to define the essence of counselling as it functions in the educational framework in general and in the elementary school system in particular in order to understand the workings of affective education, which is intensively delivered in the Israeli elementary school system.

COUNSELLING AND AFFECTIVE EDUCATION

Educational counselling in the western world has gone through a developmental process since its beginnings in the 1950s. Havinghurst (1952) defined school counselling as emphasizing developmental tasks, the successful achievement of which led to happiness, while failure led to unhappiness. The role of counselling was to facilitate individual movement along the developmental path. Later, in the 1960s and 1970s, the counselling role developed and Glanz (1974) described counselling in the educational framework as an applied social science which specifically dealt with human growth and development. Herr (1974) indicated that school counselling took on the additional role of career and vocational guidance in order to provide the individual pupil with the ability to make both personal and career decisions that would lead to realization of potential as well as to self-actualization.

According to Hansen, Stevic and Warner (1986), during the 1980s school counsellors began providing the individual pupil with a wide variety of therapeutic services and training programmes which responded to the changing demands of a sophisticated and complex society. This radically changed the counsellor's traditionally more narrow developmental role to one responsible for all aspects of the individual pupil's psychological well-being, including well-being in the social context. They also defined modern counselling as a growth process through which individual pupils are helped to define goals, make decisions, and solve problems related to personal, social, and educational concerns. Gysbers (1993) described counselling in the United States as the area in education which has traditionally dealt with personal adjustment and development. According to Young (1993), the primary goal of counselling in Canada is to facilitate development in three areas of the pupil's life, namely educational, vocational, and personal social. In England, where counselling tends to be seen as part of pastoral care, the National Association of

Pastoral Care in Education (NAPCE, 1986) defined the major issues dealt with by counsellors as those which focus on personal, social, and moral development of the pupil as well as the teaching of interpersonal skills. Arnott (1993) perceived counselling in New Zealand as a wide range of services which include personal and social education.

Lang (1995) postulated that affective education is deeply embedded in the counselling model common to many educational systems in the western world. In the United States, Canada, England, Denmark, the Netherlands, Germany, Belgium, Sweden, Spain, Portugal, Malta, Italy, and New Zealand affective education covers the personal, social and developmental aspects of education with the goal of fostering a healthy, moral, and democratically robust society. Thus affective education is intrinsic to the counsellor's role and is perceived as a major aspect of counselling in the educational framework.

COUNSELLING AND AFFECTIVE EDUCATION IN ISRAEL

According to Klingman and Aizen (1991), counselling in Israeli elementary and high schools is based on the English, European and North American traditions. Klingman (1982), who defined the role of the Israeli school counsellor, stated that there are three main areas where the counsellors are expected to concentrate their efforts. The first focus of the counsellor's role is in dealing with pupils, the second centres on the needs of teachers and the third aspect of the counsellor's role is that concerned with parents. Regarding affective education, the pupil focus is of paramount importance. Here the counsellor is expected to instruct pupils in adapting to the needs of both school and society; to help the individual acquire self-awareness and inter-personal skills; and to assist the pupil to actualize his or her abilities and aptitudes in both learning and societal contexts. Katz (1994) described counselling as the area in education which calls for a focus on the psychological soundness of pupils and for the promotion of a healthy school learning and social climate. In addition, the counselling process is designed to assist pupils in their personal and social development as well as in the solution of their problems. The counsellor is trained to deal with issues that are essentially part of the affective educational domain. These issues include awareness and prevention programmes which focus on alchohol abuse, drug abuse, physical abuse, and sexual abuse which are hazards that pupils are exposed to in modern day Israeli society. Thus the school counsellor is traditionally viewed as the educational professional entrusted with the promotion of affective education as well as psychological well-being in the Israeli school system. The Israeli school counsellor's role is particularly applicable to the elementary school, where the pupil population is usually non-selective, socio-economically heterogeneous and multi-ethnic. The elementary school counsellor is the professional responsible for the development of a socially cohesive pupil body capable of realizing its potential both in the cognitive and affective domains.

THE ISRAELI COUNSELLING AND AFFECTIVE EDUCATION MODEL

The Israeli counsellor uses a number of structured educational and psychological strategies in order to fulfil his or her professional role competently. The major thrust of the counsellor's role is to ensure that the school provides a healthy atmosphere for cognitive and affective development with particular emphasis on the personal, social and developmental aspects of education. The following are the strategies pertinent to the counselling process:

- consultation
- preventative counselling
- crisis intervention
- group counselling
- organizational counselling
- career development
- moral and ethical development
- community education and development.

Consultation

The counsellor in the educational framework is unable to deal effectively with all aspects of the counselling role on an individual basis. In an average size elementary school the counsellor does not have time to enter the different classes on a regular basis. Therefore, in order to fulfil his or her role effectively, the counsellor is obliged to act as a trainer and supervisor of class teachers who implement counselling policy and affective education. Thus, out of necessity, the school staffroom becomes a training centre in which the counsellor prepares class teachers as educators who engage in affective education in addition to their main roles as promoters of scholastic achievement. The counsellor closely supervises and oversees the affective aspects of the class teachers' work and serves as a consultant and advisor to the school staff in order to increase effectiveness and efficiency. The strategy of consultation places the responsibility for pupils' affective well-being in the school situation on the shoulders of those in constant inter-personal contact with the pupil population, namely teachers. The counsellor is always on the alert in order to assist teachers in their efforts to provide for pupils' needs, but will be much less involved with the pupils than the teachers.

Preventative counselling

According to Caplan's (1980) preventative counselling model, the counsellor is perceived as the lynchpin in the 'school support' system. The aim of this system is to provide information and assistance to both teachers and pupils regarding problems that plague modern society. Information, emphasizing the dangers of alchohol, drugs and sex abuse, is usually disseminated by the counsellor or by other professionals who work in close liaison with the counsellor. In addition the counsellor is the staff member who is best able to assist at-risk pupils and parents in their attempts to overcome the temptations to misuse alchohol, drugs and sex. The counsellor is at the forefront of the struggle in Israeli schools against the spread of violence, bullying, and other social and educational difficulties that undermine the morals and values of society – following the model of affective education described by Lang (1995). The counsellor's role also includes the introduction of structured prgrammes dealing with the teaching of life skills, and stress prevention methods, as well as the implementation of inter-personal teacher–pupil and pupil–pupil strategies that contribute to the improvement of the school climate and atmosphere. The counsellor professionally provides the training, methodology, and support to teachers involved in prevention as well as feedback based on scientific evaluation of the preventative counselling process.

Crisis intervention

Crisis intervention is usually a short-term 'first-aid' procedure designed to assist the pupil threatened by an immediate and pressing problem that obstructs normative and routine functioning. Crisis intervention is taken because no other effective alternative exists, and its main goal is to remove the immediate obstruction and to allow the pupil to return to rational and normative routine after which well-planned intervention can take place. As opposed to planned counselling and assistance, which deal with all aspects of the problem at hand, crisis intervention focuses on the 'here and now' in order to reach a situation that will allow for future intervention not bound by the parameters that led to the crisis. Sudden family and social crises, illness, death, injury, unexpected academic failure are typical examples of areas where crisis intervention by the school counsellor is imperative in order to restore routine and normative behaviour. Thus affective education encompasses the specifics of crisis intervention, because crisis can affect pupils usually characterized by normative behaviour and not only those considered maladjusted.

Group counselling

Group counselling is designed to enrich the affective worlds of the group's members within the educational framework. The development of a well-rounded personality, able to function within normatively imposed societal limits, is the major aim of this aspect of counselling. Inter-personal relations, social sensitivity, consideration for others, tolerance, and empathy, which all promote improved integration, esprit de corps and a feeling of belonging to society are just a few of the major topics that can be dealt with in group work. In addition, self-esteem, self-confidence, self-awareness, and independence are discussed and promoted in the group. The group becomes a social entity in which day-to-day situations are discussed and analysed, and where valuable and transferrable affective experience is gained.

Organizational counselling

The basic premise of this aspect of the counsellor's role is that the school is essentially an organization just as is a factory or a departmental store (Hanson, 1979). Professional methods designed to ensure the smooth running of the organization are of paramount importance to the realization of the school's educational aims. Clear definition of school aims, accepted methods to achieve these aims and paradigms of control are essential for school success. The establishment of a clear administrative hierarchy, mechanisms for supervision and conflict management and control, channels for inter-personal communication among the school management and teachers and between teachers and pupils and teachers and parents are also of the utmost importance for the smooth running of the school. The school counsellor, being responsible for the psychological well-being of all members of the school organization, is a key staff member in the organizational efforts to ensure self-actualization by teachers and pupils alike. Thus the counsellor is expected to make a significant contribution to all aspects of organizational development by working hand-in-hand with the school principal and staff in an on-going concerted effort to promote school improvement and effectiveness.

Career development

School is one of society's major agents in career development. Despite the fact that in modern society pupils do not enter the work force immediately after completing elementary school studies, career development is an intrinsic activity undertaken by the elementary school in order to provide a sound basis for future career satisfaction (Hansen *et al.*, 1986). The elementary school prepares its pupils for secondary education which, in Israel and other western countries, leads directly to the provision of future career opportunities. Thus preparation of pupils for a secondary education that is best suited to their individual needs from the academic and social point of view poses a major challenge to the counsellor. Development of academic selection processes, psychometric testing of pupils, organization of workshops with pupils and parents in which information about different types of secondary schools is provided are all integral aspects of career development and counselling. Exploration of the specific needs of individual pupils is also part and parcel of the career counselling process designed to assist with the placement of each pupil in a suitable secondary school in which his or her learning and social potential may be optimized.

Moral and ethical development

Western society in general and Israeli society in particular is at the crossroads of a moral and ethical crisis. Social abuses and delinquency increasingly characterize the pre-adolescent school-going community. As a result, the educational authorities have delegated high priority to the emphasis of moral and ethical development in the educational process. One of the central educational figures involved in moral and ethical education is the counsellor. In this area of counselling, the aim is to clarify moral and ethical dilemmas that are part and parcel of everyday life. Emphasis on moral and ethical reasoning, coming to terms with moral issues, and the provision of a healthy moral and ethical atmosphere are major motives of affective education. The presentation of real-life ethical and moral problems to pupils and their attempts to provide suitable solutions to these dilemmas are integral features of moral and ethical counselling, which is usually undertaken in the classroom in the form of a series of activities initiated and led by the counsellor. Democracy, human rights, racial, religious and ethnic equality, and assistance to the old and needy are just some of the issues that come to the fore in this aspect of counselling.

Community education and development

The involvement of parents and community agencies in the educational process lies at the basis of the counsellor's work. The school cannot be divorced from the mainstream of community life and parents must be encouraged to share responsibility for the formal education of their children. Parental and community needs are analysed by teams of counsellors, social workers, psychologists and educators who then involve representatives of the school parent body in discussions regarding the implementation of community education in the school. The school, in its educational activities, should mirror the concerns of individual parents as well as those of the community in order to develop healthy community-oriented behaviour by the pupils. Volunteering for community service is also encouraged by the school and the counsellor typically co-ordinates projects in which pupils contribute to different needs of the community. Parent–school interaction and partnership as well as community–school dialogue are necessary if the pupil is to understand the centrality of the community in the citizen's life and the positive contribution of a well-balanced community to affective well-being.

CONCLUSION

This paper examined the different aspects of affective education in the Israeli elementary school and described the affective education model commonly implemented by the counsellor. According to Ministry of Education and Culture authorities, affective education is entrusted to the counsellor because his or her training and professional skills serve as an appropriately sound basis for the co-ordination of this area in the educational process. The counsellor deals with the different aspects of affective education, namely personal and social development, inter-personal skills, and the general health and soundness of the school's pupil population. Thus the concern for the psychological well-being of the individual is perceived as a pivotal issue in affective education and all educational interventions initiated and undertaken by the counsellor are designed to achieve this end.

Consultation, preventative counselling, crisis intervention, group counselling, organizational counselling, career development, moral and ethical development, and community education and development are the major component areas of affective education in the Israeli elementary school and are typically accepted as those fields of endeavour which characterize the counselling role (Klingman and Aizen, 1991). The relative contribution of the school to the psychological well-being of the individual pupil as well as that of pupil society will depend on the counsellor's ability to implement the different aspects of affective education in the school curriculum. Effective counselling methods, efficiently implemented by the school counsellor, are the main vehicles which promote improved affective education and prepare the pupil to fulfil a valuable role in society, thereby actualizing one of the major goals of the Israeli elementary educational system.

REFERENCES

Arnott, R. (1993), 'A whole school approach to pastoral care: A New Zealand perspective', in P. Lang, R. Best and A. Lichtenberg (eds), *Caring for Children: International Perspectives on Pastoral Care and Personal and Social Education*, London: Cassell.

Bar-Lev, M. and Katz, Y. J. (1991), 'State religious education in Israel: a unique ideological system', *Panorama: International Journal for Comparative Religious Education*, 3(2), 94–105.

Caplan, G. (1980), 'An approach to preventative intervention in child psychiatry', *Canadian Journal of Psychiatry*, 25, 671–82.

Glanz, E. G. (1974), *Guidance Foundations, Principles and Techniques* (2nd edn), Boston: Allyn and Bacon.

Gysbers, N. (1993), 'Developmental counseling and guidance programs in the school: developments in the USA', in P. Lang, R. Best and A. Lichtenberg (eds), *Caring for Children: International Perspectives on Pastoral Care and Personal and Social Education*, London: Cassell.

Hansen, J. C., Stevic, R. R. and Warner, R. W. (1986), *Counseling: Theory and Process* (4th edn), Boston: Allyn and Bacon.

Hanson, E. M. (1979), *Educational Administration and Organisational Behavior*, Boston: Allyn and Bacon.

Havinghurst, R. J. (1952), *Developmental Tasks and Education* (2nd edn), New York: Longman's Green.

Herr, E. L. (1974), *Vocational Guidance and Human Development*, Boston: Houghton Mifflin.

Katz, Y. J. (1994), 'Chaplain and counsellor in the Israeli elementary school: overlapping or complementary roles', *Pastoral Care in Education*, 12(2), 39–41.

Klingman, A. (1982), *Educational Counseling in the School*, Jerusalem: Ministry of Education and Culture, School Counseling Service (in Hebrew).

Klingman, A. and Aizen, R. (1991), *Psychological Counseling* (2nd edn), Tel-Aviv: Ramot Publishing House (in Hebrew).

Lang, P. (1995), 'International perspectives on pastoral care (affective education)', in R. Best, P. Lang, C. Lodge and C. Watkins (eds), *Pastoral Care and PSE: Entitlement and Provision*, London: Cassell.

NAPCE (1986), *Preparing for Pastoral Care: In-service Training for the Pastoral Aspect of the Teacher's Role*, Oxford: National Association of Pastoral Care.

Young, R. (1993), 'A systems perspective on whole school guidance – pastoral care programs', in P. Lang, R. Best and A. Lichtenberg (eds), *Caring for Children: International Perspectives on Pastoral Care and Personal and Social Education*, London: Cassell.

PART 3

Examples of European Research and Initiatives in the Affective Domain

CHAPTER 15

Dealing with stress in the elementary school

Yaacov Katz

INTRODUCTION

Stress is a psychological construct that mitigates against rational behaviour. Elementary school pupils unable to cope with stressful situations find it difficult to realize their cognitive potential and the cognitive achievement of pupils suffering from stress is usually negatively correlated with their classroom performance. This paper deals with a stress prevention programme designed to provide Israeli elementary school children, who experienced stressful situations during their daily lives, with the ability to cope effectively with stress in order to promote their psychological well-being and to give them the opportunity to realize their cognitive potential.

STRESS AND COPING BEHAVIOUR

During the past few years a growing number of theoretical papers have been written and empirical studies conducted on the subject of stress and coping behaviour. Stress can be conceptualized as an adaptive response that is a consequence of any external action, situation or event that places special physical or psychological demands upon a person (Ivancevich and Matteson, 1980; Schuler, 1980). The consequences of stress include subjective effects, behavioural effects, cognitive effects, physiological effects, and organizational effects (Cox, 1978). Lazarus and Folkman (1987) indicated that general self-belief may influence stress, coping, and health indicators when individuals are faced with stressful and demanding problems and situations over periods of time. External locus of control, inability to cope with distressing experiences, fear of undesirable consequences, worry, and anxiety resulting from living in an environment fraught with danger are significantly related to a feeling of hopelessness and despair (Bandura, 1989; Brown and Siegel, 1988; Cooper, Sloan and Williams, 1988; Seligman, 1991). On the other hand, individuals with strong general beliefs, internal locus of control, trained in coping strategies, characterized by the personality trait of coherence, and confident in their ability to overcome the stressful situation are more competent in their ability to buffer against distress and stressful experiences (Cooper *et al.*, 1988; Hobfoll, 1989; Korotkov, 1993; Lazarus, 1991).

Coping behaviour may be defined as an individual's cognitive, psychological, and behavioural efforts to reduce, minimize, master, and tolerate the internal and external demands of a stressful situation. In addition, there are two distinct major coping strategies: problem-focused, designed to manage or solve the problem by removing or circumventing the stressful situation; and emotion-focused, designed to regulate, reduce or eliminate the emotional arousal associated with the stressor (Lazarus and Folkman, 1984). Carver, Scheier and Weintraub (1989) suggested that problem-focused coping comprises planning, taking action, seeking assistance, discounting irrelevant activities, and even a self-imposed delay to facilitate planning before undertaking a particular coping action. Emotion-focused coping may be broken down into responses such as seeking of social support in the face of stress for emotional reasons, ventilation of emotions, denial of the existence of the stressor, and positive reinterpretation of the stressful situation.

There is considerable empirical evidence that problem-focused coping behaviour directed towards stress-inducing threats is associated with psychological well-being, rationality, and efficient stress dissipation. Sarason and Sarason (1981) indicated that problem-focused coping, which actively confronts the source of stress, is positively related to well-being, rationality, and stress solution, and inversely related to anxiety. Zeidner (1994) suggested that a coping style based on avoidance and denial, which is closely related to emotion-focused coping, will be accompanied by a failure either actively to confront the stressful situation or to use problem-oriented coping strategies which are significantly more efficient in dealing with the stressor. Nezu and Carnevale (1987), Solomon, Avitzur and Mikulincer (1989) and Solomon, Mikulincer and Avitzur (1988) found that, among military veterans, the severity of post-traumatic stress disorder symptoms is positively correlated with 'weaker' personality characteristics and negatively associated with 'stronger' personality traits. Thus, trait-anxiety and external locus of control, and emotion-focused coping strategies are related to more severe PTSD symptoms on the one hand, and optimism and internal locus of control, and problem-focused coping behaviour correlated with less severe PTSD symptoms on the other. Thus problem-focused strategies seem to contribute to more efficient coping than emotion-focused methods, a supposition confirmed by Cornelius and Caspi (1987) as well as by Endler and Parker (1990).

The degree of control of the stressful situation also appears to be an important factor that contributes to the ability of the individual to cope with the stressor. Although most stressors elicit both emotion- and problem-focused coping (Folkman and Lazarus, 1985), the preferred coping strategy usually depends on the perceived manageability of the situation (Lennon, Dohrenwend, Zautra and Marbach, 1990). Thus problem-focused coping tends to predominate when the individual feels confident that something constructive can be done to counter the stressful situation and that the stressor can be brought under control. On the other hand, emotion-focused coping will be used when the individual displays a lack of confidence regarding his or her ability to neutralize stress, is convinced that little can be done to control the stressor or to counter the stressful situation. Carver *et al.* (1989) confirmed that active coping with stress and behaviour rationally planned to counter the stressor are positively related to control of the stressful situation, whereas ventilation of emotions, denial, anxiety, and lack of confidence are associated with pessimism regarding the ability to overcome the stressor.

STRESS AND COPING BEHAVIOUR IN ISRAEL

Because of the Israeli–Arab conflict that has generated violence and terror since the establishment of the State of Israel in 1948, the Israeli Ministry of Education and Culture has encouraged the compilation of stress prevention programmes. Over the years these programmes have been developed specifically for school pupils living near the Lebanese border and those living in the administered territories of Judea and Samaria. In both regions terrorist attacks are frequent occurrences and on a number of occasions schools and school buses have been specific targets. In order to combat stress that develops because of the need to travel to school through high-risk areas as well as the importance of dealing with stress in the aftermath of attacks, the Psychological Services affiliated to the Ministry of Education and Culture have commissioned stress prevention and intervention programmes to be undertaken in Israeli elementary schools in the sensitive areas (see Ayalon and Lahad, 1990; Klingman, 1991; Levin, 1991).

Klingman (1991) indicated that psycho-educational prevention programmes are of paramount importance for a school-going population threatened by on-going stress. An intervention programme should take the different aspects of coping behaviour into consideration when preparing the population for a successful struggle against stress. Kalish (1994) suggested that the most suitable type of intervention programme designed to combat stress at the elementary school level is one based on a prevention model. Prevention is designed to limit, or at very least delay the negative outcome of a stress-induced crisis. Guttman and Levy (1983) suggested that because Israelis have had considerable experience with war, terror and violence over the years, they have undertaken contingency planning in order to cope with stress and to provide the ability to control any stressful situations that may arise. Thus Israelis have the potential to prefer problem-focused coping strategies over emotion-focused coping methods.

Lahad (1993) built a problem-focused stress-prevention model especially designed to improve the capacity of Israeli elementary school pupils to cope with the threat of terror. In this model each of the letters making up the acronym 'basic-ph' stands for a major psychological component to be used in the individual's confrontation with stress. The components included in the basic-ph model are as follows: B – belief, A – affection, S – social, I – imagination, C – cognition, and Ph – physiology–behaviour. According to the model, two stages of training are provided, during which the school counsellor and an anti-terror expert demonstrate to the class how psychological components included in the model can be used to produce effective problem-focused coping behaviour in a stressful situation. In the first stage of training, different scenarios, based on terrorist attacks that actually took place against Israeli targets, are analysed by the instructors and the pupils and alternative methods of effectively dealing with the scenarios are suggested. In the second stage, the anti-terror expert organizes mock terror attacks on the pupils, who are then expected to react according to the best alternative previously discussed. The basic-ph model attempts to emphasize problem-focused coping strategies and to eliminate coping strategies that are emotion-focused. Thus training encourages active involvement by school pupils in developing psychological components and behaviour designed to hone their coping skills and ability to focus on the problems generated in the stressful situation.

The aim of the present study is to examine the efficiency of a problem-focused stress prevention programme designed for use in the Israeli elementary school. In order to ascertain the efficiency of the intervention programme, pupils attending two elementary schools, both situated in high-risk areas where the threat of attack on school transport was a daily possibility, were investigated. The pupils at both schools had participated in stress prevention programmes, but while School A provided a problem-focused experiential programme, School B used a non-experiential classroom-based discussion programme. The research hypothesis clearly stated that pupils attending School A, where the problem-focused prevention programme was conducted, would be better equipped to cope with stress than pupils who attended School B, where stress prevention was dealt with by non-experiential methods.

METHOD

Subjects

The research sample consisted of 230 sixth grade pupils attending two elementary schools (114 attended School A and 116 attended School B) situated in the southern region of the Greater Jerusalem school district. The pupils were resident in towns and villages south of Jerusalem in the province of Judea, situated in the territories administered by Israel since the 1967 Six-Day War, and came from middle- to upper middle-class families and socio-economic backgrounds. All the pupils travelled to school by armoured school bus and were subject to frequent stone-throwing incidents during their daily trips to and from school.

Instruments

One 15-item research questionnaire, based on the Coping Styles Questionnaire (Roger, Jarvis and Najarian, 1993) and modified for use with an elementary school sample was administered to the research sample. All questionnaire items dealt with different aspects of problem-focused coping behaviour in the situation of stone-throwing at a school bus. The subjects were asked to indicate how they would react to the stressful situation. The reliability coefficient of the questionnaire, computed by the Cronbach alpha method, reached the .80 level.

Procedure

Stress prevention intervention programmes were initiated in two Jerusalem district schools soon after it became clear that stone-throwing at school buses that passed through Arab villages and towns in the Israeli administered territories of Judea was a daily stress-producing problem. Although the buses were fitted with armoured windows, the experience of being a passenger on a school bus involved in a stone-throwing incident appeared to be traumatic for pupils on their way to and from school, and the school authorities decided that pupils should undergo a stress prevention programme at school in order to minimize the effects of the stress experienced.

School A conducted a week-long stress prevention 'survival' course, organized by psychologists who had specialized in stress prevention and an anti-terror expert. During the stress prevention course the psychologists dealt with the basic-ph principles of problem-focused coping behaviour in stressful situations (following Lahad, 1993) and the anti-terror expert instructed the pupils how to react in the event of the school bus being involved in a stone-throwing incident. In addition to the theoretical discussions conducted by the psychologists and the anti-terror expert, pupils were subject to mock stone-throwing attacks on their school bus and their coping behaviour was monitored. After each mock attack, the pupils participated in debriefing sessions, chaired by the anti-terror expert, in order to discuss their coping behaviour and to improve their coping reactions in future stone-throwing incidents.

School B invited expert psychologists to conduct a week-long stress prevention programme at the school in order to acquaint all pupils with relevant procedures in the event of the school bus being stoned on its way to and from school. The team of experts conducted lectures, used videos of stone-throwing incidents and discussed ways and means of defending the bus in a stone-throwing incident. This programme, however, did not include specially designed problem-focused coping behaviour instruction during which the pupils would be specifically taught how to deal with the problematics of being caught up in a stone-throwing attack.

The stress prevention courses were conducted simultaneously in both schools and, on their termination, the research questionnaire was administered to the 230 sixth grade pupils who served as the research sample in this study.

RESULTS AND DISCUSSION

A t-test designed to examine inter-school differences on the problem-focused coping behaviour factor was computed (see Table 1). In the t-test comparison designed to examine differential inter-school levels of problem-focused coping behaviour, statistically significant results were indicated. Pupils attending School A, who participated in a problem-focused stress prevention programme, reported significantly higher levels

Table 1: t-test results of comparison between pupils attending schools A and B on the problem-focused coping behaviour factor

Group	Variable	N	M	S.D.	T	D.F.	P
School A		114	31.04	6.11			
	PFCB*				2.26	228	0.03
School B		116	29.50	7.38			

* PFCB=problem-focused coping behaviour

of problem-focused coping behaviour when confronting a stressful situation, such as being involved in a school bus stoning, than pupils attending School B who participated in a general stress prevention programme that did not emphasize problem-focused and rational coping behaviour. The mean level of problem-focused coping behaviour attained by School A pupils was 31.04, as opposed to a mean level of 29.50 on the problem-focused coping behaviour factor achieved by pupils of School B.

The results of the statistical analysis clearly indicate that those pupils who participated in the problem-focused stress prevention programme were better equipped to cope with stressful situations, such as the stoning of school buses, than their peers who participated in a stress prevention programme that did not particularly emphasize the problem-focused or rational behaviour aspects of coping. These results confirm the suppositions enunciated by Cornelius and Caspi (1987), by Endler and Parker (1990) and by Carver *et al.* (1989), namely that problem-focused action-based coping strategies are superior to other strategies used to combat stress. The results also confirm the observations of Guttman and Levy (1983) and Lennon *et al.* (1990), who intimated that perceived manageability of the stressful situation contributes to the utilization of superior coping behaviour patterns. It appears that pupils who participated in a stress prevention programme designed to be as similar to the realities of the stressful situation as possible and to give the participants a feeling of being in control of the stressful situation were more capable of utilizing the coping strategies learnt in the programme effectively and rationally than pupils who participated in a general stress prevention programme that did not specifically promote problem-focused coping behaviour.

The outcome of the research described in this chapter indicates how an affective education stress prevention programme carried out in Israeli elementary schools can have important implications for elementary school pupils who are routinely exposed to stressful situations. The pupils who attended School A, where a prevention programme based on proven principles of problem-focused coping with stressful situations was delivered to them by expert psychologists and instructors, were characterized by higher levels of coping when confronted with descriptions of the stressful situation of being involved in a school bus stoning incident. The rational and efficient coping behaviour typifying the pupils indicates the importance and effectiveness of conducting affective education prevention programmes where necessary in order to promote the psychological well-being of the participants in such prevention programmes. Thus affective education programmes appear to be vital to the educational process and, on the basis of the research detailed above, it is suggested that teachers, educational counsellors and other educational personnel in the elementary school conduct affective education programmes for the psychological benefit of their pupils, thereby complementing the cognitive education provided in the school system.

REFERENCES

Ayalon, O. and Lahad, S. (1990), *Living on the Border*, Haifa: Nord Publishers (in Hebrew).

Bandura, A. (1989), 'Perceived self-efficacy in the exercise of personal agency', *The Psychologist: Bulletin of the British Psychological Society*, 10, 411–24.

Brown, J. D. and Siegel, J. M. (1988), 'Attributions for negative life events and depression: the role of perceived control', *Journal of Personality and Social Psychology*, 54, 316–22.

Carver, C., Scheier, M. F. and Weintraub, J. K. (1989), 'Assessing coping strategies: a theoretically based approach', *Journal of Personality and Social Psychology*, 56, 267–83.

Cooper, C. L., Sloan, S. G. and Williams, S. (1988), *The Occupational Stress Indicator: Management Guide*, Windsor: NFER-Nelson.

Cornelius, S. W. and Caspi, A. (1987), 'Everyday problem solving in adulthood and old age', *Psychology and Aging*, 2, 144–53.

Cox, T. (1978), *Stress*, London: Macmillan.

Endler, N. S. and Parker, J. D. A. (1990), 'Multidimensional assessment of coping: a critical evaluation', *Journal of Personality and Social Psychology*, 58, 844–54.

Folkman, S. and Lazarus, R. S. (1985), 'If it changes it must be a process: study of emotion and coping during three stages of a college examination', *Journal of Personality and Social Psychology*, 48, 150–70.

Guttman, L. and Levy, S. (1983), 'Dynamics of three varieties of morals: the case of Israel', in S. Breznitz (ed.), *Stress in Israel*, New York: Van Nostrand Reinhold, 102–13.

Hobfoll, S. E. (1989), 'Conservation of resources: a new attempt at conceptualizing stress', *American Psychologist*, 44, 513–24.

Ivancevich, J. M. and Matteson, M. T. (1980), 'The coronary-prone behaviour pattern: a review and appraisal', *Social Science and Medicine*, 21, 337–51.

Kalish, N. (1994), *Coping with 'Hope'*, Jerusalem: Eitanim Publishers (in Hebrew).

Klingman, A. (1991), *Psycho-education Intervention During Calamity*, Jerusalem: Psychological Counselling Services, Ministry of Education (in Hebrew).

Korotkov, D. L. (1993), 'An assessment of the (short-form) sense of coherence personality measure: issues of validity and well-being', *Personality and Individual Differences*, 14, 575–83.

Lahad, S. (1993), 'Basic-ph: the story of coping', in S. Lahad and A. Cohen (eds), *Community Stress Prevention*, Vol. 2, Kiryat Shemona: The Community Stress Prevention Centre.

Lazarus, R. S. (1991), *Emotion and Adaption*, London: Oxford University Press.

Lazarus, R. S. and Folkman, S. (1984), *Stress, Appraisal and Coping*, New York: Springer.

Lazarus, R. S. and Folkman, S. (1987), 'Transactional theory and research on emotions and coping', *European Journal of Personality*, 1, 141–69.

Lennon, M. C., Dohrenwend, B. P., Zautra, A. J. and Marbach, J. J. (1990), 'Coping and adaptation to facial pain in contrast to other stressful life events', *Journal of Personality and Social Psychology*, 59, 1040–50.

Levin, Y. (1991), *Living in Peace with War and its Aftermath*, Tel-Aviv: Motive-Orion Publishers (in Hebrew).

Nezu, A. M. and Carnevale, G. J. (1987), 'Interpersonal problem solving and coping reactions of Vietnam veterans with post traumatic stress disorder', *Journal of Abnormal Psychology*, 96, 155–7.

Roger, D., Jarvis, G. and Najarian, B. (1993), 'Detachment and coping: the construction and validation of a new scale for measuring coping strategies', *Personality and Individual Differences*, 15, 619–26.

Sarason, I. G. and Sarason, B. R. (1981), 'Teaching cognitive and social skills to high school students', *Journal of Consulting and Clinical Psychology*, 49, 908–18.

Schuler, R. S. (1980), 'Definition and conceptualisation of stress in organisations', *Organisational Behaviour and Human Performance*, 25, 184–215.

Seligman, M. E. P. (1991), *Learned Optimism*, New York: Knopf.

Solomon, Z., Avitzur, M. and Mikulincer, M. (1989), 'Coping resources and social functioning following combat stress reactions: a longitudinal study', *Journal of Social and Clinical Psychology*, 8, 87–96.

Solomon, Z., Mikulincer, M. and Avitzur, M. (1988), 'Coping, locus of control, social support, and combat-related post-traumatic stress disorder', *Journal of Personality and Social Psychology*, 55, 279–85.

Zeidner, M. (1994), 'Personal and contextual determinants of coping and anxiety in an evaluative situation: a prospective study', *Personality and Individual Differences*, 16, 899–918.

ACKNOWLEDGEMENT

This chapter is based on a paper sponsored by the Institute for Community Education and Research, School of Education, Bar-Ilan University.

CHAPTER 16

The development of altruism: an alternative to Kohlberg's model

Victoria Gordillo

THEORETICAL INTRODUCTION

The research described in this chapter sought to demonstrate that the development of moral reasoning is intimately connected with the development of understanding of what is involved in a relationship, and that moral development reflects processes of affective bonding to significant others. The study used promise-keeping as an example of a fundamental principle regulating human interaction in terms of fairness and care. Promise-keeping represents one of the moral issues assessed by Kohlberg as an important aspect of moral reasoning.

Like Keller (1988), we argue that the contextualization of moral rules in the specific conditions of a situation is an important factor in eliciting the reasons or motives for upholding them. Youniss' research (1980), in agreement with Piaget's early work, provides clues that the power structure of relationships is a factor affecting moral action. While in authority relationships (e.g. parent–child) obedience to rules is the dominant regulating pattern, relationships of equality (e.g. peer relationships) are characterized by reciprocity. Given these findings, the assessment of moral reasoning in a situation that is not structured in terms of power or authority is of special importance in broadening our understanding of the developmental roots of the morality of promise-keeping.

Cultural variations may therefore provide opportunities for testing the adequacy of a developmental theory. In Kohlberg's work, while the stages of post-conventional reasoning have been widely discussed, the concept of the pre-conventional and conventional stages is mostly taken for granted. A critical appraisal of these stages was the goal of the research.

In a theoretical reconceptualization of interpersonal moral reasoning, Keller and Reuss (1984) traced the interpersonal roots of moral understanding. They challenged the contention in Kohlberg's system that loyalty and moral feelings such as empathy, or prosocial concerns and non-instrumental affective bonding to others, are exclusively a phenomenon of conventional morality and thus are not manifested before stage 3. Their findings show that a genuine concern for morality and relationships is evident in Icelandic children's social and moral reasoning about promise-keeping in friendship. This criticism is consistent with results of other studies (Turiel, 1983; Damon, 1984). For example, Eisenberg (1982, 1986) concluded that pre-school children frequently use non-egoistic need-oriented and empathic reasoning which in terms of Kohlberg's theory should not occur before stage 3 in early adolescence.

According to Kohlberg (1984), the individual at the pre-conventional level has not yet really come to understand and uphold rules, expectations, and conventions of authority and society. Only the conventional self is identified with or has internalized the rules of others, authority and society. The cognitive structural difference between the two levels is described in terms of the underlying social perspective. Stage 2 is characterized by a specific or isolated individualistic perspective. In this stage, each person will put his or her own interest first, and this leads to an emphasis on 'instrumental exchange'. There is no room at this stage for a genuine care for the other's concern. For Kohlberg, stage 3 is the 'third-person' or 'member of a group' perspective. Individuals perceive situations from the point of view of the relationship of caring, trust and respect. Moral norms and expectations are generalized across persons and situations, with an emphasis on being a good, altruistic, or prosocial personality. Genuine moral feelings of gratitude and loyalty as well as conscience are major constituents of the conventional level.

In short, interpersonal concerns at level 2 are interpreted as basically instrumental and egoistic. They become socially and morally transformed at level 3, when the individual is concerned with a good relationship 'for its own sake', i.e. without a self-serving instrumental interest.

In our research we sought to demonstrate the existence of precursors of genuine moral and interpersonal reasoning in young children. Our hypothesis is based on previous findings. A series of studies evidenced that on the one hand, children around the age of seven express a non-questioned rule orientation when reasoning about promise-keeping in a friendship, while a concern with punishment as motive for upholding the rule is practically absent. On the other hand, genuine morality or fairness concerns as well as non-instrumental motives are expressed in the age group between seven and twelve. Based on these findings, we argued against the contention in Kohlberg's theory that moral reasoning about fairness issues at the pre-conventional stage 2 level can be characterized as an exclusive instrumental exchange. Children's moral arguments at this stage seem to reflect the process of affective bonding to others and their growing awareness of what it means morally to stand in a relationship.

Through perspective-taking the person gains access to his and the other's subjective worlds. Selman (1980) has shown that the ability to differentiate and co-ordinate perspectives of self and others develops in a hierarchical sequence in which each step is a logical prerequisite for the next. The achievement of a new level of perspective-taking leads to the reorganization of the understanding of aspects of social reality, e.g. to take into account the effects of one's actions on the welfare of others.

In our research we chose two topics: how people come to understand the contractual norm of promise-keeping; and relationship norms, referring to the question of how people come to understand friendship as a relationship that involves morally relevant expectations and obligations about how we ought to act towards each other and take the other's welfare into account. The consistency between moral judgement and action will be approached by analysing the process of decision-making in an action dilemma involving promise-keeping in the context of a close friendship. Like Keller and Edelstein (1990), we do not want 'to argue for an exclusive role of peer-relations in the development of moral reasoning, but we see friendship as an illustration of how cognition and affect are related'.

THE EMPIRICAL RESEARCH: METHOD AND SAMPLE

Socio-moral understanding was assessed in a study of 277 subjects (139 male and 138 female), aged seven, nine, twelve and fifteen. All were at private school or public school in Madrid. 96 came from upper/middle-class families, 105 from working-class families, and 76 were gypsies. A longitudinal sample was also involved composed of 34 boys interviewed in 1991 and again in 1993 as a two-year follow-up.

Subjects were interviewed about an everyday action dilemma occurring between friends based on Selman's friendship dilemma, with minor modifications. The main character in the story promises to meet their best friend on their special meeting day. Later, the protagonist receives a more attractive invitation to a movie from a third child who has only recently moved into the neighbourhood. Various psychological details are mentioned that complicate matters further, for example that the best friend has problems they want to talk about and that they do not like the new child.

The story contains conflicting interpersonal and moral obligations:

- the moral obligation of the promise
- interpersonal obligations related to the friendship
- altruistic obligations related to the situation of the new child.

Within the domain of friendship, the issue of conflict resolution refers to children's and adults' ideas about how friendships are maintained in the face of difficult situations, methods or procedures for rectifying discord and disagreement within a friendship, and notions of the kinds of conflict that are seen as natural and expectable in friendship.

Seven variables formed the basis of analysis in the study:

- problem definition
- motivation for the decision
- consequence for the protagonist
- consequence for the friend
- moral evaluation
- promise-keeping
- concept of friendship

In relation to this the objectives of our study are to describe:

- the ages at which the average child is capable of the kind of altruism characterized by each stage
- the differential growth rate according to school, and what these differences might mean about the social *experiences* of the child
- the differential growth rate in socio-moral development in three broadly defined socio-economic groups
- the susceptibility of development of altruism[1] through planned stimulation.

The following are the descriptions of significant characteristics of each level according to Selman (1980):

- Level 0: *Momentary friendships and physical solutions to conflicts.* There is no differentiation between the subjective perspectives of self and other. The viewpoints of the self perspective are also constitutive of the perspective of the other.
- Level 1: *One-way friendship and unrelated solutions to conflicts.* Subjective perspectives of self and other are differentiated in terms of given needs, interests and feelings. Conflicts are viewed essentially as a problem that is felt by one party and caused by the actions of the other.
- Level 2: *Bilateral friendships and co-operative solutions to conflicts.* The conflict is still not seen to originate within the relationship itself. Rather, some external circumstance or event is seen to be the cause of the disagreement and hence its removal is the source of resolution. The violation of obligations and responsibilities is acknowledged by the self who is aware of the necessity of regulatory strategies even though such strategies may be morally deficient (lying).
- Level 3: *Stability of friendships and mutual solutions to conflicts.* The individual understands that certain friendship conflicts reside within the relationship itself, in the interaction between the parties, rather than in external annoyances to each party individually. Being a 'good friend' in the sense of being a loyal, trustworthy and dependable person is the superordinate viewpoint guiding action choices. At level 3 criteria of precedence are established that determine why it is 'more right' to go with the friend than to accept the invitation of the new child, while acknowledging responsibility towards the new child as well.

Levels vary from the lowest, level 0, to the highest, level 3, with transitional levels (0/1, 1/2, 2/3). The responses of our subjects were coded and categorized at each of the seven levels for the different issues of problem definition, motivation for the decision.

The interview involves descriptive social and prescriptive moral reasoning. That is, the subject has to define the action problem in a preliminary way. Later he or she has to make a hypothetical choice for the protagonist and give the reasons for the choice as well as for the alternative option. These considerations are reflected in the anticipation of the consequences of the choices from the perspective of those concerned (protagonist, best friend, new child). Regulative strategies are then explored in order to avoid or compensate unwanted consequences for self and others. Finally the action choice is evaluated in terms of moral rightness. The variables of the study in each interview are: problem definition, consequences for actor, consequences for friend, moral evaluation, together with two other topics: the concept of promise-keeping and of friendship.

The friendship dilemma

A very important aspect in research about moral development is to verify how the seven variables listed above are constructed across the age groups. In our empirical study we show how the development of moral responsibility is evidenced in general reasoning about moral obligations and responsibilities towards a close friend. The question of personal commitment to obligations and responsibilities is approached by analysing the use of moral and friendship reasoning in the interpretation of a morally relevant dilemma in a close friendship.

In the sample made up of seven-year-old children, the variable scoring was very low. In the problem definition, 23 per cent were in level 0/1 and 1, which means that they have no understanding of the interpersonal dimension of the conflict. Sometimes the conflict is seen as an option between two more or less attractive alternatives: 'Because he told Peter he would go with him and with Oscar too' (168/7) (numbers refer to subject's identification and age).

Ironically, the same percentage appears at level 2, which could mean there are a number of subjects for whom promise-keeping and interpersonal relationships are seen as something obligatory: 'David doesn't know where to go but he had promised Oscar to come' (150/7).

Unlike the German researchers, we do not consider separately the decision 'movie' from the decision 'friend' (to go with friend and not to the movie with the new child), because the decision 'friend' does not always show a higher stage of moral development. Also, Keller and Edelstein indicate that, sometimes, going to a movie is more moral when it implies a concern for the new child. In our sample, almost one quarter of the subjects fall into level 1, where the reasons for the decision rely on the attraction of each offer. However, and this is essential regarding altruism at this age, 26 per cent of the above-mentioned subjects fall into level 2 (the compulsiveness of the promise and the relationship can be considered as evaluating criteria). This means a less selfish and hedonistic decision than was expected by previous research. The same attitude is verified when evaluating the consequences for the friend. Equally surprising is the number of those who are concerned with how the friend will feel: 'He will be sad' (173/7), 'he will get angry because he is his best friend' (161/7).

As is natural at this age, the moral evaluation of the situation shows a greater sensibility than that needed to understand the concept of promise. Nevertheless, the interpersonal relationship implied by the promise also plays an important role. The fact that two subjects reach the highest level presupposes a good guess (or even a mistake in codification) more than that they actually attain level 3.

The concept of friendship in seven-year-olds mainly lies at level 2 (42.9

per cent): friendship as an exchange of mutual interests. However, the question is even simpler for a good number of subjects (37.7 per cent): friends are just playmates. The global evaluation of moral development as far as this dilemma is concerned scores a transitional level (1/2). There is not a real change from a subjective and selfish perspective to a reciprocity one. But the number of those reaching level 2 (27.3 per cent) supports this second perspective, where normative and interpersonal motivations are taken into account.

At the age of nine, the 68 subjects of the sample are more capable of defining the problem: 27.9 per cent already attain level 2, and four subjects level 2/3, where feelings are considered and obligation is internalized. As for the variable decision, level 2 dominates (33.8 per cent) and there are ten that pay attention to the emotional needs of the friend in the first place (level 2/3). In the case of the variable consequences for the friend they mostly focus on the negative feelings unfairly induced in the friend (level 2). There are also nine subjects related to internal processes and trust (level 2/3): 'he will have a guilty conscience because he didn't go with Oscar' (182/9). This also happens in the variable moral evaluation since promise and relationship stand out as criteria (about 51.5 per cent in level 2): 'he must go with Oscar, because he is his best friend and he promised to do so' (201/9).

The highest scores are in the concept of friendship, with 67.6 per cent in level 2, characterized by reciprocity: 'because she is my best friend and I am hers' (003/9), 'because you can tell him about your problems' (024/9).

Globally, the level of moral development of this group seems to be between 1/2 (39.7 per cent) and 2 (35.3 per cent). What makes them different from the former age group is that nobody is in the lowest level, and only nine subjects have a position below level 1.

The level that the majority reaches in the variable moral evaluation is particularly significant in the case of the 12-year-old group. 69.1 per cent are in level 2, scoring only 14 subjects higher and only seven lower. The levels are the lowest in the variable problem definition because more than half of the subjects do not reach level 2. Friendship is also a value acknowledged by most of these children. Eleven of them obtain the highest scores, which is why this variable stands out from the rest. The concept of friendship as a reciprocal relation, which speaks for security and total trust, influences the negative consequences expected for the protagonist if not remaining with the friend (almost all are in level 2 or higher). The consequences anticipated for the friend if left alone are similar: 'she will feel bad, because she left her and went with a new friend' (220/12).

In general, respondents at this age are at level 2 – total reciprocity – although there are ten subjects at a superior level.

Finally, the sample of 15-year-old subjects manages to define the problem clearly and take into account the feelings and relationship with the friend (less than one third of the sample is above level 2). The motivation for the decision is between level 2 and 2/3, i.e. friendship is seen as something that bears obligations. And the same occurs with the moral evaluation, since breaking a promise means to deceive, to endanger friendship, and to feel guilty. The consequences for the friend are even more altruist than those regarding the protagonist. In the concept of friendship 34.4 per cent is in level 3: friendship as a deep relationship, where there is total trust and security in the other person. The concept of promise is between level 2 and 2/3, and the consequences of not keeping a promise are emphasized: 'no-one would trust him, of course' (248/15).

Achieving the highest level is not easy, and in our sample this happens only in relation to the concept of friendship. There are only two children at level 0 (seven years old). However, at level 0/1 there are another two who are nine years old. At level 1 there is only one 15-year-old and 11 seven-year-olds. Level 1/2 is possibly the most appropriate for seven-year-old children, but in our sample we only find there 43 per cent of the subjects. In level 2 the percentage of nine-year-old subjects is slightly above the seven-year-olds (35 per cent against 27 per cent), but the sample of 12-year-olds are the most adequate to this level. In the highest level there is also a proportional representation of all ages, although the 15-year-olds are mostly (39 per cent) in this level.

The expectations in relation to social class have been fulfilled in general, but there are data that are interesting to analyse.

The longitudinal study

Of the sample of 43 seven-year-old subjects interviewed in 1991, we were able to follow 34 that we interviewed again in 1993 at the age of nine. In order to verify if significant changes had taken place in those two years, we analysed the data through a t-test. We also obtained the Mann-Whitney U for non-parametric assumptions.

There were statistically significant differences between the two groups in all variables, so we could assume that a change had taken place and that it had been positive. The global level of the children interviewed in 1991 rose from level 1 to 1/2 and 2. We did not find gender differences across the age group. In the male group there were two variables which were non-significant: motivation for decision and promise-keeping. However, there was some difference in favour of the nine-year-old group. In the female group, the non-significant variable was friendship concept (*cf.* Table 1).

DISCUSSION AND CONCLUSIONS

The purposes of research

It is reasonable to suggest that as a result of this study, our knowledge of the characteristics of the moral development in the different age groups researched has improved.

In spite of the advisability of repeating it in further research carried out on different samples (e.g. other towns, rural settlements, etc.), we have identified a significant point in development. Early childhood seems to consist basically of a unilateral positioning or a reciprocity in action. Later on it will focus more on interaction as the subject succeeds in combining their own perspective and that of others in relationships with others. Finally, in adolescence the subject's theory of relationships will be based on the understanding of each person's expectations.

Table 1: Test comparisons at 7 and 9 years (N=34)

Variable	Time 1		Time 2		
	mean	std.dev	mean	std.dev	t
Problem definition	2.97	1.40	4.18	1.23	3.74 (1) ms
Choice motivation	3.38	1.53	4.54	1.43	3.20 (2) ms
Consequence for protagonist	3.02	1.69	4.60	1.32	4.24 ms
Consequence for friend	3.61	1.32	5.09	0.94	5.22 ms
Moral evaluation	3.61	1.41	4.96	0.88	4.68 ms
Promise-keeping	3.55	1.39	4.75	1.22	3.73 (2) ms
Friendship concept	3.50	1.67	5.21	0.99	5.07 ms
Global	3.55	1.30	4.87	0.89	4.81 ms

(1) Statistically non-significant in the female sample
(2) Statistically non-significant in the male sample

Interpersonal moral responsibility is a process which is present at as early an age as seven, as soon as the subject is capable of an incipient perspective-taking of the situation of the other. This capacity of perspective-taking certainly increases with time, but it may be accompanied by a certain cynicism lacking in childhood. We therefore agree with Selman that the changes within the relation between thought and feeling, or feeling and action in the same person are necessary criteria for perspective-taking as a rating of socio-cognitive development. Moral responsibility as an essential element of social personality should include not only cognitive aspects – attainment of new perspectives, transcending of subjectivism – but also affective aspects, the necessary change of attitude to accept and respect the other.

The hypothesis underlying our research has been confirmed both by our empirical data and by the theoretical development we have undertaken. Contradicting Kohlberg's hypothesis and statements obviously demands more abundant data than we are presenting here, but the way is open. Altruism exists in childhood and it implies perceiving the other as another self and applying the 'golden rule' of reciprocity in all its aspects and possibilities. Personal and cultural variables interact throughout this evolving process giving place to different configurations.

As for exploring the relationship with oneself, that is to say in order to find individual differences within, all we have done is apply a different moral content (the dilemma of the relationship with authority). Nevertheless, consequences could also be drawn from the opinions of a subject concerning the matters dealt with in the interview. The connection between problem definition and the concept of friendship, or the moral assessment given to the action of the protagonist and the concept of friendship, are some of the possibilities that could be analysed not only statistically, but also qualitatively, by means for example of a study of cases – the latter perhaps the more convenient here.

Regarding individual differences between subjects, we would like to point out the absence of differences between the two sexes, a fact that in principle could be considered surprising given that girls are considered to have greater sensitivity in interpersonal matters. Although Selman did appreciate a certain difference, other researchers closer to us, such as Keller and Edelstein, did not. This leads us to think that the instrument that has been applied may not capture adequately the different aspects mentioned.

The differences due to social status appear as a serious question. It is true that they have also been found in other research, but if in the case of Selman such differences disappear or lessen with age, that is not so in our case. We have seen under the corresponding heading that it did not seem to make much 'evolutionary' sense that 12- and 15-year-old subjects were surpassed in their moral thought by younger peers from a higher social status. In our sample the subsample of gypsies has a great weight, a fact that leads us to two different questions: in the first place, the need to form this group so that it may stand at the appropriate level from an evolutionary point of view, and secondly the need of a better understanding of their own culture. There is no doubt that in this group the concepts of friendship or promise are approached differently to other social groups, which implies a different way of conceptualizing the problem and solving it in a 'moral' way.

It is also surprising that seven- and nine-year-old children belonging to what we have called a 'low' social status reach higher scores than those belonging to the high social status subgroup, even if later on this does not occur. It seems clear in this case that the influence of the socialization processes have helped the development of these variables more in some cases than in others.

As for the differences due to the type of school, it is the private school students that reach higher average scores, possibly because these schools have traditionally made a greater emphasis on moral education. Fortunately, the moral education of students is now a major goal in state schools and this will lead in the future to lessen such differences. Besides, when crossing this variable with the social status, it is not always the higher social class that comes out best: it is the students of private schools belonging to the lower social status that reach the highest average scores in the conceptualization of friendship. One possible way of interpreting this fact is giving the socialization process such a decisive weight that it eliminates social origin. As could be expected, age establishes statistically significant differences at all times and in all variables. It is therefore verified that socio-moral thought grows parallel to the general development of the subject. Other findings suggest non-variation of the sequence, the total structure of each stage and the hierarchic order.

Both our own data and that from similar researches carried out in other countries show the possibility of developing moral attitudes and values at an early stage of development, as there is a predisposition towards the other that makes it possible to grasp – even if in a very elementary manner – such difference in perspective. Therefore our initial hypothesis has been confirmed: contrary to Kohlberg, the subjects in our sample show certain characteristics which are those of an incipient morality reaching beyond the distinctive features of a pre-conventional stage. Even at the age of seven, action is decided by something more than fear of punishment or unquestioning obedience to established rules. The justification and moral assessment of the action are clearly superior to the 'instrumental morality' which according to Kohlberg goes with these ages.

It is also true that as far as friendship is concerned, a morality of fairness – typically masculine – as different from a morality of caring – typically feminine – do not appear in the subjects researched. Such differences may develop at later ages and may be a consequence of specific socialization processes, but our data does not allow us to reach any conclusion which could point at two different moralities, a typically masculine and a typically feminine one. The differences in socio-moral reasoning can be due to cultural variables – as we have pointed out in relation to social status, type of school or even country – but in no case has the gender been a variable that has established a difference in the analysed sample.

Although we have worked on a hypothetical moral dilemma, we have always been aware of the importance of action in morality. That is why the questions have tried to combine opinions, feelings and choices in a consistent manner and based on personal commitment. Because purpose and responsibility are two basic aspects of human action, everything concerning goals, the means to reach them and the resulting consequences are matters that should be analysed in detail. Our aim in doing so is to assess the capacity of the subject to combine what concerns him or her and what concerns others, what one may wish at a given moment and the socially necessary principles to maintain an adequate interpersonal relationship.

The last section of this chapter will deal with the final aim we had set ourselves with our research, namely to design actions that would promote moral development in school environments. But before that we shall describe the methodology followed in this research.

The methodology

One common criticism of research carried out on the basis of hypothetical dilemmas refers to the possible difference between a hypothetical reasoning and reasoning in reality. Can the same level be expected in both situations? The question raised has to do with the difference between capacity and performance, for even if it is difficult to define the level of development – or capacity – of a subject under actual circumstances, predicting its performance is even more so. No matter how well understood the other's perspective is and the social rules governing personal relationships, there are many other attitudinal and affective variables that will condition the decision to act in one way or another.

On the other hand, the concept of stages in itself does not seem suitable to grasp the complexity of the evolutionary development of a subject in the psycho-social area. It has been proved that the influence of variability due to context or content can contradict the concept of stage. And at the same time it must be remembered that such situational variability may affect one subject more than another.

Because it is so difficult to explain the complex interaction of the cognitive and the affective processes in the child, we have tried to establish different methods that can bridge the gap between the research and the reality of the classroom.

Naturalist observation helps to make up for the shortcomings of previous methods in as much as it supplies contrasting elements to theoretical statements in actual and multiple contexts. At the same time it is a way of including teachers in the planning and carrying out of the research. Within the model we are submitting, the task of teachers would be to provide a critical analysis of this model from their own experience and practical activity in the classroom and thus test both its limits and the possibilities of applying it in new contexts. The aim is not that the child should necessarily show the same level of thought and action, but that the organization appropriate to each area has similar evolutionary and hierarchic characteristics. That is to say, subjects with a high level would be capable of performing at a lower level, but not vice versa.

For Selman to determine whether certain responses reflect truly qualitatively distinct levels requires both empirical evidence of sequence and a logical argument that points to hierarchical relations among different concepts. Models based primarily on empirical evidence without an examination of the logic of categories are prone to confuse content with structure. Models based too heavily on underlying formal logic without adequate attention to empirical connections are prone to be too abstract, unmeasurable, and incomplete (1980, p. 297).

The aim in educational research is not only to assess or define levels, but also to foster their development by means of promoting the adequate context and incentives. Maturity is known to be the capacity to choose among different alternatives the one best suited to a specific circumstance, rather than the capacity to perform at a high level. We shall therefore refer to some educational proposals deriving from our research.

Consequences for education: the development of altruism

Because one of the main features of the moral self is the need of consistency between judgement and moral action, it is for teachers to guide the activity of the subject leading to the choice of a morally correct action. The subject must be able to do it, know how to do it and want to do it. And this requires the development of certain assumptions – the capacity to act morally, certain knowledge (what this kind of behaviour is about, and a motivation) and wanting to do so. The aim of our research is basically to prove that such 'assumptions' are found in children since early childhood. The capacity of a child to act in an altruist manner – allowing the other's good to come before their own – clearly shows the capacity to act morally. Starting from this point we can define aims for moral development (prior study of the evolutionary characteristics of socio-moral thought throughout the different ages) and propose certain actions. Lickona (1991) and Wynne and Ryan (1993), for example, have reminded us recently that the aims of education have remained the same for centuries: help people to be wise and good. Today we may have to turn back to this second aim of education, to what has also been called the 'formation of the character'; and restore the role of the teacher and the school in this task. For Lickona there are two values which are the core of this public morality which is for the school to teach: respect and responsibility. The former as the passive element of morality, the latter as its active element. Such responsibility includes caring for others, the carrying out of our own responsibilities, contributing to the community, relief of suffering and the making of a better world. Most of these can be included under 'altruism' given that they imply the opposite to individualism and selfishness. If we want to say it in a more positive manner: they foster solidarity.

The data from the research described in this paper suggests that empathy is an affective skill which can be developed from an early age. At a cognitive level this skill is closely related to the capacity to take the perspective of others. Therefore it is necessary to create situations which will encourage the development of this capacity in children. The schoolroom environment is morally so rich and so dense (Wynne and Ryan, 1993, p. 98) that the teacher is hardly aware of it. But even so, the nature of school exists and it conditions the formation of character. In the light of this and the findings of the research, schools should:

- Create a positive moral culture in the school, developing a total school environment (a school-wide sense of community, a moral community among adults, and time for addressing moral issues) that supports and widens the values taught in the classroom.
- Foster caring beyond the classroom, using inspiring role models and opportunities for school and community service to help students learn to care by giving care.
- Recruit parents and the community as partners in values education, encouraging parents to support the school in its efforts to foster good values; and seeking the help of the community in reinforcing the values the school is trying to teach.

Within the classroom this approach calls upon the teachers to:

- act as caregiver, model and mentor, supporting pro-social behaviour and correcting hurting actions.
- create a moral community in the classroom, helping students to know, respect and care about each other, and feel valued members in the group.
- practise moral discipline, fostering moral reasoning, self control and a generalized respect for others.
- create a democratic classroom environment, involving students in decision-making and shared responsibility, thus making the classroom a good place to be and learn in.
- teach values through the curriculum, using academic subjects as a vehicle to examine ethical issues.
- use co-operative learning to teach children the disposition and skills for helping each other and working together.
- develop the 'conscience of craft' by fostering students' academic responsibility and their regard for the value of learning and work.
- encourage moral reflection through reading, writing, discussion, decision-making exercises and debate.

- teach conflict resolution so that students have the capacity and commitment to solve conflicts in fair, non-violent ways.

In short, it is all about treating students as we want them to treat others, bringing to light the hidden content of the curriculum and teaching through our own subject a set of values and an approach to learning. It has been said (Gordillo, 1992, p. 40) that rather than giving courses on moral education, the role of the teacher is to help students to face the moral implications of the subject taught and make them understand that knowledge is a form of power, which – like all power – can be used for better or worse. One way of fostering altruism in students will be to encourage them to use their knowledge in the service of others. Obviously, this implies a less 'independent' and competitive way of acquiring knowledge than has traditionally been practised in our classrooms.

If teachers can develop in students altruism as a moral attitude, even more so as guide – whether teacher-guide or simply tutor – for it is ultimately their responsibility to form values and attitudes (see Ministerio de Educación y Ciencia, *La Orientación Educativa y la Intervención Psicopedagógica*, 1990), they can provide both for the group and the individual opportunities to render actual services to others. Thus they develop selfless, empathic, compassionate attitudes, all of which are basic elements in moral education and essential for altruism. The child should not only have a knowledge of moral principles, but should also be encouraged to act in a certain way, a way of acting which is elicited by the right feelings (pain for the sadness of others, compassion for the suffering that cannot be relieved, tenderness for weakness, joy of beauty, etc.). A key feature of the teaching of the theory of guidance in recent times has been to conceive empathy as something that can be learned. One suitable way to acquire such a notion could be to bring the suffering of other members of society before the students, giving them the opportunity, no matter how small, to relieve such suffering. In order to promote altruistic feelings in students, it seems useful to include this sort of true experience in the curriculum, instead of utopian or impracticable ones.

At a different level, but also concerning the fostering of positive attitudes and feelings, we have story-telling as a means of moral education. The psychiatrist Coles (1989) has drawn our attention to the powerful influence of stories in the configuration of our own lives. Stories capture our imagination and move our hearts, they suggest rather than compel, which is why they have always been a means of moral education which is being rediscovered today. 'The telling of stories is a particularly good method of moral education, for stories have the power of eliciting sentiments. That is not the case in the discussion of dilemmas or in the clarification of values, where questions are merely intellectual problems rather than human problems loaded with emotions' (Gordillo, 1992, p. 134). Not only that, discussions which are supposed to be morally neutral may turn into desensitizing processes about what is right and what is wrong. The student needs criteria in order to form a judgement. The adult cannot deprive the pupil of moral wisdom, but can show it without imposing it. The need to carry out certain behaviours in order to learn them is part of that experience.

Finally, the education of altruism also requires models. Having mentioned the need of action and the fostering of the right sentiments as essential elements in this development, we must not forget the tremendous influence of modelling. The teacher-guide should incorporate the behaviour he or she wants to teach: the student will learn not from words, but from actions.

Altruism is indeed acquired by living in a community that puts it into practice, rather than through exhortation or discussion. School is, together with the family, the micro-society where the life of the student takes place. If it loses its own aims and goals as a society and merely reflects the society that surrounds it, it will not fulfil its formative function. When this happens, says Coleman, the child only spends a few hours there, instead of living there. That is why it is easy for the child to escape from the need to help others, or from the consequences of not being honest, or of breaking a promise. According to this author, the reason why the values that have to do with helping others and contributing to a common effort and mutual respect are not promoted (Coleman in Wynne and Ryan, 1993, p. iv) is because most of the aims at school consist in an individualistic achievement of goals with hardly any common aims. But if such values are not fostered, the opposite attitudes are bred. Therefore, because the teacher is not the only agent in education, it is of the utmost importance to plan what we want to teach and by which means.

The atmosphere at school reflects what is valued in it. More decisive than any programme for the teaching of values are the kind of relationships existing between teachers, managers and students, the rational quality of discipline, cleanliness, order, the rules about what is allowed and what is not. All of which confirm a set of values whose presence or absence promotes a positive or negative learning in students. If the curriculum is the knowledge, capacities and attitudes taught and promoted at school, it is indeed achieved in an explicit manner, but also in an implied manner through the hidden curriculum, also called *null curriculum* or curricular void, which has not received much attention in moral education programmes. It concerns aspects deliberately not taught and it affects the potential of the curriculum. It also implies the exclusion of certain ways of thinking about things, which accounts for its danger in moral education. The desirability of developing altruism and modelling behaviour, whether or not it is explicitly part of the curriculum, is taught through the hidden curriculum. But a mistaken conception of the person and their development could make such work be seen as pointless, leaving it explicitly outside the educational goals pursued. It would then result in a curricular void due to a mistaken theoretical interpretation. That is precisely what we have tried to avoid in this research.

NOTE

1. Altruism can be defined for the purposes of this chapter as 'a situation where an individual acts taking regard of the benefits to the other/s before the benefit to themselves'.

REFERENCES

Coles, R. (1986), *The Moral Life of Children*, New York, Atlantic Monthly Press.

Coles, R. (1989), *The Call of Stories*, Boston: Houghton Mifflin.

Damon, W. (1984), 'Self-understanding and moral development from childhood to adolescence', in W. Kurtines and J. Gewirtz (eds), *Morality, Moral Behavior and Moral Development*, New York: Wiley.

Eisenberg, N. (ed.) (1982), *The Development of Prosocial Behavior*, New York: Academic Press.

Eisenberg, N. (1986), *Altruistic Emotion, Cognition, and Behavior*, Hillsdale: Lawrence Erlbaum.

Gordillo, M. V. (1992), *Desarrollo Moral y Educación*, Pamplona: EUNSA.

Keller, M. (1988), *The Development of Interpersonal Moral Reasoning: Three Studies on the Conception of Preconventional Morality*, Berlin, Max Planck Institute for Human Development.

Keller, M. and Edelstein, W. (1990), 'The development of a moral self: Consistency and inconsistency from childhood to adolescence', paper presented to the *Conference on Morality and the Self*, Ringberg.

Keller, M. and Reuss, S. (1984), 'An action-theoretical reconstruction of the development of social cognitive competence', *Human Development*, 27, pp. 211–20.

Kohlberg, L. (1984), *Essays on Moral Development. The Psychology of Moral Development*, vol. 2, San Francisco: Harper and Row.

Lickona, T. (1991), *Educating for Character*, New York: Bantam Books.

Ministerio de Educación y Ciencia (1990), *La Orientación Educativa y la Intervención Psicopedagógica*, Madrid: MEC.

Selman, R. L. (1980), *The Growth of Interpersonal Understanding*, New York: Academic Press.

Turiel, E. (1983), *The Development of Social Knowledge. Morality and Convention*, Cambridge: Cambridge University Press.

Wynne, E. A. and Ryan, K. (1993), *Reclaiming our Schools*, New York: Macmillan.

Youniss, J. (1980) *Parents and Peers in Social Development*, New York: A. Sullivan.

CHAPTER 17

Upbringing: a domain of the school?

Kirsten Reisby

WHY IS UPBRINGING ON THE AGENDA REGARDING SCHOOLING TODAY?

The word 'upbringing' is cognate with Germanic or Scandinavian words (such as the Danish *opdrage*), and means 'to rear', or 'the manner or action of bringing up', that is, to bring the child from a state of nature to the dignity of the fully developed human being. Upbringing and education were later understood as a process of civilization: the child was to be introduced, 'led into', the moral basis of society, its norms and systems of knowledge, and would in this way develop character traits acceptable to society. In Denmark, the family played a central part in this process. It was not only the right, but also the duty of the family to take charge of the upbringing of the child, that is to say to take care of the child, accept responsibility for its behaviour and ensure that it both grew in knowledge and was instructed in the tenets of Christianity.

In the 1960s and '70s, in professional circles that adopted a critical stance towards society, the term 'upbringing' was replaced by the term 'socialization'. This latter term was actually a statement of intent, marking the central position of the state and of society in relation to the family. The state and society had taken over many of the functions that had previously been the responsibility of the family, including part of the function of reproduction. To an increasing extent, caring for and looking after children became a public task. Institutions such as kindergartens and schools were to contribute to the process of adapting the child and bringing it to accept the way society was organized and the conventional ideologies. The school was one of society's most important agents of socialization. This meant that the mandate to bring up children was not held by the family alone: there were many agents of socialization, both formal and informal.

The conditions and forms of family life had also changed markedly when the second wave of industrialization swept through Denmark in the 1950s. As production increased, so did the demand for workers, and women entered the job market in increasing numbers; wages rose, and so did consumption. So what does the 'traditional' family look like today, forty years on? The situation can be indicated by some figures taken from recent statistics. Only 3–4 per cent of the mothers of small children are housewives (Christoffersen, 1993), so the housewife at home is in fact becoming an historical phenomenon. If both parents are working, their working hours overlap considerably – six hours a day on average (Thaulov, 1993) – which means that children have to be cared for outside the family in the daytime. In other words, the family needs child-care institutions, which in turn leads to the institutionalization of children's lives, split up between the school and such institutions as school kindergartens and youth clubs, free-time activities, and so on. The Danish family has been called 'the time-manager family' (Jørgensen *et al.*, 1986): time spent together as a family is plotted into the plan of the week like other activities.

The question arises, therefore, whether the nuclear family remains a reality at the present time, or whether it too has become an historical phenomenon. In Denmark it can be difficult to form an overall view of the situation of the family. It has become normal for couples to live together without getting married, even after they have had children, but it is also normal for couples to get married later at some point or other. A couple living together are not registered, however: father and mother will appear in the statistics as singles. On the other hand, divorce figures show that about a third of all children will experience the separation or divorce of their parents before they reach the age of 18 (Christoffersen, 1993). In the face of all these figures, the basis for regarding the family as the primary factor in upbringing would appear to be very unstable. The fact that society is increasingly interested in the school taking an active part in the upbringing of children has to be seen in relation to these changed family conditions; teachers are expected to care for children and strengthen their individual and social development.

'IN CO-OPERATION WITH PARENTS'

The new role expected of the school became clear with the 1975 Education Act for the Danish Folkeskole. The introduction to the statement of aims paragraph was as follows: 'It is the task of the Folkeskole in co-operation with parents to …', after which the text goes on to list all the developmental and teaching tasks faced by the school. This introduction has been preserved in the revision of the Act made in 1993. The statement of aims concludes with the requirement that 'the daily life of the school should be built on freedom of thought, equality of worth and democracy'. Taken literally, this statement of aims calls for very close co-operation with all parents regarding, for instance, the all-round development of the child. On the other hand, this statement of intent, that school and home should co-operate, has not developed in practice, and for this reason the Danish parliament took the initiative in supporting development projects aimed at promoting this co-operation and offering teachers better opportunities for establishing closer contact with the individual child. The intention behind school–home co-operation may be seen as a way of really underlining the democratic obligations of the school, as well as a desire to counteract tendencies to polarization between the state and the population. At the same time, this passage is also a recognition of the fact that school is moving into the domain of the parents by explicitly being given responsibility for the all-round development of the child.

This chapter, however, will take a closer look at the way some teachers and parents respond to the question of who is responsible for the upbringing of children. What do these two parties expect, and what demands do they make on each other in terms of caring for and bringing up children?

'THERE'S A WORLD OF DIFFERENCE BETWEEN MY SCHOOLING AND MY CHILDREN'S'

This comment was made by the father of a pupil in grade 2. Even though he had only left school himself 15 years earlier, he felt there had been enormous changes. He, and other parents interviewed in connection with the evaluation of development work in the Danish Folkeskole, stress the fact that teaching has changed, and are especially aware of the radical changes which have taken place in the teacher–pupil relationship. The 'old' authoritarian class teacher[1], as they knew him or her, has gone, and the 'new' type of teacher expends a lot of time and energy on building up a close personal relationship with every pupil and a good social climate within the group of children in the class.

Many parents have shown some surprise at these changes, but most of them are satisfied with the process the school has been through; they feel it has become more 'human'. The 'teacher with a human face' has meant that in general their children feel more secure and happy in school. Even so, of course, parents also have many critical comments.

The statements from parents referred to here are taken from material collected in connection with a research and evaluation project carried out by a group of researchers (Harrit *et al.*, 1992; Reinsholm *et al.*, 1994; Reisby *et al.*, 1994). The evaluation was requested by the government and the aim was to collect experience gained in the course of a number of local development projects, initiated by teachers, which went under the general heading of *Expanded functions of the class teacher*. The development projects were funded by central government, and formed part of a countrywide governmental programme of development in the Folkeskole entitled *The school as a local cultural centre*. The purpose was to gain experience from innovations covering a wide range of areas, as a basis for the revision of the Education Act relating to the Folkeskole.

The development work in the Folkeskole and the research and evaluation project took place in the years 1989–92. The project included a questionnaire and a qualitative study of 15 selected development projects. The qualitative study was organized as a case study, building, for example, on semi-structured interviews with heads, teachers, parents and pupils from classes involved in each development work. During the interviews we asked the participants for their views on the 'good class teacher', and the responsibility of the school with regard to the upbringing of children.

'THERE ARE CERTAIN ASPECTS OF UPBRINGING WHICH THE SCHOOL IS BOUND TO BE INVOLVED IN, BUT THERE MUST BE A CONSTANT DIALOGUE WITH THE PARENTS'

The quotation above is from an interview with one of the class teachers of a grade 2 class in a wealthy area on the outskirts of Copenhagen. The development project involved a double class teacher system, which meant that the teacher of mathematics and the teacher of Danish shared the tasks and responsibility of the class teacher. It also included close co-operation with parents on a parents' council, an increased flow of information, conversations with parents, parents and family evenings and family excursions.

The justification for the whole project can be summarized in the description given by the teachers of the group of parents they were dealing with: they are all newcomers and have no social network where they live. Both parents are hard-working publicly employed academics or fill high positions in private industry. They are interested in what their children do at school, but as the children grow older interest tends to be concentrated on high academic standards. Their everyday lives are very systematized and tend to follow a fairly strict timetable. The children have a lot of spare-time activities, and they are fetched and brought by car. As one of the class teachers put it:

> Everything tends to be timed. They don't like to mess around, and whatever they do together with their children has a touch of quality about it. They like things to be efficient and done quickly, and this is also reflected in some of the things we do together with them ... We often have to take a lot of stick from parents if we don't live up to their expectations.

Faced with children whose daily lives are of this nature, teachers feel that it has become their responsibility to create emotional security and cohesion in the children's lives, and to a certain extent this also includes the question of upbringing. Parent–teacher meetings have been used to discuss attitudes and norms and thereby create a set of common rules for the social life of the class, for the general framework of the children's lives, and so on.

Teachers also accept responsibility for the physical and mental development of the child. If something is wrong, they contact the parents immediately, and create an atmosphere of security. The children:

> ... know that they can come in and talk to us about problems which may arise among themselves. Nor do we mind hearing about private matters, and in fact we have an agreement with the parents that we and the children should get to know each other well, even though this means invading the privacy of the home.

This quotation is an example of the direction in which the school has changed, and how teachers explain the necessity of this change. The conditions affecting family life are such that the school must take on a caring role, and contribute to the emotional stability of the child and social education within the class, as well as to parents' reflections on the norms that they apply to upbringing in the home. According to the statement of aims paragraph, however, all this must take place in co-operation with parents, and the teachers referred to here admitted on several occasions that this was not without problems.

The private sphere would seem to be a dangerous area: 'The children can tell us about private matters … even though this means invading the privacy of the home'.

WHAT DOES PRIVACY MEAN?

The opposite of private is public, and what the teachers are saying is that there is a gap between the public and private spheres, that the school belongs to the former, that the teachers represent the public sphere and cannot therefore invade the privacy of the home without further ado. Talking about private matters means relating something that has happened within the family, something that belongs to the sphere of intimacy which we do not talk about. This is of course a tautology: the private sphere is the absence of the public sphere. In one of his earlier works, the German social philosopher Jürgen Habermas presented a description of the development of the classic 'bourgeois public sphere' in certain European countries since the era of the Enlightenment (Habermas, 1976). The bourgeois public sphere presupposed the right to private property and acted as a critical control on the activities of the state. The growth of capital and the increased co-operation between capital interests and the state (the system) has led to a structural change – a decline – of the bourgeois public sphere. Habermas outlined the forms of imagination characteristic of the bourgeois public sphere, and inspired by this we may say that in the 19th century and nearly up to our time, there was a consciousness gap between the private and public spheres. Within the private sphere also, however, people differentiated between the social and the intimate sphere. The family as an institution belonged to the sphere of intimacy: feelings, sexuality, and married life were themes cut off from the social sphere. The latter was concerned with economic matters and was confined to work places. In short, it was not *comme il faut* to talk about work or financial matters at home, or about intimate matters at work. Moreover, the whole of the private sphere was cut off from culture and politics, which was what public life was about. Habermas emphasized that this division into separate spheres was more or less broken down as the boundaries between the state, capital and the market gradually disintegrated. At the same time, the family was deprived of some of its traditional functions. As we said in the introduction, many tasks related to reproduction have been taken over by the public sphere, and the only things that keep families together are feelings and consumer activities. According to Habermas, the 1950s were characterized by a polarization of the social and intimate aspects of the private sphere; the world of work and organizations became 'public', and the family more private (1976, p. 141).

However, the boundaries of the intimate sphere in Denmark are also changing. The slogan of the women's movement in the 1970s, 'Private is Public', was a crossing of the boundary and seen as provocative at the time. So was 'confessional writing' in the literature, which was precisely a question of bringing the personal, intimate sphere into the public arena. It was just 'not done', and represented a breach with a moral code widely supported by people at of all levels of society.

Today, these boundaries of consciousness have been eroded in many ways and indeed the boundaries themselves have shifted. The teachers, however, take for granted that they have not disappeared completely, and therefore find it important that agreement/consensus be reached within the teacher–parent group both as regards the fact that teachers are involved in upbringing, and that their caring task may mean that they become involved in people's private lives, in the terminology of Habermas: in the intimate sphere.

The question is now whether the teachers are right in thinking that parents experience a boundary line between the school as part of the public sphere and the family as part of the sphere of intimacy.

'MAKING CHILDREN INTO REASONABLY ACCEPTABLE PEOPLE IS BASICALLY THE RESPONSIBILITY OF PARENTS'

In the research mentioned earlier we interviewed one couple, and a father and a mother separately. All the parents corroborated the statements made by the teachers, agreeing that the development project had been a success. The couple stressed that the class teacher has a caring role:

> They have to be able to see when there's something wrong with a child. They must ask the child what's wrong, and they must have the right to tell the parents if they think a child has problems, even though they might be family problems.

Using almost the same words as the teacher, this couple is saying that the fact that a child has problems allows the teacher to step over the invisible boundary line and enter the world of the family.

There is full support for the idea that teachers should take care of the social life of children – in school. The parents emphasize that it is important to create common norms and rules, that there is discipline and that standards are set for children's behaviour and for their work in school and at home. One mother said that she felt that the teachers had struck a good balance between fixed rules and freedom, and that at the same time they had established a good relationship with the children. But the child's integration of values and norms is basically a matter for the parents.

My conclusion is that the teachers and the majority of parents agree that the teachers are responsible for caring and upbringing in school, and that they agree on where the line is to be drawn between school and home. Some of the possible problem areas have been discussed at parent–teacher meetings, but many have not. This is not strictly necessary, however, because of the general agreement.

'THE SCHOOL WILL HAVE TO TAKE RESPONSIBILITY FOR UPBRINGING. MANY CHILDREN LIVE ARTIFICIAL LIVES'

These are the words of a male class teacher, who teaches in a school in a provincial town where the parents are of very mixed social, economic and cultural backgrounds. There is a fair amount of unemployment in the town. He, too, forms a class teacher team for a grade 2 class along with a female mathematics teacher.

He has two arguments for the view that the school must take over the task of upbringing. The first one is that parents have no idea what a family is and what upbringing entails. Family life is marked by instability: a high divorce rate, more alcohol consumption than in previous times and a lack of emotional energy, all of which means that the child is left to its own resources and to the entertainment provided by the media – an 'artificial life'. What is needed is a 'family teacher'.

The second argument is that the teacher is the only factor linking the life of the child together:

> Today, the class tutor is the chain holding together children's lives. This may sound ambitious, perhaps even insulting to parents, but in fact it is we who have to co-ordinate whatever action has to be taken when a child has problems in life. No one else can do this. Social workers or psychologists can be brought in, but nothing happens; there has to be a teacher there all the time, or else nothing gets done.

Both class-teachers see it as their responsibility:

- to support families that need it by keeping in close contact with them
- to establish a close emotional contact with each child and to be a kind of substitute parent
- to create norms and rules for social behaviour in the class
- to take care of the child's psycho-social and health welfare
- to create shared experiences for child and family and for families together and to establish common norms.

Here there is no border between the public and intimate spheres. As the teachers see it, the state, and they themselves as representatives of the state, must go in and compensate for unsatisfactory conditions and forms of family life. They also try to resurrect some kind of local cultural community for and together with the parents as a compensation for the dissolution of traditions and of the conditions of life typical of society in the past.

'I HAVE TO ADMIT I AM DELIGHTED WITH THE WORK THESE TWO TEACHERS PUT IN'

This is also a statement made in the course of the interviews with parents. The couple quoted both praised the efforts made by the teachers on behalf of their children, their deep involvement and the work they had done to enable parents and children to do things together. In their opinion all were also agreed, however, that there were considerable social and cultural differences within the parental group, and that this cannot be overlooked; some parents, for example, had never taken part in anything.

The father thought that this had meant that a particular group of parents had done the lion's share of the work. While admitting that 'his style of life was probably more conservative' than that of the teachers, he nevertheless agreed with their long-term goals for the children's development. Nor did he have any objection to the teachers' 'interfering' in his own family life if they felt that his son had problems, but stressed that this was because they were competent teachers whom he trusted. It would appear that this father's views about the responsibility of the school and the nature of parent–teacher co-operation had changed. He still maintained the boundary between family life and school, but the boundary may be crossed because the teachers are competent.

Another parent, a mother, was also enthusiastic about the teachers' work. She was convinced that teachers must become involved in upbringing and in caring for children. If the teacher discovers that a child has problems, then it is best to approach the parents and talk to them about it:

> But for this to be possible you need to be on the same wavelength as the class teacher, to have more or less the same attitude to things, and to be able to talk to him or her.

Maybe it was just the social and cultural differences between parents that prompted her to stress that upbringing is a question of norms, and that a certain measure of agreement in this respect is a prerequisite for talking about private problems. The couple touched on precisely this point as being central to the reservations they had about the development project. As they put it: 'We are still basically positive, but we still send out warning signals'. In their view, the parents as a group 'both financially and as regards attitudes to life' were split up into three groups with conflicting interests: those socially involved with an active family life and a circle of friends; the single parents without such a social network; and parents of a lower social status with many problems. The latter group did not participate. For the second group the primary aim of activities was social contact; activities with the children were of secondary importance. Their own group (group 1) preferred activities relevant to the children. In their view the teachers had allied themselves too much with the second group – the beer and wine drinkers.

What the couple was saying was that they were not quite on the same wavelength as the teachers, nor did they have the same opinion on the border line between school and home as regards upbringing:

> The teacher should keep well away from the private sphere, the internal problems of the nuclear family and such like, which might come to his notice. He should be careful what he gets involved in as far as the privacy of family life is concerned.

These are strong words. Later in the interview they said that the class teacher should take care of an unhappy child in school, and that if the child had persistent problems the teacher should contact the parents.

Towards the end of the interview they said that the class tutor might be obliged to approach the parents if the child is unhappy as a result of conditions in the home. In this case he can be the disinterested third party who can get the parents to start working on their internal conflicts.

This couple are an interesting source because they try to maintain a clear boundary around the intimate sphere, knowing well that there are families with problems that affect the children. In these cases the teacher is forced to contact the family, but if the family opens its door to him, then he is no longer the advocate of the child, but a neutral third party.

UPBRINGING – A QUESTION OF PROFESSIONALISM

This data from our research provides examples of teachers who are trying to accept the consequences of the conditions that threaten the life of the family, and the break-up of norms and traditions that lead to uncertainty and insecurity.

These projects took place in a Danish setting, and may appear strange and possibly irrelevant to other European contexts. The justification for presenting them here is that they can cast light on one of many possible ways of taking the affective dimension seriously. These teachers have become involved in the personal and social development of their pupils; they have involved the parents in co-operation on a wide front; and they have received the complete or partial support of the parents to make caring and upbringing matters in which the school must be involved. At the same time, however, the parents who were interviewed stressed that the school cannot interfere in questions of upbringing without reservations; they expect the class teacher to arouse confidence and display competence.

Competence is a question of professionalism, and in this respect most forms of teacher training are inadequate. The professional competence necessary to care for children, to interrelate with parents and with the social and health systems, calls for insight into these systems, but also for ethical principles and reflective awareness of one's own feelings. The affective dimension in the work of the teacher has many facets, and it is very important that it be integrated into the general processes of teaching. In consequence, there is a need to take a long, hard look at the question of professionalism and teacher competence.

NOTE

1. For an explanation of the term 'class teacher' and a description of the class teacher system in Denmark, see Chapter 12.

REFERENCES

Christoffersen, M. N. (1993), *Familiens ændring – en statistisk belysning af familieforholdene*, Rapport 93: 2, Copenhagen: Socialforsknings-instituttet.

Habermas, J. (1971), *Erkenntnis und Interesse*, Frankfurt am Main: Suhrkamp.
Habermas, J. (1976), *Borgerlig offentlighed. Henimot en teori om det borgerlige samfund*, translated from *Strukturwandel der Öffentlichkeit. Untersuchungen zu einer Kategorie der bürgerlichen Gesellschaft.* (German edn, 1962), Denmark: Fremad.
Harrit, O., Kryger, N., Moos, L., Reinsholm, N. and Reisby, K. (1992), *Klasselærere: Tradition og fornyelse*, Copenhagen: Royal Danish School of Educational Studies. English summary of evaluation report as 'Form teachers: tradition and renewal', for the Innovation Council of the Folkeskole, Copenhagen. Copenhagen: Royal Danish School of Educational Studies.
Jørgensen, P. S. *et al.* (1986), *Efter skoletid*, Copenhagen: Social-forskningsinstituttet.
Reinsholm, N., Kryger, N., Moos, L. and Reisby, K. (1994), 'Caring, upbringing and teaching – the Danish class teacher system', in P. Lang, R. Best and A. Lichtenberg (eds), *Caring for Children: International Perspectives on Pastoral Care and Personal and Social Education*, London: Cassell.
Reisby, K., Kryger, N., Moos, L. and Reinsholm, N. (1994), 'The tasks of the class teacher – tradition and renewal. An evaluation of development projects carried out in the Danish Folkeskole', *Pastoral Care in Education*, Vol. 12, No. 1, pp. 27–33.
Thaulow, I. (1993), *Børnefamiliernes arbejdstider – en analyse af fleksible arbejdstider i staten*, Rapport 93: 3, Copenhagen: Socialforsknings-instituttet.

CHAPTER 18

Teachers' understanding and emotions in relation to the creation of boys' masculine identity

Niels Kryger

INTRODUCTION

The background of this chapter is some research work I have done on masculinity in the Danish Folkeskole: how masculinity is considered and treated in an educational context. The work involved two studies:

- *Gender, School Culture and Male Teachers – Big Boys in School – A Qualitative Study of the School's Role in the Formation of Gender identity in a Group of Adolescent Boys* (PhD study) (Kryger, 1988a)
- 'progressive' male teachers' ambiguous attitudes to femininity and masculinity (Kryger, 1992)

THE SHAPING OF A MASCULINE IDENTITY IN A CULTURAL AND SOCIAL CONTEXT

The shaping of a gender identity plays an important role in the formation of an identity as a whole. However, this shaping of gender identity is often difficult in our societies because the division of labour is based more and more on androgynous values. At present, the ideal is that most tasks in the labour market can be and should be conducted by females as well as males. This is one of the most fundamental cultural changes of the last three or four decades. Today, Danish school culture and teaching mainly support these androgynous values.

In former times, the gender identity was shaped through the distribution of tasks in society. Furthermore, for working class men gender identity was bound up with physical manual work. Today, this kind of work is disappearing. At present the shaping of a gender identity is a task mainly related to leisure time activities. Mass media, fashion, sports, etc. offer gender models (often traditional models) to fulfil this task. In school or at the workplace, of course, individuals are working on their task of shaping a gender identity, but mainly as subordinated activities and in school often as sub-cultural or counter-cultural activities. Consequently, the shaping of a gender identity is often a process that takes place in spite of the nature of official school and workplace cultures.

In progressive movements in education and the labour market, many traditional masculine values are considered reactionary values that should be opposed and combated, particularly those masculine values that are connected with a traditional working class culture: physical manual work, bodily vigour, power and strength. In boys' search for masculine identity, however, these values are still active in their consciousness and activities.

Generally, issues connected with gender and the shaping of a gender identity constitute one of the most important emotional and affective areas in the Danish school of today. It is an area that reflects cultural changes and an area that often evokes ambiguous and ambivalent attitudes and emotions. In particular, many teachers frown on boys' search for a masculine identity.

THE BIG BOYS IN SCHOOL

Big Boys in School is a qualitative study of the school's role in the formation of gender identity in a group of adolescent boys. The empirical materials originate from a class in a Danish Folkeskole that I followed periodically during grades 8, 9 and 10 in the 1980s. I focused my attention on a specific group of boys in the class and those factors which were of significance in the formation of their gender identity.

The study consisted of classroom recordings, interviews with teachers and pupils, observations in and outside the classroom (the boys' extracurricular activities, for example), recorded in diary entries. This plurality of data and data types was used consciously to register changes of viewpoint, for example between teacher planning viewpoints and pupil viewpoints, particularly in connection with the analysis of various conceptions of the gender problem, and in the analysis of the management of male and female life spheres.

In the interpretation of my data, I have tried to distance myself from two research positions that would at first sight seem to be opposed, but often show similarities in practice. The first is rooted in an objectivistic tradition that finds its purest form in positivism. In this tradition, all conditions associated with the researcher's subjective consciousness are deemed sources of error, and must be eliminated. The second position is not represented in the same way by a scientific tradition, but is a tendency in parts of qualitative research to establish the concepts concerning development and emancipation with which 'phenomena are measured' in a normative manner. The basis of such a procedure might be one's own subjective development, or a given research or emancipatory movement. The latter approach draws on an aspect of research recognized by the scientific tradition itself, namely, that the subjectivity of the researcher cannot be kept out of the research process. In both positions, the researcher is given the role of omniscient 'narrator' and interpreter, the voice of truth (as in positivism), or the chooser of normatively determined concepts. The researcher manifests himself or herself in this way only indirectly, namely as a writing and interpreting subject. I did not wish to present myself to the group of boys I worked with as an omniscient researcher, who could conjure up objective concepts of development and emancipation without ambiguity. Ambiguity and lack of clarification were part of the 'researcher subject' I bore within me through the research process. Therefore, the research process could not be understood without reflecting on and attempting to formulate something about ambiguities in myself as a person and researcher with regard to the project. I was not simply the observing eye or the interpreting subject, but became, by way of my participation in the social life of the class, a part of the class's social dynamics.

In getting a theoretical and methodological grip on these complex problems, the concept of projection has come to hold a central place in my analysis. In its most unreflective form, projection is synonymous with attributing our own development to the people we meet, as well as interpreting their actions on the basis of our own life experience. I do not consider projection as a source of error, but on the contrary as a way to the understanding of and insight into others and thus as a valid subjective starting point for the researcher/interpreter. An unreflective projection can, however, prevent us from seeing and recognizing that the people with whom we are dealing can differ from our expectations. In this approach, it is advocated that present historical conditions make it particularly important for the researcher/upbringer to co-reflect, and make manifest, his or her projections when deciding on the attitude to adopt with regard to the formation of gender identity in children and the young. Many adults who are responsible for child upbringing today have experienced conflict and uncertainty where sexuality is concerned earlier in their life. This makes them prone to project without reflection their own course of development onto the child/young person, and further use this projection as a norm for his or her 'emancipation'.

AN EXAMPLE – PETER

To illustrate the boys' attitudes and understanding I quote from an interview with one of the boys:

Niels: There has been a lot of talk about women going out to work, and that men should stay at home. Do you think this is reasonable?
Peter: Yes, let them pave the roads. They'll not bother with that anyway. Or to be dustmen. The rough work is for the men to do. And as you can see, women have no muscles.

Peter was at that time 15 years old. I will make a short analysis of his statement seen in the light of the socio-cultural point of view. Peter is – like many of the boys I observed – son of a father who is a manual worker. One of my points is that the sometimes desperate insistence of these boys on hard, muscular work must be seen as an attempt on their part to maintain the ideals of their own culture, that is, ideals of a primarily working class culture. Consequently, there is a tendency for them to make use of these ideals mainly in connection with their leisure activities where they lay stress on physical power. That includes, for example, their involvement in the mass media and sports.

In school, these boys build up a sub-culture distinct from an intellectual and, as the boys see it, female world. The distinction is sustained by means of 'tough' attitudes and forms of behaviour. Consequently, I have chosen to call the boys participating in this sub-culture the 'tough guys'. Their female class teacher frowns on these boys' attitudes concerning gender issues. She looks on them as male chauvinists. She is provoked because her understanding of gender issues is based on thoughts about liberation and progressiveness inspired by the liberation movement of the 1970s. Her aim is to develop a new understanding of sex roles. She was unable to look at boys' search for masculinity as potential to be developed. On the contrary, she considered their search as a disturbance to her world.

FINDINGS IN THE RESEARCH PROJECT

The socialization process in boys

My investigation confirms the results of studies which adopted a developmental-psychological and psychodynamic point of view to the sexual development of boys. These studies have shown that many boys use stereotypic forms of manliness to explore their sexual identity during puberty and the period immediately preceding it (Nielsen and Rudberg, 1991). The forms of manliness in question are traditional, at least when seen from a transformational point of view. In my analysis, I supplement these developmental/psychological results with a socio-cultural analysis showing that several of the forms of manliness used by the boys are difficult to practise in a social context, primarily because of the changes that have taken place in family patterns and on the labour market. It is precisely in this area of tension between the necessity of changing a number of the traditional forms of manliness (of which the boys are also conscious), and the more immediate task of forging a boy/male identity, that my analysis of the boys' development potentials unfolds.

The gender socialization of boys whose fathers are manual workers

Most of the boys observed are sons of fathers who perform manual work, mainly skilled and unskilled workers, but also small independent craftsmen. I have already suggested that the insistence of these boys on hard, muscular work must be seen as an attempt on their part to maintain the ideals of their primarily working class culture. However, contrary to the English working class 'lads' described by Paul Willis (1977), the boys in my study are well aware of the difficulty of deploying such ideals in connection with their future jobs. Consequently, the tendency is for them to make use of these ideals, stressing physical prowess mainly in connection with their leisure activities (including, for example, their involvement in the mass media and sports) and school, where they give substance and form to a boy sub-culture distinct from an intellectual and, as the boys see it, female world. The distinction is sustained by means of 'tough' attitudes and forms of behaviour.

Progressive education and questions pertaining to sexuality

In my study, the term 'progressive education' covers educational thinking inspired by cultural positions that have their source in the emancipation movements of the 1970s (for example, the women's movement and the somewhat smaller men's movement). I argue both that this type of 'progressivism' lies behind many of the ideas that determine the attitude adopted towards questions pertaining to sexuality within education, and that a very negative picture of men has been drawn within this emancipatory tradition, particularly of men from the lower stratum of society, where physical expression is intimately tied to the idea of maleness. By way of a kind of negative projection, the emancipatory movements, which are primarily middle class movements, have fragmented the ideals of working class culture, because these male ideals are looked upon as threatening, not only in the form they take among working class people, but also for what they represent for the middle class itself. One of my conclusions is that we who have roots in middle class movements must shake off the negative connotations of these boy/man images if we are to meet 'the tough guys' on a footing permitting us to see and encourage their development potential and possibilities, especially with regard to their search for male identity.

GENDER, SCHOOL CULTURE AND MALE TEACHERS

In my other study I focused on the male teacher. It was undertaken at the beginning of the 1990s, and reflects what I would call the beginning of a new understanding of masculinity in the educational world. The aim of this investigation was to evaluate developmental projects in Danish primary school, implemented to promote equality between the sexes. In this study I focused attention on some male teachers who wanted to develop new gender roles, both among pupils and among adults. It was a qualitative study. My data came mainly from interviews with four of the male teachers.

These male teachers felt a need to develop alternative masculine behaviour in their job as teachers. Especially they felt pressure from their female colleague to drop some of the traditional masculine attitudes and practices. However, this pressure was often mixed with ambiguity because female teachers at the same time profited from the respect that traditional masculine authority creates. It works in practice when it is about maintaining order in school. At least it does on the surface. Sometimes it results in a kind of double communication: at one level the message is: be a man, use your (traditional) masculinity. At another level the message is: Drop the traditional masculinity. Find new ways to exercise your authority. Be a progressive man! In ideological discussions on equality and education, of course, it is mainly the last statement that is accentuated.

Male teachers often get such double and ambiguous messages from their female colleagues. This external ambiguity, however, corresponds to an inner ambiguity in many of those male teachers who consider themselves as progressive teachers. In their search for new masculine roles, these male teachers have to confront traditional male roles as they appear in the school, and they have to interact with traditional male types.

Before I describe these two types I will comment on my theoretical method: these types should not be considered as 'labels' that can be applied to specific individuals, but should be seen as polarities on a topological continuum from which teachers try to detach themselves, while at the same time entering into dialogue with them. These polarities are the patriarch and the anonymous technocrat.

THE PATRIARCH AND THE ANONYMOUS TECHNOCRAT

The patriarch is a visible authority. In his teaching he is concerned with social relations with the pupils. His historical root is the father figure in the bourgeois family from the 19th century. In exercising authority he symbolizes order, decency (decorum), justice and rationality. He represents the old world order. He was a symbol of mastery of the bourgeoisie, and he was (and is?) a symbol of male dominance.

Seen in a psychodynamic light he was (and is) the symbol of repression of needs. To be a reasonable man implies repression of needs. At the same time, however, the patriarch has a likeable quality: he is concerned with social relations. He is not only a person who uses his power. He is also a person who protects and takes care of his children and family and in the school: the pupils.

The anonymous technocrat is characterized by escaping from work with human relations. As a teacher he can keep the pupils at a distance by escaping into the subject, for example maths. In Denmark he is often called 'the subject teacher' (e.g. maths teacher) as opposed to the class teacher. In exercising authority he does not make his own person visible. He typically refers to rules and procedure coming from outside. Those male teachers who want to depart from a traditional male authority have to relate themselves both to the patriarch and to the anonymous technocrat.

SEARCH FOR A NEW MALE TEACHER ROLE

Most of the teachers we met in the developmental projects emphasized the importance of working on human and social relations with the pupils. Therefore 'our' teachers reject the anonymous technocrat as a model, for example as he appears in the role as a traditional subject teacher, because he does not undertake work within social relations.

One of the teachers said: 'It is too easy to be a maths teacher. It only involves working with textbooks. There is no discussion. It is tailor-made for us men. And all "talk" we hand over to the women.' Their attitudes to the patriarch as model are more ambiguous. He undertakes the work concerning social and human relations. And when it works it appears to be effective. But they criticize his authority because at the ideological level it represents the old world order, first of all because he represents male dominance.

Sometimes, however, some of the teachers undertake a role that draws elements from patriarchal patterns. In these cases, for example, they accept using their authority if female teachers have given up on maintaining order. And sometimes, but not always, they succeed. But first of all these male teachers try to find new models in their teaching work. In this search for new model male teachers we have collaborated in formulating two possibilities:

- using the female teacher as a model
- rediscovering the boy in his own mind and life story.

FEMALE TEACHERS AS MODELS?

A little surprisingly for me, male teachers nearly totally rejected female teachers as models. They accentuated many negative points in the female teachers' exercise of authority. I shall mention three of them.

They are anxious about losing control of the situation in the classroom. Male teachers accentuate the fact that this fear results in female teachers often intervening in social situations too soon. One of the male teachers expressed it in this way: 'Many of them are afraid of losing control. So they cut off much earlier than us. Often much too soon.'

The second thing they emphasize is that female teachers do not have the intuition and knowledge to understand the boys' social interaction and their search for male identity. A male teacher formulated it in this way: 'I often fight with boys. We are scrapping. The female teacher doesn't like it. She thinks it's a strange thing to do.'

The third thing the male teachers say is that female teachers are not able to take a liberal view of things. They do not use humour as a tool in their interaction with the pupils. These considerations among the male teachers are of course not their final judgement on their female colleagues. Of importance, however, is to find out why the male teachers need to distance themselves from the female teachers. All of them had chosen to work together with female teachers in the developmental projects dealing with gender and equality, which I and other colleagues were evaluating.

My interpretation is that they had earlier tried to use femininity as a model in their teaching work. But today they reject femininity as a model because they look at it as treachery to themselves as men and to the boys in the school. And, at a more general level, as treachery to masculinity.

RE-DISCOVERING THE REPRESSED BOY IN YOUR OWN MIND

These male teachers have rejected the anonymous technocrat as a model. They have also rejected the female teacher as model, and partially the patriarch. They try to develop a practice that is sensitive to the boys' search for a male identity. During the project about gender and equality, they became aware that they had in many respects repressed 'the boy' in their own mind. As one of them said: 'The school romanticizes a traditional girl behaviour, especially girls' neatness. Often male teachers refer to this neatness to maintain order among the boys.' This teacher admitted that he earlier regarded the boys' behaviour as foolish, but his attitudes changed during a course where the class was segregated into a boy group and a girl group: 'This course gave me a feeling of freedom. In the boys being together, I felt an enormous dynamic I never found among the girls.'

Two conditions had to be fulfilled before this teacher was able to consider the boys' social behaviour as a constructive force. The first condition was that he gave up a traditional teacher authority and tried to be a companion to the boys. The other condition concerned his own relationship to masculinity. To be sensitive to the boys and their social behaviour, he needed to re-discover his own childhood. This discovery, however, is not without ambivalence. He had to discover some repressed feelings and experiences. He said: 'I wasn't a very good football player, but I tried to be. I still remember the tough talk in the locker room and I remember the feeling of defeat.' This male teacher re-discovered the forgotten manliness during the course together with the boys. He found it in activities such as going fishing, body-building and old-fashioned male gymnastics.

Generally we see here a new trend among male teachers as they reflect on issues of gender in their teaching.

REFERENCES

Kryger, N. (1988), *Drengene i 8. x og forestillinger om mandligt og kvindeligt i den progressive pædagogik*, Danmarks Lærerhøjskole (PhD thesis, only available in Danish).

Kryger, N. (1988a), *Big Boys in School – a Qualitative Study of the School's Role in the Formation of Gender Identity in a Group of Adolescent Boys*, Copenhagen, Royal Danish School of Educational Studies.

Kryger, N. (1988b), *De skrappe drenge og den moderne pædagogik* (The Tough Guys and Modern Pedagogics), Copenhagen: Unge Pædagoger.

Kryger, N. (1992), 'Køn, skolekultur og den mandlige lærer (Gender, School Culture and Male Teachers)', in G. Pedersen and K. Reisby (eds), *Ligeværd og Mangfoldighed*, Copenhagen: Denmark's Lærerhøjskole.

Nielsen, H. J. and Rudberg, M. (1991), *Historien om piger og drenge. Kønsosialisering i et udviklingspsykologisk perspektiv*, Copenhagen: Gyldendal.

Willis, P. (1977), *Learning to Labour*, London: Saxon House.

CHAPTER 19

'Boys and girls': a gender-fair educational film?

Christiane Vandenplas-Holper and
Anne Ghysselinckx-Janssens

The study presented here was inspired by the first author's participation in the *Commission pour l'Egalisation des Chances des Garçons et des Filles dans l'Enseignement*, set up in 1979 by the Belgian *Ministère de l'Education Nationale et de la Culture Française*. This committee recommended *Filles et garçons* (Boys and girls), a film produced by Paulo Van den Hove and Myriam Flore for the educational TV sponsored by the Ministry, as a tool for gender-fair education in the classroom. No educational guidelines, however, were available as to how to use the film and educational psychologists who had used it were unable to describe how children reacted to it. A pilot study suggested that Van den Hove and Flore could be regarded as having a highly developed clinical flair for children's development. When invited to discuss their film with educational psychology students, they said that they had been guided by Belotti's (1974) pleas against sex-role stereotyped child-rearing techniques. Since neither of them had had formal research training in children's development, they did not provide a detailed rationale for their construction of the film or guidelines concerning its educational use in the classroom.

Our purpose when studying *Filles et garçons* was twofold. At first sight, the film seemed well-balanced educational material in which stereotypic and counter-stereotypic actions were alternated. We first devised a conceptual and methodological tool in order to analyse the film and decide whether it could be regarded as 'gender-fair' or not. We then described children's reactions when watching *Filles et garçons*.

Parson (1969, in Mussen, 1985) states that in most societies, the role of men is 'instrumental' while that of women is 'expressive'. Generally, the male's status is more highly valued than the female's. This general statement is documented in empirical studies. Chombart de Lauwe and Bellan (1979) as well as the numerous studies reviewed by Maccoby and Jacklin (1973), for example, have shown that due to this differential status, girls identify with male persons and/or value male activities while the reverse is not necessarily true for boys. Koblinsky, Cruse and Sugawara (1978) have shown that fifth-grade children possess a clear set of expectations about the characteristics of boys and girls. In general, boys are viewed as active, powerful, adventurous, and resourceful whereas girls are perceived as nurturant, dependent, polite, and interested in domestic duties.

Content analysis of fairy tales (Bierhoff-Altermann, Brandt and Dittel, 1982) and of children's readers (Denmark and Waters, 1977) has shown that the latter reflect adults' and children's stereotypes. Women and girls appear far less frequently in children's books than men and boys. When females do appear, they are more likely than males to be portrayed in a negative fashion (Scott and Feldman-Summers, 1979). In reaction to this state of affairs, over the past decade, some progressive teachers have been designing educational material whose aim is to present more egalitarian sex-role activities (*Changeons les livres*, 1982; Guttentag and Bray, 1976; Smith and Pasternak, 1977). Experimental research has shown that children's sex-role stereotypes may be modified by story-telling which presents non-traditional sex-roles (Berg-Cross and Berg-Cross, 1978; Flerx, Fidler and Rogers, 1976).

The question arises, however, as to what can be regarded as educational material for a non-traditional sex-role training. Experimental non-traditional or 'gender-fair' material consists in using role-reversals or counter-stereotypic presentations in which males are featured in stereotypically female actions (e.g. the boy is baking) and females in stereotypically male actions (e.g. the girl is playing football). Since children are highly stereotyped with reference to sex-roles (Maccoby and Jacklin, 1973), the relevance of such role-reversing material for educational purposes may be questioned with respect to cognitive developmental theory. Indeed a schema functions as an anticipatory structure that leads the individual to search for a certain type of information or to be ready to receive information consistent with the schema. Perceptual information that is inconsistent with the schema may be ignored or transformed (Martin and Halverson, 1981, in Huston, 1983, p. 399; Vandenplas-Holper and Jenart, 1989). Despite some contradictory or mixed results (Jennings, 1975), most experimental studies have confirmed this general statement (Cordua, McGraw and Drabman, 1979; Koblinsky, Cruse and Sugawara, 1978; Liben and Signorella, 1980). Children who were shown different kinds of material – a film, stories or pictures – in which sex-roles were traditional or counter-stereotypic remembered traditional sex-role activities better than counter-stereotypic ones. When sex-roles were presented as counter-stereotypic, children often recalled them as stereotypic. The recall of the agent performing a sex-role-related action is, however, a crucial element if gender-related educational material is expected to be efficient in changing children's sex-role stereotypes.

The present study proposes and empirically tests the concept of 'gender-fair' educational material, a more differentiated concept than the dichotomy 'stereotypic/counter-stereotypic', used in experimental studies. This concept is grounded on considerations of the psychometric approach and on cognitive developmental considerations.

Some decades ago, psychometricians constructed 'culture-fair' tests. They were characteristically designed to rule out several major cultural parameters, including not only language but also knowledge and intellectual skills specific to any given culture or subculture. Containing only the elements common to all the cultures and subcultures they were designed for, they were supposed to disadvantage none of them (Anastasi, 1968, pp. 242–3; Demangeon, 1976, p. 87; Reuchlin, 1972, pp. 75–80). By analogy to the concept of 'culture-fair tests', we propose the concept of 'gender-fair educational material'. This material is supposed to portray male and female characters in such a way that neither gender is disadvantaged with respect to the other.

With respect to cognitive developmental theory, counter-stereotypic presentations of sex-roles may be regarded as highly discrepant from the children's sex-role schemas. An egalitatarian presentation in which a stereotyped activity is presented in a sex-role appropriate as well as in a sex-role inappropriate way, featuring both male and female agents (e.g. the boy and the girl are baking; boys and girls are playing football) may be considered as only moderately discrepant from the children's schemas. With respect to the optimal mismatch hypothesis (Turiel, 1973), moderately discrepant but not highly discrepant stimuli, may be expected to unbalance children's sex-role schemas and call for accommodation to more flexible schemas.

The present chapter has several aims. Firstly it describes the main features of the content analysis which has been conducted in order to assess whether *Filles et garçons* can be considered as 'sex-role-fair'. This analysis can easily be carried out by practioners with respect to other educational materials. Secondly, it describes how children reacted to the film while watching it. This analysis illuminates the processes which underlie the children's processing of the film and can guide practitioners while discussing materials concerning sex-roles with children.

In an experimental context, the operationalization of the concept of 'gender-fair' material would be rather easy. Within the framework of the present study, however, based on a 'real-life' film which was not made for an experimental purpose, a long and complex analysis was required. A last aim of this chapter is thus to introduce the interested reader to some of the details of the content analysis and to test some additional hypotheses.

The chapter first explains the different steps which were necessary to describe the film in a conceptually coherent framework. The content analysis of the film's scenario combines several main categories: the gender of the agents featured by the film; the positive or negative scores of actions; and the stereotypes of actions (actions may be stereotypically male, stereotypically female or neutral). Furthermore, the content analysis had to cope with such minor aspects as pronouns as well as negative or positive forms which are expressed by words such as 'yes' or 'no' and have to be referred to the preceding context. Indicators of children's 'subjective values' referring to sex-role related actions were also considered.

The study tests empirically whether *Filles et garçons* may be considered as gender-fair educational material. The different presentations of sex-role related actions made by the film have been weighted differentially. A stereotypic presentation which reflects the children's stereotypes has been given a score of 1; an egalitarian presentation which represents a moderate discrepancy from these stereotypes has been given a score of 2; a counter-stereotypic presentation which represents a high discrepancy from children's sex-role stereotypes has been given a score of 3. According to this rationale, a weighted score of sex-role related content has been devised. An overall gender-fair presentation of all the actions featured in the film corresponds to a score of 2 which is obtained by a mixture of egalitarian presentations and a balancing of stereotypic and counter-stereotypic presentations. If *Filles et garçons* is indeed a sex-role-fair film, the mean score of the actions featured in the film should be not significantly different from 2. A comparison of the mean score of the actions featured in the film and the 2-norm is carried out for the film as a whole and for each of the sequences it includes.

In a first analysis, the scores which compare the weightings of the presentations to the scenario to the 2-norm only take into account the fact that an action has or has not been performed by an agent. This analysis is made by the 'action only' coding frame. In some of the statements of the film, however, specific linguistic markers refer in addition to the child's competence or incompetence, to the easiness or difficulty of the task and its appeal or lack of appeal.

These dimensions have been taken into account in a 'subjective values' coding frame. It was assumed that the latter, which refers to more subtle cues of stereotyping than the 'action only' coding frame, would bring about a lower mean score than the 'action only' coding frame. Indeed, if the film features actions in an egalitarian and a counter-stereotypic way, it might be expected that boys and girls would consider nevertheless that actions not appropriate to their gender are less easy and less pleasant to perform and that they perform them with less competence.

Finally, research on sex-roles reveals that – due to the differential prestige of men and women in our society – there is considerably more resistance to the notion of non-traditional roles for males than for females (Vandenplas-Holper, 1987, pp. 196–9). The same applies to sex-roles in teaching material (Scott, 1986). Two additional hypotheses can be derived from this general state of affairs. Although the film as a whole could be considered as gender-fair, it might be that this gender-fair nature is stronger when stereotypically female actions are featured than when stereotypically male actions are featured; and that it is stronger when the statements of female speakers are considered than when those of male speakers are considered. If, on the other hand, the authors of the film have been wholly consistent in their gender-fair options, stereotypically female actions should be expected to be presented in a way which is just as sex-role-fair as the way in which stereotypically male actions are presented, and units of analysis spoken by male speakers should be presented in a way which is just as sex-role-fair as the way in which units of analysis spoken by female speakers are presented.

Sixteen groups, each composed of four children – one 7- and one 8-year-old boy and two girls of the same age – were videorecorded when watching the film. A preliminary assessment had shown that they were highly sex-role stereotyped. Systematic observation was carried out in order to analyse the children's reactions while watching the film. These reactions are described for each of the five sequences of the film. A very detailed microanalysis is further carried out for one of the sequences.

METHOD

Five sequences of the film *Filles et garçons,* with a total projection time of 21 minutes, were selected for our study. They feature different actions performed by boys and girls. Some of these actions may be considered stereotypically male; others stereotypically female; and others neutral, likely to be displayed by boys and girls alike. The first sequence is presented according to a guessing game procedure. The camera presents an array of nine toys and the female commentator's voice asks the spectators to guess if the different toys will be chosen by a boy and/or a girl. The camera then shows the child who has chosen the toy and the commentator's voice labels the gender of the child who has made the choice. The second sequence shows boys and girls busy with housekeeping. The third sequence shows children, guided by a male or a female adult, involved in their hobbies. The fourth sequence first shows a girl afraid to go into an unknown place; the same sequence is then performed with a boy as the agent. The last sequence shows boys and girls in a playground. In most of the sequences, the children comment on some of their actions. Some actions are further commented on by an adult speaker. Four of the five sequences are finally introduced and/or closed by an owl which makes sex-role-fair statements referring to the different actions which have been featured.

THE DIFFERENT STEPS OF THE CONTENT ANALYSIS OF THE FILM

Definition of actions and stereotypes

The different sequences were each cut down into smaller units. Eighteen different actions were singled out for the five sequences. On the basis of Maccoby and Jacklin's (1973) review of children's sex-role development and of a catalogue of sex-role stereotypes identified in children's educational material (*Changeons les livres,* 1982), each of the 18 actions which make up the film was classified as: stereotypically male, i.e. likely to be displayed by boys; stereotypically female, i.e. likely to be displayed by girls; or neutral, i.e. likely to be displayed by boys and girls alike. Table 1 gives a detailed overview of the 18 actions and their classification in function of stereotypes.

Coding of actions, agents and speakers

A transcript of the total verbal content of the film was made and a content analysis carried out. Since the film does not meet the criteria of controlled research material, it was not possible to include the cinematographic, non-verbal material into a systematic analysis. The latter was only considered occasionally, when the verbal content of the film could not be made unambiguous without taking the non-verbal context into account. The transcript was broken down into different units of analysis, each containing one to three of the following elements: the agent; the action; the circumstances. The first two represent the critical elements for our analysis, which is based on the matching between the agent and the action combined with stereotypes. The different steps of the content analysis are as follows.

Table 1: Structure of the film *Filles et garçons*

Sequences (S) and actions (A)	Stereotypes (1)	Number of units of analysis
S1: Toy choices		
A1: puzzle	N	1
A2: 'plasticine' toy	N	1
A3: ball	M	1
A4: drawing set	M+F	1
A5: construction set	M	1
A6: skipping-rope	F	1
A7: cowboy costume	M	1
A8: iron	F	1
A9: question–answer toy	N	1
S2: Housekeeping		
A10: laying/clearing the table, cleaning the room	F	10
A11: giving orders, criticizing	M	3
S3: Hobby		
A12: doing woodwork	M	2
A13: knitting	F	20
A14: cooking	F	2
S4: Unknown place		
A15: being afraid	F	12
A16: taking initiative	M	7
S5: Playground		
A17: playing football	M	15
A18: skipping with a rope	F	4
Total number of units of analysis		84

Note: M represents actions likely to be displayed by males, F represents actions likely to be displayed by females and N represents neutral actions likely to be displayed by boys and girls alike.

The 18 action categories

Each of the different units of analysis of the film was classified in terms of one of the 18 different actions[1]: 'Sometimes I lay the table' (*Des fois je mets la table*) operationalizes action 10 (A10); 'Girls are always afraid' (*Les filles ont toujours peur*) operationalizes A15; 'Let's go ahead' (*On y va*) operationalizes A16. Some of the units of analysis had to be related to their preceding linguistic context in order to be coded: 'Sometimes I give my place to my brother' (*Des fois je laisse ma place à mon frère*) is coded as 'sometimes my brother lays the table', since it follows the statement 'sometimes I lay the table'. 'Catherine stayed in the girls' playground' (*Catherine restait du côté des filles*) is recoded as 'Catherine did not play football' (A17). Units of analysis which do not refer to any of the 18 actions were not taken into account (e.g. 'I like waffles. I have to confess that I am very fond of nice food'.).

Agents
Agents are the people who perform the action. Singulars or plurals of the nouns referring to agents are not differentiated. The gender of the agent is coded as: *male* if the action is explicitly attributed to one or several male agents – 'Boys are funky' (*Que les garçons, c'est froussard*) (A15); *female* if the action is explicitly attributed to one or several female agents – 'Girls are always afraid' (*Les filles ont toujours peur*) (A15); or *egalitarian* if the action is explicitly attributed to one or several male and one or several female agents – 'There are schools where boys and girls are equally skilful at playing football and basketball' (*Il y a des écoles où les filles et les garçons jouent avec autant d'adresse au football qu'au basketball*) (A17).

In many cases, the agents are not explicitly referred to by the labels 'boys' or 'girls' but by the personal pronouns 'I' or 'you'. These personal pronouns are coded as male or female according to the gender of the speaker or the person being spoken to: e.g. 'I am doing my first piece of knitting' (*Moi je suis à mon premier tricot*) (A13) is coded as male since the statement is made by a boy; 'I sometimes lay the table' (*Des fois, je mets la table*) (A10) is coded as female since the statement is made by a girl. 'You should not be afraid to stay alone' (*Alors tu ne dois pas avoir peur de rester seule*) (A15) is coded as 'female agent' since the person spoken to is a girl.

Actions and subjective values of actions
The 'action only' coding frame considers only the fact that each of the 18 actions has or has not been performed by an agent. The 'subjective value' coding frame considers the positive or negative forms of the child's competence/incompetence, of the easiness or difficulty of the task and its appeal or lack of appeal.

In some of the statements made in the film, these subjective values are explicitly expressed by specific linguistic markers. In 'I like to hammer nails into planks' (*J'aime bien planter des clous dans des planches*) (A12) and in 'In the beginning I was not very fast [when I was knitting]' (*Au début, je n'allais pas très vite*) (A13), 'I like to' and 'I was not very fast' are considered as explicit markers of the appeal and the competence dimension respectively. The actions containing markers of subjective values are first coded according to the 'action only' coding frame; they are then coded according to the 'subjective value' coding frame.

Positive and negative scores of actions and subjective values
A positive or negative score has been given for each action and for each 'subjective value'. Actions are given a positive score if the action has been performed ('Sometimes I lay the table') or should be performed. They are given a negative score if the action has not been performed or should not be performed ('Then you should not be afraid to stay alone'/*Alors tu ne dois pas avoir peur de rester seule*) (A15).

Before they are coded, agreements and disagreements expressed by 'yes' and 'no' are always related to the preceding action they refer to. Some actions, although presented in a positive surface form, refer to the fact that one of the 18 actions has not been performed or is no longer performed, e.g. 'I stop' [playing football] is given a negative score for A17 (playing football).

With respect to 'subjective values', ' to be easy' or 'to do well' are considered as positive forms of the easiness/difficulty or the competence/ incompetence dimension respectively. 'To be difficult' or 'to go slowly' are considered as positive forms of the appeal dimension; 'I like to' or 'it is fun' are considered as positive forms of the appeal dimension; 'to be fed up with' or 'to have aching legs' (after having played football) are considered as negative forms of this dimension. When units of analysis contain explicit linguistic markers of negative subjective values, they are given a positive score within the 'action only' coding frame. Indeed 'not going quickly when knitting' (A13) or 'not liking to skip with a rope' (A18) presuppose that the actions of knitting and jumping have been performed.

The status of the speakers

The label 'speaker' refers to the person who speaks either as an agent in the different sequences of the scenario or as a commentator, introducing or commenting on the different sequences. Speakers are classified according to their age status (child or adult) and according to their gender (male or female). An additional category refers to the owl.

The weighted score of sex-role-related content

According to a 'syntactic transformation system', based on the combination of the gender of the agents featured in the film, the positive or negative score for actions and subjective values and the stereotyping of the actions, the actions on the one hand, the subjective values on the other are regarded as presented in a stereotypic, counter-stereotypic or egalitarian way and different weights are given to these presentations. Table 2 gives a synoptic overview of all possible combinations and of the different weights which are given to each. Examples of units of analysis drawn from the transcript are presented below as illustrations of the different cells of Table[2]. Each example is followed by its code, given in Table 1, and the code of the examples, given in Table 2.

Stereotypic presentation

- matching of a male or female agent with a positively scored action or subjective value and a stereotypically male or female action: 'I [male agent] have fun in playing football' (A17; a); 'Girls are always afraid' (A15; e).
- matching of a male agent with a negatively scored action or subjective value and a stereotypically female action, or matching of a female agent with a negatively scored action or subjective value and a stereotypically male action: 'Catherine did not play football' (A17; h).

Egalitarian presentation

- matching of male and female agents referred to in either a conjunctive or a disjunctive way with a positively or negatively scored action

Table 2: Weighting of the different combinations of agents, positive and negative forms of actions and subjective values and stereotypes

Agents	Positive or negative scores of actions or subjective values	Stereotypes	Presentations of sex-roles by the film	References to examples	Weights
M	+	M	Stereotypic	a	1
		F	Counter-stereotypic	b	3
M	-	M	Counter-stereotypic	c	3
		F	Stereotypic	d	1
F	+	F	Stereotypic	e	1
		M	Counter-stereotypic	f	3
F	-	F	Counter-stereotypic	g	3
		M	Stereotypic	h	1
M+F	+	F	Egalitarian	i	2
		M	Egalitarian	j	2
	-	F	Egalitarian	k	2
		M	Egalitarian	l	2

Note: For agents and stereotypes, M refers to male, F refers to female agents or stereotypes.

or subjective value and a stereotypically female or male action: 'There are schools where boys and girls are equally skilful at playing football and basketball' (A17; j). 'At home, who are more helpful, boys or girls?' (*Et à la maison, des garçons ou des filles, qui rend le plus de services?*) (A10; i).

Counter-stereotypic presentation

- matching of a male agent with a positively scored action or subjective value and a stereotypically female action: '[a male agent chooses] a skipping rope' (A6; b) or matching of a female agent with a positively scored action or subjective value and a stereotypically male action: 'Some girls are good at football' (*Il y a des filles douées pour le football*) (A17; f).
- matching of a male agent with a negatively scored action or subjective value and a stereotypically male action or matching of a female agent with a negatively scored action or subjective value and a stereotypically female action: 'I [male agent] give up playing football' (*J' abandonne de jouer au football*) (A17; c).

According to the rationale which has been specified, the different types of actions were weighted in the following way: a score of 1 was given for a stereotypic unit of analysis, a score of 2 for an egalitarian unit of analysis and a score of 3 for a counter-stereotypic unit of analysis. The neutral actions were given a weight of 2, irrespective of the gender of the agent.

The male and female status of the speaker and the male and female stereotyping of the actions featured in the film were the two main independent variables. The adult/child status of the speakers is considered in a secondary way since only a small number of items refer to them.

The mean weightings of the different combinations of agents, positive and negative scores and stereotypes make up the weighted score of sex-role related content. This score is computed according to the 'action only' coding frame for all of the units of analysis and according to the 'subjective value' coding frame only for those units of analysis that have specific linguistic markers. These two scores make up the two dependent variables.

Two coders coded the transcript of the scenario. Several steps were followed: a) identification of the units of analysis referring to each of the 18 actions; b) identification of the units of analysis containing explicit markers of 'subjective values'; c) coding of positive and negative scores within the 'action only coding frame'; d) coding of positive and negative scores within the 'subjective value coding frame'; e) coding of the gender of the agents; and f) coding of the gender and the adult/child status of the speakers. Intercoder reliability assessed by Cohen's K coefficient was high. The coefficients were .97 for a, .95 for b, .80 for c, .95 for d, .96 for e and 1 for f respectively. The few remaining disagreements were solved by discussion before further analyses were carried out.

SYSTEMATIC OBSERVATION OF THE CHILDREN WATCHING THE FILM

The videorecordings which had been made while the children were watching the film were analysed by systematic observation. Several observers have recorded the children's reactions on an electronic observation device by categorizing them into three broad categories: verbalizations, surprise reactions and non-verbal communication. In accordance with Inhelder, Sinclair and Bovet (1974), Miller (1973) and Vandenplas-Holper (1996), surprise reactions are considered as reactions to the discrepant stimuli provided by the film and disrupting the child's stereotypic sex-role schemata. Since the watching of the film occurred in a group setting, verbalizations and non-verbal communication were also considered.

The overall analysis of the film was made according to the following categories and criteria.

Verbalizations
Speaking to a peer

- The child asks a question, answers a question or engages in a dialogue; his or her verbalizations are understandable to the observer.
- The child is oriented towards a peer by rotating his or her body or arms, by looking at him or her, by speaking to him or her even if the verbalizations are not audible.

Speaking without addressing a particular peer

- The child answers the questions asked by the commentator of the film
- The child speaks without being orientated towards a peer; his or her verbalizations are not understandable to the observer
- The child speaks to himself or herself while watching the film.

Non-verbal communication with a peer

- The child looks at a peer; taps on his or her shoulder; touches his or her body.

Surprise reactions

- Laughter and expressions like 'hi, hi'; smiles are not considered.
- Astonishment and surprise: verbal exclamations like 'ah', 'oh', 'hein'; non-verbal behaviour such as opening the mouth in astonishment, raising eyebrows or putting a hand in front of the mouth.

The children's reactions while watching the five sequences of the film were recorded according to these broad categories and summed across categories for each sequence and for each child. Since this analysis revealed some interesting features, a still more detailed microanalysis of the 'toy' sequence was carried out.

This 'toy' sequence is constructed according to the following procedure. The camera presents an array of nine toys and the voice of the commentator asks the spectators to guess if each of the toys will be chosen by a boy or a girl. The presentation of each of the nine toys then proceeds in two phases. In the anticipation phase, the camera shows one of the toys which is labelled by the voice of the commentator who says for instance: 'a skipping-rope' (A6) or 'a cowboy costume' (A7). Spectators are supposed to guess who will choose the toy which has been presented. In the confirmation phase, the camera shows the face of the child – either a boy or a girl, a boy and a girl for A9 – who has chosen the toy which has been shown. The voice of the presenter mentions the child's gender: 'a boy' for A6 and 'a girl' for A7. In order to illuminate the way in which the children process the information conveyed to them in this sequence, the children's reactions have been analysed separately for the anticipation and the confirmation phase of each of the nine toys according to criteria which are more detailed than those which have been used for the overall analysis by the three broad categories described above.

According to the analysis which has been presented in Table 1, the eight first toys have been divided into two blocks. It is considered that A1 to A4 confirm the children's stereotypic anticipations since A1, A2 and A4 are neutral and A3 is presented in a stereotypic way. A5 to A8 are all presented in a counter-stereotypic way which is supposed to invalidate the stereotypic anticipations which the children have made overtly or covertly only. A9 again presents a toy which has been considered as neutral.

The children's verbalizations have entirely been transcribed and classified according to three microcategories:

- the references to the gender (RG) of the child ('a boy' or 'a girl') who is supposed to choose the toy which has been presented in the anticipation phase or who has chosen the toy in the confirmation phase;
- the expressions of surprise (S) defined according to the criteria used for the overall analysis of the film;
- the comments (C) in which no reference is made to the gender.

Due to technical constraints, the microanalytic observation of the 'toy' sequence has been carried out only on 12 groups.

RESULTS

The first part of this section presents the results of the content analysis of the film; the second part presents the results of the systematic observation while the children were watching the film.

The content analysis of the film

Eighty-four units of analysis have been coded in the 'action only' coding frame. The number for each of the sequences is given in the last column of Table 1. The overall mean score for the 84 units of analysis based on the weighting described is $2.27, SD = .90$. This mean score and the mean scores for the different sequences have been compared using t-tests to the norm of 2 which corresponds to completely sex-role fair material. The t-tests are two-tailed since no hypothesis is made in either direction. The overall mean is significantly different from the 2-norm: $t(83) = 2.80; p < .01$. For S1, S2, S4 and S5, means are respectively 2.33, 2.23, 2.16 and 1.89; the corresponding standard deviations are .71 .83, .96 and .99. None of these means differs significantly from the 2-norm. For S3, however, the score is significantly higher than 2: $M = 2.67, SD = .76; t(23) = 4.29, p < .001$.

Thirty-three units of analysis have specific 'subjective value' markers. If these units of analysis alone are considered, it appears that the 'action only' score is significantly higher than the 'subjective values' score; $M = 2.36, SD = .90 v. M = 1.94, SD = .97; t(32) = 2.51, p = .005$, one-tailed. Nine out of the 33 units of analysis had different codings for the 'action only' and the 'subjective value' coding frames. For eight out of these nine different units of analysis, the action was counter-stereotypic from the 'action only' point of view and stereotypic from the 'subjective values' point of view. The difference is significant according to a binomial test at $p = .01$, one-tailed.

As to the comparison of stereotypically male and stereotypically female actions, 29 units of analysis refer to stereotypically male actions and 48 items to stereotypically female actions. With respect to the gender and adult/child status of the speakers featured in the film as agents and commentators, it appears that 41 units of analysis have male speakers and 38 have female speakers. The owl is the speaker for five units of anlysis. Comparisons between stereotypically male and stereotypically female actions and between statements made by male and female speakers are made separately by t-tests for independent measures. As predicted, the 'action only' score is significantly higher for stereotypically female than for stereotypically male actions: $M = 2.58, SD = .74 v. M = 1.93, SD = 1.00; t(76) = -3.14, p = .001$, two-tailed.

For male speakers, whether adults or children, the 'action only' score is slightly higher than for female speakers, but the difference is not statistically significant: $M = 2.41, SD = .89 v. M = 2.13, SD = .93; t(78) = .17$, two-tailed. If only the 36 items which have male child speakers and the 19 items which have female child speakers are considered, it appears that the male speakers have higher scores than the female speakers: $M = 2.38$, $SD = .90\ v.\ M = 2.15$, $SD = 1.01$, but the difference is not significant either.

The mean 'action only' score for the owl is 2.20, $SD = .45$. It does not significantly differ from the 2-norm.

Children's reactions while watching the film

Children's reactions while watching the film were observed for the 16 groups on which this study is based. If all of the children's surprise reactions are considered, it appears that they were most frequent for the 'toy' and the 'hobby' sequences. For the 'toy' sequence, each child showed about four reactions, for the 'hobby' sequence about three reactions and about one reaction for each of the other three sequences[3]. The 'hobby' sequence has been the sequence which has the highest weighted score of sex-role related content. It depicts boys who are knitting, a heavily stereotypically female activity, and the camera focuses on them for a long time. The toy sequence which elicited the highest number of reactions but which did not differ from S2, S4 and S5 with respect to the weighted score of sex-role related content was submitted to a more detailed analysis in order to elucidate the processes leading to this high number of reactions.

A first analysis has summed all the reactions across categories, across the anticipation and the confirmation phase and across the 48 children on which this analysis has been carried out. The results are presented in Table 3.

Table 3: Sum of references to gender, of expressions of surprise and comments for each of the nine activities of the 'toy' sequence; anticipation and confirmation phases confounded

Neutral toys and stereotypic presentations				Counter-stereotypic presentations				Neutral toy
A1	A2	A3	A4	A5	A6	A7	A8	A9
3	15	13	23	33	45	56	57	23

It appears that the counter-stereotypic presentations elicit by far more numerous reactions than the stereotypic and the neutral presentations. Table 4 presents the same analysis detailed according to the three categories and for the confirmation phase only. It appears that the children's

Table 4: Detailed analysis of reactions in the confirmation phase of the 'toy' sequence: sum of reactions according to each microcategory

	Neutral toys and stereotypic presentations				Counter-stereotypic presentations				Neutral toy
Microcategories	A1	A2	A3	A4	A5	A6	A7	A8	A9
RG				1	1	0	1	1	3
S		2	6	1	8	11	31	34	44	3
C					1	0	3	2	1

RS: reference to gender; S: surprise; C: comments

reactions which occur in the confirmation phase are nearly always reactions of surprise and astonishment and that their number increases for the counterstereotypic presentation from A5 to A8.

DISCUSSION AND EDUCATIONAL IMPLICATIONS

To sum up, it appears from the content analysis of *Filles et garçons* that the film has, in general, a weighted score of sex-role related content which exceeds the 2-norm corresponding to sex-role fair material. A closer look at the score for the different sequences reveals that S3, the 'hobby' sequence, has the highest score, differing most from a sex-role fair presentation. The analysis of the children's reactions when watching the film shows that S3, which mainly features boys knitting and commenting on their knitting, brings about most surprise reactions. For this sequence, the children's reactions thus paralllel the results of the weighted score for sex-role related content. The microanalysis of the 'toy' sequence shows that the children react heavily by surprise and astonishment mainly in the confirmation phase of the counter-stereotyped presentations. Overall, these results show that the children who are sex-role-stereotyped process the film in a way which can be considered as a reaction to the discrepancies introduced into their stereotypic gender schemata by the counterstereotypic presentations of the film.

Some other conclusions can be drawn from the content analysis of the film. Since in general, stereotypically female actions have higher scores than stereotypically male actions, the producers of *Filles et garçons* mirror the fact that social norms are more flexible about girls engaging in counter-stereotypic actions than boys. Nevertheless, the units of analysis spoken by male and female speakers are equally gender-fair. Furthermore, the units of analysis spoken by the owl which introduces and closes some of the film's sequences are completely gender-fair. Finally, the weighting of the film's content within the 'subjective values' coding frame brought about lower scores than the coding within the 'action only' coding frame. Thus, even if boys and girls are performing actions which are counter-stereotypic, they like performing them less than stereotypic actions and/or feel less competent in doing so.

Several criticisms have to be made about the present study. The most important may be that sex-role stereotypes have been defined by the researchers on the basis of literature in the field of sex-typing, but the children's sex-role stereotypes referring to the actions featured in the film have not been assessed directly. This aspect should be considered in future studies. The identification of 'subjective value' markers seems interesting. We should nevertheless point out that, since subjective markers were present in less than one third of the units of analysis, the different dimensions of 'subjective markers' – easiness/difficulty, competence/incompetence, and appeal/lack of appeal – had to be confounded. If the present analysis were to be expanded to a larger 'corpus', these different dimensions should be analysed separately. Finally, due to the fact that *Filles et garçons* is a 'real-life' film and not material constructed for research purposes, the number of units of analysis for stereotypically male and stereotypically female actions as well as the number of units of analysis spoken by male and female speakers are fairly unequal. This state of affairs could be considered unacceptable from a strictly experimental perspective, but has to be come to terms with in studies on 'real-life' educational material.

The content analysis we carried out required the definition of a large number of coding rules for a relatively small corpus to be analysed. We nevertheless think that the tool we have devised is a heuristic one and can be generalized to other material by applying the criteria which are presented synoptically in Table 2.

The rationale behind the construction of the weighted score of sex-role-related content calls for some qualifications. The mean 2-norm may be obtained by a constellation of several combinations:

- egalitarian statements in which stereotypically male and/or female actions are matched with a male and a female agent, e.g. 'There are schools where boys and girls are equally skilful at playing football and basketball'
- neutral actions likely to be performed by boys and girls alike, e.g. choosing a question–answer toy
- balancing of stereotypic presentations, e.g. 'Boys are funky' and counter-stereotypic presentations, e.g. 'Girls are always afraid'.

An ideal ratio for the construction of sex-role fair material might be one third neutral actions, one third stereotypic presentations and one third counter-stereotypic presentations, with stereotypically male and stereotypically female actions being presented in equal proportions. With these considerations in mind, practitioners can easily analyse the educational material which is provided to them in readers, story books or films. They can also construct their own educational material according to sex-role fair criteria. Experimental studies (Cordua, McGraw and Drabman, 1979; Vandenplas-Holper and Jenart, 1989) have shown that young children transform counter-stereotypic information into stereotypic information. A gender-fair presentation can be supposed to have a better chance to change the children's stereotypes than a totally counter-stereotypic one, since it is less discrepant from the child's sex-role schemata. This supposition has nevertheless to be validated by empirical research.

The 'toy' sequence is particularly interesting. The analysis which has been carried out by the researchers shows that *Filles et garçons*, which has been produced by practitioners, has been very skilfully constructed. It can inspire other practitioners to design their own guessing games which will appeal highly to the children. The watching of a film like *Filles et garçons,* of other gender-fair educational material or other educational material referring to affective education should be followed by a discussion in order to enhance its influence on the children's development. In other studies, we have presented story books to the children and conducted a discussion in which children were asked to recall what happened in the story, to take the role of the different characters of the story and to say if they would or would not have acted in the same manner and give justifications of their answers. They were also given some counter-suggestions and asked to refer the content of the story to their everyday life (Vandenplas-Holper, 1987, pp. 111–15).

Children's gender development and affective education depends on a variety of influences which are due to parents, teachers, peers, other adults and mass media. Adequately designed educational material and discussions are one of the tools that can enhance children's personal growth.

NOTES

1. The most important examples for content analysis are first presented in their English translation, then, in brackets, in the original version of the script. The French quotation is followed by its reference to one of the 18 action categories, labelled A1 to 18. The complete coding manual contains some additional minor rules which cannot be given here.
2. One example is given for most cells of Table 2. The transcript did not contain an example for each of them.
3. These means are given approximately, since the duration of the five sequences is not equal.

REFERENCES

Anastasi, A. (1969), *Psychological Testing* (3rd edn), New York: Macmillan.

Belotti, E. G. (1974), *Du côté des petites filles*, Paris: Editions des Femmes.

Berg-Cross, L. and Berg-Cross, G. (1978), 'Listening to stories may change children's social attitudes', *The Reading Teacher*, 31(6), 659–63.

Bierhoff-Altermann, B., Brandt, S. and Dittel, A. (1982), 'Die Darstellung geschlechtstypischen Verhaltens in Märchen: eine Inhaltsanalyse', *Psychologie in Erziehung und Unterricht*, 29, 129–39.

'Changeons les livres scolaires et les livres d'enfants', Groupe de travail (1982), *L'image des femmes et des hommes dans les manuels scolaires*, Brussels.

Chombart de Lauwe, M. J. and Bellan, C. (1979), *Enfants de l'image*, Paris: Payot.

Cordua, E. D., McGraw, F. O. and Drabman, R. S. (1979), 'Doctor or nurse: children's perceptions of sex-typed occupations', *Child Development*, 50, 590–3.

Demangeon, M. (1976), 'Les tests indépendants de la culture: "Culture-free" ou "Culture-Fair tests"', in M. Reuchlin (ed.), *Cultures et conduites*, Paris: Presses Universitaires de France, 85–100.

Denmark, F. L. and Waters, J. A. (1977), 'Male and female in children's readers: A cross cultural analysis', in H. Poortinga (ed.), *Basic Problems in Cross-cultural Psychology*, Amsterdam: Swets and Zeitlinger, 190–7.

Flerx, V. C., Fidler, D. S. and Rogers, R. W. (1976), 'Sex role stereotypes: Developmental aspects and early intervention', *Child Development*, 47, 998–1007.

Guttentag, M. and Bray, H. (1976), *Undoing Sex Stereotypes: Research and Resources for Educators*, New York: McGraw-Hill.

Huston, A. C. (1983), 'Sex-typing', in P. H. Mussen (ed.) (1985), *Handbook* of *Child Psychology*, Vol. 4, *Socialization, Personality and Social Development*, New York: Wiley.

Inhelder, B., Sinclair, H. and Bovet, M. (1974), *Apprentissage et structures de la connaissance*, Paris: Presses Universitaires de France.

Jennings, S. A. (1975), 'Effects of sex typing in children's stories on preference and recall', *Child Development*, 46, 220–3.

Koblinsky, S. G., Cruse, D. F. and Sugawara, A. I. (1978), 'Sex role stereotypes and children's memory for story content', *Child Development*, 49, 452–8.

Liben, L. S. and Signorella, M. L. (1980), 'Gender-related schemata and constructive memory in children', *Child Development*, 51, 11–18.

Maccoby, E. E. and Jacklin, C. N. (1973), *The Psychology of Sex Differences*, Stanford, CA: Stanford University Press.

Miller, S. A. (1973), 'Contradiction, surprise, and cognitive change: the effects of disconfirmation of belief on conservers and nonconservers', *Journal of Experimental Child Psychology*, 15, 47–62.

Reuchlin, M. (1972), 'Les facteurs socio-économiques du développement cognitif', in F. Duyckaerts, C. B. Hindley, J. Lézine, M. Reuchlin and A. Zemplini (eds), *Milieu et développement*, Paris: Presses Universitaires de France, 69–150.

Scott, K. P. (1986), 'Effects of sex-fair reading materials on pupils' attitudes, comprehension, and interest', *American Educational Research Journal*, 23, 106–16.

Scott, K. P. and Feldman-Summers, S. (1979), 'Children's reactions to textbook stories in which females are portrayed in traditionally male roles', *Journal of Educational Psychology*, 71, 396–402.

Smith, M. and Pasternak, C. (1977), *Breaking the Mould. Lesson Aid Plans to Explore Sex Roles, K-8*, Toronto: Ontario Institute for Studies in Education.

Turiel, E. (1973), 'Stage transition in moral development', in R. M. V. Travers (ed.), *Second Handbook of Research on Teaching*, Chicago: Rand and McNally, 732–58.

Vandenplas-Holper, C. (1987), *Education et développement social de l'enfant*, Paris: PUF (2nd revised edn).

Vandenplas-Holper, C. (1996), 'Intraindividual and interindividual cognitive conflict, related variables and relations with cognitive development', *Swiss Journal of Psychology*, 55 (2/3), 161–75.

Vandenplas-Holper, C. and Jenart, A. (1989), 'Children's recall of familiar and discrepant descriptions of adult–child relations', *Archives de Psychologie*, 57, 33–51.

ACKNOWLEDGEMENTS

Anne-Françoise Désirant and Isabelle Montulet took part in various preliminary phases of the present research. Joëlle Goethals served as a second coder. Jean-Marie De Ketele made useful comments on a first version of the manuscript. We gratefully acknowledge these various forms of help.

CHAPTER 20

A pupil with conspicuous behavioural problems receives the support he needs

Klaus Winkel

Gerd Kohl completed the tenth form of the Göttingen-Geismar Comprehensive School with the Secondary Level 1 Leaving Certificate, entitling him to continue on to any other secondary level 2 school; following a year of general vocational education, he then went on to complete successfully an apprenticeship as a roofer. There is nothing in his curriculum vitae to indicate a problematic school career; in his records from the 9th and 10th forms nothing suggests that his completion of school was at one point very much in question, that he had once been on the threshold of failure. It is this near failure and the fact that he overcame it that is the subject of this chapter. It is meant to illustrate that school can indeed help pupils with learning and social difficulties, when teachers as in Göttingen-Geismar Comprehensive are put in a position to seek and provide pedagogical answers instead of compelled to respond administratively and bureaucratically to pupils in difficulty.

The example of Gerd Kohl demonstrates that impending failure is reversible when teachers have the opportunity to observe, reflect on, and influence their pupils' social, emotional and cognitive development. The organizational structure of the team/small group model, as it was developed and practised at Göttingen-Geismar, offers this opportunity and demands of teachers that they act pedagogically. Gerd's story clearly demonstrates the effect of this school model. Nonetheless, caution is advised in drawing conclusions; there have been other cases in the school (Behrendt, 1980).

However, pupil experiences with the team/small group model have been for the most part positive (Schlömerkemper and Winkel, 1987). Its essential structural features have a supportive effect, as in Gerd's case. This is also supported by the study cited above, which analysed the responses of pupils and parents to questions about these features.

The first part of the study outlines the aims and structures of the team/small group model, as it was developed at Göttingen-Geismar Comprehensive School. Of the structural features, emphasis should be given to the tutor system as well as learning diagnosis and support, because they were especially important for Gerd's development. According to what we know about Gerd, his family and elementary school experience were not the cause of his difficult behaviour in school; however, since his experience of the comprehensive school was in contrast to that of his family and village, these areas will be briefly described in the second section. The third section of the chapter describes his difficult behaviour and suggests its possible causes. The range of options available to his teachers (primarily his tutors) and the ones they employed to help Gerd out of his difficult situation are outlined in the fourth section.

In reporting on Gerd's learning history two sources will be used:

- Learning diagnosis material: primarily the learning progress reports prepared each semester by the tutors and the observation records kept as part of the learning diagnostic process
- an interview conducted by the author with Gerd, lasting several hours and comprising 73 pages of written material.

In the fifth and final part I draw a number of conclusions from Gerd's case meant to stimulate critical thought about the teaching and learning conditions in our regular schools, but also in reform schools such as Göttingen-Geismar Comprehensive School.

AIMS AND STRUCTURAL FEATURES OF THE TEAM/SMALL GROUP MODEL

The Integrated Comprehensive School of Göttingen-Geismar, in which Gerd was enrolled, is organized according to the team/small group model. The primary aims of the model are to bring teachers and pupils into close contact with each other over a long period of time, and in so doing to create conditions for an intensive and holistic teaching and learning process. Teaching is not to be the task of departmental specialists, nor should learning always be an individual and competition-oriented task. Individuality should be complemented by the collectivity of the teacher team or the group of pupils. In contrast to diffuse 'class' association and instruction given by a continuously changing variety of teachers representing their disciplines, a clearer and more stable social structure with denser interaction allows the individual and the classroom community to develop alongside each other. The learning progress of each pupil can be better observed and supported. Instructional content can be better geared to the individual needs of the pupils (or the group) than in the conventional class, which must learn at a seemingly uniform pace. Pupils and teachers are free to shape their own learning and teaching.

These aims can be achieved through a basically very simple organizational structure: a group of 90 pupils (three classes) are taught by a team of teachers of appropriate size (about six to eight teachers). In principle, the members of this team share the sole responsibility for the instruction of 'their' pupils. Therefore the team represents the greatest variety of expertise possible. The pupils are grouped into the customary classes or 'home' groups of 30 in number, but within these groups of 30 the emergence of a complex social structure is encouraged within small groups (table groups), usually of five or six pupils, which are kept as stable as possible. These table groups play an important role in the lessons and in school life (Schlömerkemper and Winkel, 1987).

One of the most important practical changes in pedagogy concerns the tutorial function of all the team members. Each home group is assigned two or three 'tutors' who take on, in addition to administrative duties, important tasks in the area of learning diagnosis, learning support, parental involvement, and above all, as confidant for their group of pupils with whose social, emotional and cognitive development they are especially concerned. In everyday schooling this pupil–tutor relationship is given special consideration by means of a series of provisions (*cf.* Winkel, 1984).

- During the first week of school the pupils are taught and looked after almost exclusively by their tutors.
- The tutors teach as much and as long as possible in their home group. If there must be any teaching by non-specialists it is normally done by the tutors.
- The tutor's lesson observation requirements are fulfilled in his or her home group.
- A teamroom which is always open makes teachers available to their pupils.
- The tutors travel with their pupils on home group trips. Often they undertake other activities together, e.g. weekend excursions.

Regarding learning diagnostic activities, these are the most important tasks of the tutor:

- The tutor compiles all available observations, information, and experiences gained from lessons, home life and free time, for the purpose of obtaining the most accurate and detailed picture of the pupils as possible.
- The team of tutors meet regularly once a week, to discuss conflicts and possible learning support measures and to consider different approaches they might use.
- The tutors conduct 'table group evenings'. On these occasions the observations, experiences, and information gathered by themselves and other team teachers are discussed with parents and pupils and together they consult on further steps to be taken in instruction.
- The tutors write learning progress reports for their group of pupils. They gather observation records and learning cards. They get pupil feedback, they speak with parents and thus are very well informed about each pupil.
- In the group of tutors teamwork is developed in a specific way. It allows a teacher to respond personally to each individual pupil (Winkel, 1979).

It would be impossible to describe here the theory and practice of learning diagnostics and support as they were developed in Göttingen-Geismar Comprehensive, in all their complexity and interrelatedness. Therefore the reader is referred to the collection published by Herrlitz and Schaub

(1979), in which the preconditions required for the model, its guiding principles and functions and its elements have been explained by those with personal experience. Here it is only possible to introduce the most important basics of learning diagnostics.

- So that pupils learn co-operation and do not feel that their teachers value only the individual knowledge of each pupil, it is stipulated in the school plan that no form of individual quantifying evaluation should be used.
- Assessments of work are not referenced to the class average, but rather to the pupil's personal learning progress, and they always include hints for success in future work.
- The pupils are given the opportunity from 5th form onwards to respond to their teacher's remarks about their performance. In this way they should gradually learn to evaluate for themselves their academic performance as well as their work habits. Thus the learning progress report includes a section written by the pupils themselves, in which they may comment on all the issues in their school experience that are important to them. The teachers outside the pupil's team also adhere to this principle of teacher/pupil dialogue when providing feedback on academic work.
- Performance evaluation has been supplanted by learning diagnosis. By that we mean that any observation of learning should lead to indications of the problems the pupils have with learning in the school setting and what kind of support would be helpful. The point is to find out how to enable each pupil to work successfully in the future in a way that gives him or her personal satisfaction.

In practice, the work of learning diagnostics comprises three elements:

- observation of the table group by a visiting second teacher, and that teacher's discussions with the pupils about the current task and its fulfilment
- analysis of the 'learning cards' from the written feedback of the other teachers by the tutors
- reflection on the pupils' situation during the tutorial meeting and preparation of the table group evenings; the writing of the learning progress reports by the tutors (Brandt, Klemenz and Winkel, 1980; Schlömerkemper and Winkel, 1987).

'Learning support' is understood at this school as having a dual meaning. First, in the sense of the pedagogical efforts made by teachers for the benefit of their pupils' development; and secondly, it refers to the provision of additional instruction and learning time for the pupils who need it in order to ensure equality of opportunity, which 'in some cases is only guaranteed through the granting of special opportunities' (Deutscher Bildungsrat, 1970, p. 30).

With the involvement of a second teacher and the so-called group study period, the school has developed two institutions which are dedicated to learning support in the sense of providing special opportunities (Winkel, 1985). The focus is on the pupil's social as well as academic learning.

During periods designated for group study, each tutor works with two or three table groups on a cross-disciplinary theme, i.e. a small project. In addition, these periods offer the opportunity to discuss current problems (e.g. conflicts in the table group), to review and reinforce past lesson material, or take part in some group activity (e.g. telling horror stories). But in general, in the group study periods the emphasis is on cross-disciplinary study help for the long term, while the involvement of a second teacher is meant to provide support on selective points, usually discipline related.

GERD'S SCHOLASTIC DIFFICULTIES AND THEIR CAUSES

During the first semester of the sixth form the following note was made:

> Gerd Kohl urgently needs instructional help and study group support to stabilize his behaviour. He is not helped any more by being stereotyped as suffering from academic pressure and lack of motivation. Difficulties in partner and group work, lack of confidence and withdrawal (going home crying, frequent absences), above all from the aggressive acts of other pupils (verbal stigmatization).

At the time of his enrolment in the comprehensive school Gerd is described as a strong, alert boy; aged 11, he is a little older than the average age of his classmates. There is nothing in his file from elementary school to suggest that any difficulties are to be expected.

Gerd was born in a village about 15 km from Göttingen, where he lived with his parents and five brothers and sisters during his school years. His mother had been a housewife since the birth of her first child; his father was an installer of specialized machines and worked away during the week. His two sisters, five and six years older, eventually left home to train as dental and medical assistants. His older brother, unemployed since completing an apprenticeship in carpentry, was living at home; his second brother, one and a half years younger, was attending the local Hauptschule, and Gerd's youngest brother would later attend Göttingen-Geimar Comprehensive as well.

Gerd had attended the local elementary school. At this time he had three different class teachers, and he did not like going to school. These first school years were not likely to be without problems since according to him he was given a lot of homework which he was not always able to manage without help. While taking tests, his palms were often sweaty. A glance at the record of his grades from the last two years of elementary school reveals a slight downward trend: after the first semester of the third form Gerd had a grade point average of 2.3 (on a scale of 1 to 6 where 1 is the best) and in the last grade report of the fourth form an average of 3.0. Particularly dramatic is the trend in dictation, from 1.0 in the second form to 4.0 (just passing) by the end of his time in elementary school.

Gerd felt liked by his classmates, and many of them were his playmates in the afternoon. He roamed the village and surroundings with them, they formed gangs, played practical jokes on adults and played soccer and table tennis in a club. Gerd was a member of the junior fire fighters. He knew everybody in the village and everyone knew him.

Considering this background, the alarm sounded in the tutor's note seems surprising. A year after entering the comprehensive school it is discovered that Gerd feels so bad about school that he is often absent, goes home, and cries, because his classmates harass and tease him. Gerd's academic performance causes worry for his tutors as well. They see a correlation between social recognition and scholastic achievement and therefore request help during lessons (from the second teacher) and Gerd's participation in a study group for the purpose of stabilizing his behaviour. We should first consider how Gerd got into this difficult situation and how he behaved in it.

Shortly after he enters school, as Gerd later reports, cliques form in his home group. On the one hand there is a group consisting of boys whom he perceives to be dominant and aggressive, whose members all live in Göttingen, and on the other hand, a leftover group of three boys from the village. The city group is identical to a table group; the village group changes its composition; Gerd feels he belongs together with the two other village boys. The city boys learn quickly how to act in solidarity with one another; in Gerd's group there is a lot of fighting. Accordingly they rarely manage to co-operate, while the others are often able to present good results from their work. This obvious superiority is exploited by the city boys; they try to force the village boys to the sidelines.

> You village kids can't do anything! That was really discouraging, when eight or ten people were saying that to two or three. Because who else was from the village? Ines stayed out of it anyway. And I did the most together with Hans and Peter in our free time. Me and them, I think both of them, Hans and Peter, were glad when they didn't have anything to do with them. Well, what can I say?

Even in the interview Gerd seems to feel helpless; during these school years he and the two other boys try to fend off the verbal attacks:

> You city guys! You tinned food eaters! Well we said anything and everything, and that's when it began. At first you could still defend yourself against the things they said, but then it got to be too much for me.

Gerd and his friends are not successful with this. His group is marginalized and Gerd is under individual pressure in addition. It is too much for him to be attacked and mocked on account of his unfortunate family name (*Kohl* means cabbage):

Gerd: I felt really bad for the first two years. I can still remember always running out of the classroom, on the bus, and away.

Interviewer: What happened exactly?

Gerd: I think it was between two lessons and then: 'Hey you cabbage head (*Kohlkopf*), hey you empty head (*Hohlkopf*), hey you cabbage head!' When that happened, I got out as fast as I could.

The situation grows particularly unbearable due to the fact that his troubled table group is never able to shield him but rather is also a source of these taunts. His table group mates are possibly the first to make fun of him in this way. 'I didn't like Ali always saying "cabbage head – empty head" to me', he writes in his second learning progress report. Ali, a boy from the city who is not part of the city clique, sits with him in the same table group during this time. 'And this "empty head", well, that got on my nerves or, it hurt me.' During this phase – until the seventh form – another reason for Gerd to leave the school is because he believes he has observed that the strong city kids are favoured in lessons since they speak up and are called on more often.

Gerd can think of no way out of his distress other than escape. This takes two forms: Gerd leaves his home group and spends hours with the school assistant who welcomes his help; or he flees school and goes home without telling anybody. He grows quiet during his lessons; he does not participate in lesson discussions and does not work with his table group.

Accordingly, comments in the learning diagnosis materials accumulate until eventually they become alarm signals. For Gerd and his table group intensive help must be found – and other kinds of help besides the usual ones, which for Gerd had so far consisted of resolving conflict by having those involved talk about it.

> like talking about it or something. I don't think I would even have been able to, to sit with the class and with those guys ... to talk about myself in front of thirty other people or something. Or let them talk about me. That's when I always just got away as fast as I could.

The causes of Gerd's difficulties in the school were, in the writer's view, particularly the strangeness and alienation, the inadequacy of his repertoire of behaviour, and insecurity about his abilities. Before Gerd came to the school, he lived, together with his brothers and sisters, in a familiar and for him comprehensible village environment in which he had his place as a soccer player, member of the fire department, and son of the assistant chairman of the shooting club. Being together with his friends in the school and in the afternoon was important as a daily affirmation and at the same time the most natural thing in the world.

The comprehensive school's all-day operation leads to an extremely long school day for those pupils who come from further away. Gerd must leave the house before 7.00 in the morning and does not arrive home until 5.15 or even later in the evening. When he has time to play after dinner, his old friends have to be at home; in the winter it is already dark. Gerd is separated from his old village clique; for the duration of his crisis he has little contact with his friends. Gerd is not only forced to cope with a new school, but he has been deprived of his familiar village surroundings as well.

In this environment Gerd had acquired a certain functional behavioural repertoire that was suitable there and could be employed successfully. Fistfights with his peers and gang fights were part of it, as was strict subordination to the instructions of his coach, the fire chief, or teachers, which were recognized or accepted as correct.

The school, with its new teachers and new classmates, is strange to him because there he is perhaps expected to behave differently from how he has learned to in his village; at least, Gerd does not know exactly how he is supposed to behave. It is fairly clear that conflicts are to be resolved by speaking about them together in the group. A little beating up of each other – and then everything is fine again – appears to be every bit as unlikely as a teacher or tutor laying down the law and pupils following it. Talking about conflicts, finding solutions and ways out of them together is what Gerd is not able to do. A part of his experience has been invalidated: Gerd does not possess the behavioural repertoire demanded of him.

Gerd had already become unsure of his academic performance in elementary school. The downward tendency indicated by his grades may have caused him to doubt whether he would be able to fulfil the demands of a 'city school'. Yet this idea is not corroborated by Gerd's statements; he had hoped that the change to a new school would mean relief from some academic pressure and that he would be able to meet the demands. Since in the new school there is no feedback on his performance in the form of grades or points Gerd is neither able to see his hopes fulfilled nor his fears confirmed by his teacher. Nevertheless, in the formation of pupil hierarchies in the school, academic performance plays a role which should not be underestimated.

At the beginning of his time in the comprehensive school Gerd was 'not picked up from the place where he was standing' – perhaps because the tutors and teachers did not know anything about this place. As the tutors are making their notes, Gerd's future in school is at risk: he must become integrated in his home group or he is likely to become truant.

FROM OUTSIDER TO CLASS SPOKESPERSON – PEDAGOGICAL SOLUTIONS AND THEIR PREREQUISITES

There are conditions and developments which come naturally with time which can change the long-term situation of a student like Gerd:

- The pupils grow older; other things become important to them besides angering and belittling their classmates.
- Within a group the pupils learn to like each other, when they interact with each other frequently.
- As they become older their free time shifts more and more towards the evening; Gerd again finds the time and the opportunity to meet with his village clique, which makes his school situation easier.
- His parents' consistent policy of keeping him at the Göttingen-Geismar Comprehensive School allows him no way out other than to cope with the school, get accustomed to it, and finally develop a positive attitude towards it.

This is certainly not enough to get Gerd out of his position as an outsider, to integrate him into his home group and to stabilize him so that he can relate to his classmates with self-assurance and can learn according to his abilities. Gerd needs additional help, and he and his classmates receive it, especially from his tutors.

'If it hadn't been for the tutors, I would have skipped school for sure.'
This subheading is not a strict quotation but rather a composite of the following interview statements: I ask Gerd if he had found at least his tutors

to be understanding of him and his situation:

Gerd: Yes, you could say that, yes. If it hadn't been for them, then I would have for sure gone into town every morning instead of to school.

Interviewer: Really – those boys made your life so awful that you would have started skipping school at the age of eleven.

Gerd: Yes, for sure.

In the 5th and 6th forms Gerd has three and later two tutors who accompany him through the six years of comprehensive school. Walter is chosen by Gerd to be his personal tutor; Walter writes his progress reports, speaks to his parents and takes care of him. In doing so Walter always confers with his tutors; they also prepare and conduct the home group discussions that are so terrifying and fruitless for Gerd. The alarm notice quoted above originates in one of their weekly meetings during which they also consider how Gerd could be helped to be more successful than he had been in the 5th form.

For Gerd it is invaluable that a tutor is there at all times for him. He says of Walter that he had helped him to cope with school; Walter had supported him, he could talk to Walter about anything. Walter had had time for him. 'The tutors', wrote Gerd in the pupil section of his second learning progress report, 'are very very very very good; they are not so strict.' Gerd has come to this conclusion as a result of his experiences with understanding, attentive teachers who are willing to talk with him. They do not punish him for his usually unreasonable disappearances from school, do not demand an explanation from him or hold him responsible but instead see this flight for what it is: a signal of great distress. They also see it as their task to help him find another way out of this distress than through escape.

This teacher behaviour is predicated on discussions among the tutors during which causes and correlations are considered in detail: the information and agreements in the team, which prevent interference from outside teachers without sufficient knowledge of the case; the exchange of information between tutors and parents. The most important factor is, however, the team's decision not to draw up a set of school rules prescribing, in bureaucratic fashion, specific school reactions to specific pupil behaviours and then escalating these measures with mechanical precision. Only in this way do teachers acquire the necessary discretionary scope for pedagogically based action. And so it is in the case of Gerd. Before describing the objectives of their actions and pedagogical practice we should emphasize once more that for students like Gerd – and also for most others – it is important to know that they have in their tutors a trusted adult who helps when it is necessary.

Gerd: When something went wrong – bad grades in maths, or in English, I don't know whether we asked him …

Interviewer: to help us with it

Gerd: … or he offered to do it. When he does something like that, that's really important, that he is someone who helps you?

Interviewer: Of course. But apart from helping you with some subjects, how else did he help you?

Gerd: Helping me to survive this crisis in the school, yes, and … I really don't know right now. Things don't always have to stick out in your mind to make you think it was important that Walter was there.

Interviewer: That sounds as if there was a relationship of trust which was understood.

Gerd: I think so, yes.

THE WORK OF THE TUTORS: LEARNING SUPPORT, GROUP WORK AND EMOTIONAL STABILIZATION

The tutors are already beginning to take notice of Gerd's problems in the 5th form. Their initial reaction takes the form of discussions with his parents, with Gerd, with the group of city boys and the whole home group; these bring no recognizable improvement for Gerd – probably not least because he avoids them himself, so that he cannot be involved in any verbal agreements. In the second half of the 5th school year Gerd receives academic help as part of the group study periods. His group is supervised by his tutor, who writes in his learning progress report:

> In my group study on Monday and Thursday mornings you had and used several opportunities to work on and eliminate difficulties in English and maths lessons. You especially had a lot of fun with speaking English and playing dialogues and showed that you can use the new language well. You sometimes need some additional practice in maths and English to be able to keep up with the material in the lessons, or to review the material so that you don't forget.

In the 6th form this remedial help for Gerd is rigorously continued and extended. First, Walter frequently observes Gerd's group in the maths lessons as a second teacher. Second, he helps the group in English by taking them out of the lessons occasionally and teaching them separately, and third, he works with this and another group together in the group study periods, in which they have time for various kinds of activities: construction of a model playground out of matchsticks, conference simulation discussion of table group problems, the study of ordnance survey maps of the area in which the boys live, tutor afternoon preparation, soccer and handball games, and revising and playing English dialogues from the first book, among other things.

These three support activities serve the purpose of making the students able to work in all subject areas, so that in the long term they are able to take control of their own learning. For Gerd that means above all strengthening him emotionally so that he can be confident of keeping up with academic instruction. The fact that he needs more time, that he consumes more of the teachers' time, is taken for granted and he is not blamed for it.

Gerd's table group often gets – sometimes together with other pupils – opportunities for independent group work, which can or must be done outside the home group classroom. The topics include films about the villages in the district, preparation of an agricultural exhibition in the school, and – in the 7th form – reports on the farming operations in a village. This selection shows that this 'tracking measure', for which the tutors have made available lessons in German, English, art, and social studies, aside from the training of group work skills, also has the objective of incorporating Gerd's 'other' world into the school and making his experiences relevant to instruction.

Study help and group work are always directed, aside from towards the acquisition of skills and abilities, at the emotional stabilization of Gerd: when he presents his agricultural exhibit, shows his own films, he is interesting to the home group and removed from his position as an outsider. In the independent work periods he learns, separated from the city boys, to interact playfully with other students in many ways. Eventually, the home group, including the two feuding table groups, visits the farm belonging to the parents of one of the boys, who proudly drives the tractor out of the garage. The home group cycles through the villages of the district – they 'cover' the home towns of their classmates literally. 'I think', wrote Walter, 'these activities were an important contribution to the emotional stabilization of the students, having made their change to a new school and school location easier.'

Learning diagnosis – a prerequisite for successful learning support
Since the learning diagnosis – in contrast to the assessment of a pupil using grades – also takes into consideration the pupil's social situation, Gerd's tutors are forced to form an accurate picture of him, to reflect upon the causes of his problems, and to look for solutions such as the ones described above.

> To create these learning conditions, ongoing discussions among the tutors, the regular exchange of observations, and thoroughgoing agreement on all support measures were absolutely necessary. This level of communication, facilitated by the shared workplace in the teamroom, contributed decisively to the avoidance of tracking in the conventional sense. The fact that observed learning difficulties or conflicts in the table group were always discussed immediately in the tutor meetings guaranteed that we could usually react as a team, with the consent of teachers outside the team as well. The joint learning diagnosis prevented the strict schematization of the working behaviour of the pupils in this home group and the development of rigid images of the pupils in our minds. The tutor discussion always offered the opportunity to correct our own perceptions and to notice aspects previously unobserved in the pupils' learning. We formed our working hypotheses, analysed the pupils' reactions, tested our hypotheses on the basis of these reactions, changed them, threw them out, clarified among ourselves the freedom we were willing to allow the pupils in their independent work, and the freedom the pupils needed in our opinion for the development of their independence.
>
> (Behrendt, 1979, pp. 286–7)

In this circle of hypothesis, support, monitoring, and alteration, Gerd is active as a pupil:

> The pupils became actively involved in the definition of the assignments; they even learned, at times, to negotiate with the teacher on possible assignments or to suggest topics, which demanded of them hard work because they had not been 'prepared' by the teacher. During such work the pupils were so highly motivated that they worked beyond the end of the period, whereby they often managed to interest other pupils in the subject and to involve them in the work co-operatively. As soon as we negotiated the learning conditions with the pupils, the learning diagnosis was also a subject for discussion with the pupils, not only during the table group parent meetings or in the form of the learning progress reports, but primarily in the analysis of concrete work outcomes as well.
>
> (Behrendt, 1979, p. 288)

In the semester reports the pupils are not just objects of school assessment either, because if the tutor had had to express Gerd's performance as a grade, or wanted to report to him openly and honestly, or even 'mercilessly', as is called for from time to time, Gerd would have been in even more distress and would possibly have given up in total resignation. Walter, however, writes in the first learning progress reports primarily about Gerd's social situation and its influence on his learning conditions. He emphasizes successful work with instructional material and encourages further successful learning processes. Weaknesses and failures are mentioned, yet not without suggestions for help; blame and fault-finding, on the other hand, are avoided. In the excerpt from the learning progress report cited above, Walter expresses clearly that Gerd is receiving study help in English and maths, because he needs more time than other students to keep up with the material and make it stick. This is merely stated as a fact, as something natural; that is the way it is and it is all right: whoever needs more time for his or her learning, may have it – the teacher's time included. At the same time Walter makes clear that Gerd has fun speaking English in a small group, that in fact he can deal with this language quite well, which appears to be difficult for him when he is under pressure from the city clique and in the large group. He attempts to mirror Gerd's feelings, indicates the possible sources of his difficulties, responds to him by being receptive to his criticism of the boys' clique and becomes his ally. 'Above all we must think together about what to do about this group of boys which, not only in your view, gets preferential treatment.'

At the end of the 6th school year this support and encouragement bear fruit. Gerd is accepted as a fully fledged member of his home group, he gets along with his classmates to the extent that he works together successfully with individuals from the city group from time to time. In the subjects of maths and English he participates successfully and confidently, but continues to take extra group study time. At the beginning of the new school year he is elected class spokesperson and is fully capable of fulfilling the duties of this office. The next few years pass by with relatively few problems, but they are not at all easy; he works successfully in most subjects, and procures for himself the help he needs in English and maths. He is fully integrated in his home group.

CONCLUSION

Of the 185 students who entered the Göttingen-Geismar Comprehensive along with Gerd, at the first attempt

- 164 students earned the Secondary Level 1 Leaving Certificate
- 16 students earned the Realschule Leaving Certificate
- 2 students earned the Hauptschule Leaving Certificate
- 3 students failed to earn any leaving certificate.

In the following years the number of students who left the school without any certificate stabilized between two and four – success for this school (Winkel, 1985), which has at least been confirmed by the Köln-Holweide Comprehensive School (Ratzki *et al.*, 1996), which is likewise organized according to the team/small group model. This commendable achievement is, as the example of Gerd shows, not the consequence of careless assessment or even a negligent lack of academic standards, but rather the result of the intensive pedagogical efforts of all those involved.

So that the work of teachers can be as fruitful as this, the school needs – this is also shown by Gerd's case – few but nevertheless essential changes, the primary aim of which should be the de-bureaucratization of school. This means, above all, transforming school officials who instruct, test, and evaluate without respect of person into teachers who are given curricular and administrative discretion and can exercise it competently. In this, I include, above all:

- a breakdown of the school hierarchy in favour of an organizational structure based on co-operation
- loosening of space and time strictures, within which instruction is forced, in favour of longer time periods determined by themes and subject matter, which also make it possible to leave the schoolroom
- extension of the concept of school learning to include practical, emotional, and social learning
- abandonment of grades and certificates in favour of a dialogical learning diagnosis.

When these and other demands have been met and teachers understand how to make use of the opportunities thereby opened up to them, the number of pupils with 'disturbed' or 'conspicuous' behaviour will be considerably reduced, simply because the limits of behavioural options will no longer be so narrowly and rigidly circumscribed. The school of today often creates problems which then require a great deal of financial, intellectual, and personal investment to be solved.

Gerd cannot, if he wants to continue at another school, be spared a kind of 'culture shock'. And it can happen anywhere that he meets a group of dominant, verbally aggressive classmates who drive him to flee. And the change to a new school, even to a reform school, is not the only risk pupils may encounter during the course of their school career, as learning is always a risky matter. Therefore, each and every school needs teachers who appreciate some of these risks and who are competent enough to help in mastering and overcoming them: teachers who care, who are doubly qualified in their subject areas and in pedagogy, and who have the time and the opportunity to work consistently with relatively small groups. This, then, touches on issues regarding teacher preparation and the transformation of the work of teachers. These demands and considerations have been put forth, more precisely and in more detail by competent people but with only meagre success.

Gerd Kohl's scholastic career is, in my view, a convincing example of the effectiveness of pedagogical efforts in a school which is in the process of partially fulfilling these demands. Gerd is no exception in his school. The school in Göttingen is, however, an exception. The state culture ministers established the comprehensive schools in 1982 as schools with 'ability tracking', exempting only the comprehensive schools of Göttingen-Geismar and four others which, with their pedagogical distinctiveness, enjoyed exceptional status. In 1985 the comprehensive schools of the Saarland also adopted the team/small group model, under the condition that they retain half-day operation and ability tracking as well as compulsory grade assessment. Since then, however, pedagogical reform at the comprehensive school has been stagnating. In the interest of our pupils we should raise the question why the better school must remain the exception.

REFERENCES

Behrendt, W. (1979), 'Die Tischgruppe als Differenzierungs- und Fördergruppe', in H.-G. Herlitz and H. Schaub, *Die Praxis der Lerndiagnose und Lernförderung im Team-Kleingruppen-Modell Untersuchungen und Berichte der Projektgruppe SIGS Universität Göttingen*, Vol. 4, pp. 246–89.

Behrendt, W. (1980), 'Kritische Anmerkungen und Fragen zur Lerngeschichte eines Schülers aus dem 9. Jahrgang der IGS Göttingen-Geismar', *Untersuchungen und Berichte der Projektgruppe SIGS Universität Göttingen*, Vol. 8.

Brandt, H., Klemenz, I. and Winkel, K. (1980), 'Das Team-Kleingruppen-Modell an der IGS Göttingen-Geismar – ein Weg konsequenter Schulreform', in W. Bassmann, K. Dehnbostel and G. Drenkelford (1950), *Gesamtschule – Lernen ohne Angst*, Frankfurt: Fischer Verlag, pp. 151–87.

Deutscher Bildungsrat (1970), *Empfehlungen der Bildungskommission: Strukturplan für das Bildungswesen*, Bonn.

Herrlitz, H.-G. and Schaub, H. (1979), *Die Praxis der Lerndiagnose und Lernförderung im Team-Kleingruppen-Modell*, Vol. 4 of *Untersuchungen und Berichte der Projektgruppe SIGS der Universität Göttingen*.

Ratzki, A. *et al.* (1996), *Team-Kleingruppen-Modell Köln-Holweide*, Frankfurt: Peter Lang Europäischer Verlag der Wissenschaften.

Schlömerkemper, J. and Winkel, K. (1987), 'Lernen im Team-Kleingruppen-Modell', *Biographische und empirische Untersuchungen zum sozialen Lernen in der Integrierten Gesamtschule Göttingen-Geismar*, Frankfurt: Peter Lang Europäischer Verlag der Wissenschaften.

Winkel, K. (1979), 'Team, Tutor und Tischgruppe als institutionelle Voraussetzung der Lerndiagnose- und Förderarbeit', in H.-G. Herlitz and H. Schaub, *Die Praxis der Lerndiagnose und Lernförderung im Team-Kleingruppen-Modell*, Vol. 4 of *Untersuchungen und Berichte der Projektgruppe SIGS der Universität Göttingen*, pp. 47–53.

Winkel, K. (1984), 'Die Schülerin Vera. Lernbedingungen und soziale Erfahrungen im Team-Kleingruppen-Modell', *Untersuchungen und Berichte der Projektgruppe SIGS Universität Göttingen,* Vol. 11.

Winkel, K. (1985), 'Auf dem Weg zu einer Förderung ohne Auslese', *Die Deutsche Schule*, 75, pp. 279–92.

CHAPTER 21

Affective education and teacher training in Italy: experiences and research results

Donata Francescato

WHY AFFECTIVE EDUCATION IS NECESSARY IN OUR CHANGING SOCIAL CONTEXT

Like many European countries, Italy is undergoing massive political, economic and cultural change; facing the historical transition from a production to a service economy, in which secure lifelong jobs are diminishing and unemployment, part-time work and self-employment are increasing. Traditional female and male roles are also evolving, the number of patriarchal and nuclear families is decreasing and there are now more double-career, single-parent, and step families. Separation, divorce and remarriage are becoming common (Francescato, 1995). Procreation patterns have modified, making, for example, the single-child family, once a rarity, fairly common among professionals in urban areas. Child abuse and neglect have also become more visible. These deep changes in family and work patterns have been accompanied in Italy by extreme turbulence in the political arena. Old parties have vanished, new ones are emerging[1]. Old reference points are becoming obsolete; personal and social discontent is increasing, and since the late 1970s, health and social services have been criticized and legal reforms have attempted to make them more responsive to their clients.

Educational institutions have been especially blamed, as well as parents, for doing a poor job of educating the new generation in these times of dramatic social change. Many studies have documented the poor structural and functional conditions under which many schools operate. Others have focused on the mediocre results of our schooling system (Pennisi, 1993).

Children coming from lower socio-economic backgrounds drop out of school sooner and more frequently encounter juvenile delinquency or drug addiction in their adolescence. Bullying, suicides, and fighting are increasing in both junior and senior high schools. Assessment procedures in schools create anxiety and discontent among students and parents, who rightly perceive that the quality of life of their offspring may be negatively affected by school policies and by teacher behaviour. In Italy, while theoretically all school programmes are controlled nationwide by the Ministry of Education, each teacher is 'boss' in her or his classroom. Teachers receive the same pay, are never rewarded for outstanding performance and are reproached for poor teaching.

Pupils remain with the same small group of peers for five years in elementary schools, for three years in junior high and again for five years in high schools. This could become an important structural advantage for fostering group spirit and solidarity: however, most Italian teachers are not trained in group dynamics and therefore do not always know how to promote the growth of group co-operation and collaboration among their students. Many teachers complain that they end up spending more time managing problem behaviour than actual 'teaching', and many more feel they are not properly trained to handle the psychological aspects of both pupil–pupil and teacher–pupil interactions. For instance, it is considered culturally 'normal' for students to cheat, helping each other informally; this is the only kind of 'group work' promoted or tolerated in many Italian classrooms, which provokes gross injustices in student assessment, and has negative consequences on the ethical and psycho-social development of pupils. Many teachers are at a loss as to how to handle this and other sensitive behavioural problems and need assistance from psychologists and other health professionals. These have done some very interesting experiments based on the applications of social science knowledge and skills in classroom situations to promote prosocial behaviour (Arcidiancono and Gelli, 1994; Francescato, Leone and Traversi, 1993).

In the last few years, as described elsewhere in this book (see Chapter 9 by Maria Teresa Crucillà) the Italian Ministry of Education has formally started to promote different kinds of programmes, aimed at drug abuse prevention and at the promotion of healthy and prosocial behaviour, in collaboration with the Minister of Health and local boards, which have improved the climate of many classrooms. To reform the educational system, however, requires, as community psychologists suggest,[2] working simultaneously on many dimensions (political, economical, functional, cultural and psychological), on state, local community, institutional, small group and individual levels.

In a social context like that of Italy, for instance, where individualism prevails and people have different attitudes towards traditional politics, educating people also means allowing pupils to become aware of the necessity of interdependence among individuals, groups, and natural and social environments; and of the need to take personal and group responsibility for resolving problems, instead of waiting for the state, or some other agency to take care of these issues.

As promoters of affective education have proposed, this includes revitalizing teachers and pupils who have lost hope and self-esteem and helping them exploit their strong points instead of focusing on their weaknesses. It requires focusing on their attitudes, beliefs, and emotions as central variables in the learning process. We hypothesize that modern society produces many isolated professionals, among them teachers, who often face growing behavioural and learning problems on their own in their classroom. Isolated, they become apathetic and even when they are part of big organizations they feel they are insignificant. In fact membership of unions and political parties has diminished in the last decades (Fedele, 1994). We propose that favouring group empowerment, one of community psychology's main goals, among pupils and teachers and parents could provoke lasting and beneficial changes in school settings.

About ten years ago, at the request of school teachers and health personnel, we began to experiment with various forms of school intervention, based on a blend of theoretical concepts and tools drawn from community and humanistic psychology.[3] In this chapter I will briefly describe our integrated methodology of affective education, outline in some detail our teacher training programme and discuss some research we have been conducting to evaluate the efficacy of our approach.

AN 'INTEGRATED' METHODOLOGY OF SOCIO-AFFECTIVE EDUCATION FOR PUPILS, TEACHERS AND PARENTS

From humanistic psychology we took the idea that the learning process can best take place in a context of positive interpersonal relationship and, furthermore, that classrooms should provide opportunities for the development of social and interpersonal as well as cognitive skills. Examining the literature on affective and peace education, we selected, readapted and combined some intervention strategies which had been proved effective for certain aims. We chose some of Gordon's (1974) teacher effectiveness techniques to improve the interpersonal relations between pupils and teachers. We also readapted a series of psycho-motor exercises to help students and teachers become more aware of their sensations, feelings and emotions.

Furthermore we developed a modified circletime technique, using one of the main tools of traditional affective education (Lang, 1994) to promote group empowerment, as conceived by community psychologists. Community psychologists maintain that only in groups of small size can individuals develop a sense of belonging and an awareness of their powers and limitations. One way to empower people and to improve the quality of their life is to favour their active participation in small groups. In general, this means helping individuals become more capable members of their natural groups or encouraging them to form self-help groups, or other kinds of activist social groups. In school settings it involves favouring the development of group membership among pupils, teachers and parents, empowering existing small groups and favouring the establishment of new small groups to take care of shared problems or goals (Francescato and Putton, 1995). Obviously each intervention with small groups, in different kinds of schools from nursery to high school, is planned to be specifically tailored to the target situation, and according to the specific needs and strengths of its participants; however, some objectives and some methodologies characterize our approach to small group empowerment in any school context.

Our general objectives are:

- to improve the interpersonal relations among group members
- to promote the formation of a team spirit, of belonging and inter-dependence among group members, of a climate of trust, which will favour dialogue and creative synthesis among opposite viewpoints, while respecting the diversity of group members classmates, parents, teachers, etc.[4]
- to transmit some relevant information about small group phenomena and teach some skills which allow trainees to become better partici-pants, observers and facilitators of work or discussion groups (for instance we teach them to identify the strengths and weaknesses of their own workgroup by focusing on certain tasks, processes and structural group variables, to conduct meetings, to handle group con-flicts by problem solving and creativity techniques, etc.
- to help each group to become a self-help group or a social change ori-ented group.

If the participants are a classroom of fifth grade children for instance, during weekly circle time meetings, a trained teacher facilitates the dis-cussion among classmates of a topic of their choosing (which the students may have selected through a brainstorming technique during the previ-ous meeting), or of a problem that has just arisen in the classroom and that someone has proposed for the agenda. Two or more students sit out-side the circle and observe group processes with the help of observation schemata, which have been created to fit different skills (from very sim-ple observations such as the number of times each pupil speaks, to more complex non-verbal and other group phenomena). In the last ten minutes after the discussion has formally ended, the observers describe what they noticed and teachers and students try to understand how well or poorly they did what they had decided to do: communicate, listen, propose new ideas, solve problems, take decisions, etc.

To help create a climate of mutual aid and solidarity, we try to encour-age the giving and receiving of help. For instance, in a seventh-grade classroom during one circle time on friendship, one girl revealed that as a newcomer she did not have anybody to do activities with. Some of her classmates who shared some of her interests offered to go skating with her, and go to the local bird association. In a few weeks she reported feel-ing less lonely and having acquired a few friends. In another class, during circle time in which grading was discussed, a boy stated he had difficulty studying alone, and two classmates volunteered to spend some afternoons working with him. In a senior high school a girl who discov-ered she was pregnant was helped by her classmates to tell her parents and eventually give the baby up for adoption.

We have used this integrated methodology with student groups from nursery to college level, with teacher groups and with parents and with mixed groups made up of students, parents, teachers and other school personnel. The efficacy of this integrated methodology was evaluated in several research projects using experimental and control groups. Generally, children in the experimental classes modified their self concept in a positive way, showing more self-confidence, capacity to collaborate, trust in others and a positive attitude towards the future. They also perceived themselves as more able to establish gratifying interpersonal relationships with adults and peers. Compared to control classes, pupils in experimental classes got to know each other better, reduced avoidance behaviours and increased friendly and collaborative behaviours. Moreover, both in the control and experimental groups before the intervention, boys and girls tended to choose as friends classmates of the same sex while, after having lived through at least six months of circle time, their exploratory and friendly behaviour patterns were directed at both sexes. Moreover in many instances in the experimental classes antisocial and deviant behaviour of emotionally disturbed youngsters showed a decrease in frequency. There was also an increase in their social and interpersonal adjustment, while in the control group there were no such improvements (Francescato, Putton and Cudini, 1986; Francescato and Ghirelli, 1988; Putton, 1993; Francescato, Putton, De Gennaro and Locatelli, 1995). In teachers' and parents' groups cohesion grew as well as the ability to give and receive help and to face and solve problems together (Francescato and Putton, 1995).

Once we established the efficacy of the integrated methodology in different school settings, in the last few years we have dedicated much effort to develop a training methodology for teachers which would enable them to use the integrated method (particularly our modified circle time technique) in their classroom and with time to train other colleagues to use it.

A TEACHER TRAINING MODEL

The training model we use can be applied to groups of teachers or, as we prefer, to mixed groups, for instance of teachers, parents and other mental or health personnel who maintain working relations with schools (paediatricians, school psychologists, social workers, etc). To give a better idea of what our training consists of I will describe one project in which we also did an evaluation research.

We started this intervention programme by training (in small groups) about 30 junior high school teachers and 20 psychologists, social workers and paediatricians working in community health services, who were interested in preventing drug abuse and other forms of deviance among youngsters from a town of about 100,000 people in central Italy. They were involved in about 70 hours training, meeting with us for about ten days during a two-year period. The aims of the training programme were:

- to deepen the knowledge of participants about childhood and adolescence
- to help them reflect on their own experiences as junior high students
- to enable participants to gain competence in using: some of Gordon's techniques to improve interpersonal relations between pupils and teachers (see Gordon, 1974); some psycho-motor exercises to help pupils become more aware of their feelings; a modified circle time technique to improve the interpersonal relations among students, give them a chance to discuss topics of interest to them, teach stu-

dents some group skills through observation and discussion of group phenomena, and create a mutual aid, self-help group class atmosphere.

In the first three months of training, the main skills were taught during six days of group work, conducted in three modules, at monthly intervals. During the intervals the trainees met in small groups to practise what they had learnt through simulations (pretending they were pupils and running a circle time session as they would have done in a real classroom). Their experiences were discussed in the following training modules.

The initial training days gave ample time to the exploration of the participants' childhood and school experiences using a circle time technique, and people were invited to share what we labelled 'experiential moments'. For instance, people shared good and bad memories of nursery, elementary and junior high experiences. They were asked to close their eyes and try to go back in time and see what memories they came up with. After the people who wanted to share with others had done so, discussion focused on similarities and differences between their own experiences in schools and the ones of their students. Participants were asked to pretend to be a classroom of seventh graders and discuss what they liked and disliked about schools and teachers. Observers outside the circle took notes and then people discussed their observation. At the end of each meeting much time was devoted to an examination of participants' personal attitudes and feelings towards the teaching and mental health professions, and to sharing of problems which they found most hard to face. They were also taught problem solving and other creativity techniques to be used with students when conflicts or problems arose.

After this first period of training, for the next six months trainees began using circle time in real classrooms, working in couples. One trainee, perhaps a teacher, would run the meeting, while the other took notes, for discussion during the supervision meetings. In this six month trial period trainees had four days of supervision to discuss problems and results of their experimentation. We then proceeded to evaluate the efficacy of the training method. At the beginning of the next school year 44 trained teachers or mental health workers applied circle time methodology in 44 experimental junior high classes whose 751 pupils were compared to 546 pupils (aged 11–14) attending 32 control classes.

It was hypothesized that students in the experimental group would show better self-concept and improved interpersonal relations than control pupils. Before and after the programme, both groups were given the MRO test (a four-dimensional projective technique which measures self-concept, gender role, family and interpersonal relations). After the intervention both control and experimental classes were given a sociogram. The sociogram was interpreted according to Carli and Mosca (1980) who assume that in each class exist two social dimensions: an organizational one oriented to learning (which is characterized by roles, norms and objectives); and a sub-institutional one, oriented at the satisfaction of emotional needs, affiliation, acceptance and prestige. If a teacher favours the first dimension, he or she will encourage friendships among students and favour an attitude of reciprocal avoidance. If on the other hand the teacher considers both dimensions important, he or she will encourage pupils' interactions and in this case there will be a higher degree of socialization among pupils. From the sociogram data one can derive an index of cohesion and indexes of exploratory and avoidance behaviours. An analysis of variance procedure showed that experimental pupils increased their scores in all four dimensions of MRO.

Sociogram results also showed significant differences between the two groups in the expected direction. The strongest differences were achieved with younger students who had just entered junior high school (Francescato, Putton, De Gennaro, Pirri and Brauzzi, 1995). Informal observations by teachers indicated that in the experimental classes a climate of mutual aid and feelings of empowerment were also fostered. For instance, in many classes students spontaneously helped others with academic problems by tutoring them after school; in one class one girl who had been sexually molested by her stepfather asked for help during circle time and the mother of a classmate who worked in a family clinic was able to help her troubled family. In another class, full of multi-problem children, these came up with a list of grievances about teachers' behaviour and with suggestions on how to improve their school, which was later accepted by the principal. In some classes, parents who heard about circle time meetings from their children also became involved in parents' circle time groups, giving each other support and advice. Some parents promoted new self-help groups for adoptive parents. Some teachers formed new groups designed to provide training for their colleagues during the new school year.

These training programmes have been planned and implemented by skilled community psychologists, who were themselves specially trained in community and humanistic psychology. A training programme for trainers is indispensable and generally takes about two years (250 hours of practice). Psychologists who train teachers must be knowledgeable in a variety of social and psychological topics and possess many techniques from multi-dimensional organizational analysis to community development, and from promotion of self-help groups and empowerment skills to a mastery of small group processes.[5] We found that psychotherapists were not as good as community psychologists in running these training groups, because they tended to transform them into psychotherapy groups.

Our good results may have been partly due to the fact that training was in all cases conducted with teachers or mental health workers who were volunteers and had favourable attitudes towards affective education. We are now experimenting with a variety of training techniques for teachers, who are required by law to attend some courses in order to obtain salary increases. The law has just been passed in Italy and gives us new opportunities to work with groups of teachers who may be hard to motivate. One small experiment we have started with 140 teachers in Sardinia, in a troubled high school with a very high drop-out rate, gave us hope that even with major difficulties our approach can produce some changes. Further research is needed to show which problems affective education helps us resolve, and which school problems have to be dealt with at a political, functional and social level.

NOTES

1. For the crisis of political parties in Italy, see Fedele, 1994; for other western countries, see Ginsberg and Chefter, 1990.
2. Community psychology originated in the United States (Levine and Perkins, 1987); for a good analysis, including Great Britain, see Orford (1992); for Spain, see Antonio Martín Gonzales (1996); for Italy, see Francescato and Ghirelli (1988); for an international panorama, see Hess and Stark (1995).
3. In 1982 I founded Ecopoiesis, a laboratory of research and training in community psychology. Since then we have trained about 120 community psychologists who are capable of training other professionals and who have been doing much of the experimental work described in this chapter.
4. For an acute analysis of how debates among different interest groups can produce novel solutions to complex problems, see Mansbridge, 1992, 1994a and 1994b.
5. For a theoretical description of different community psychology strategies, see Francescato, Leone and Traversi, 1993; for a description of the two year training programme, call or fax Monica Morganti Ecopoiesis on 39624401994, Via Galaezzo Alessi, 142 00176 Rome.

REFERENCES

Arcidiancono, C. and Gelli, B. (1994), *Psicologia di comunità ed educazione sessuale*, Milan: Francoangeli.

Carli, R. and Mosca, A. (1980), *Gruppo ed istruzione a scuola*, Turin: Boringhieri.

Fedele, M. (1994), *Democrazia referendaria*, Rome: Donzelli.

Francescato, D. (1992), 'A multidimensional perspective of organisational change', *Systems Practice* 5, 2, 129–46.

Francescato, D. (1995), *Hijos felices de parejas rotas*, Barcelona: Ariel.

Francescato, D. (1998), *Amore e potere. La rivoluzione dei sessi nella coppia e nella societa*, Milan: Mondadori.

Francescato, D. and Ghirelli, G. (1988), *Fondamenti di psicologia di comunità*, Rome: Nis.

Francescato, D. and Ghirelli, G. (1992), 'Continuity and creative change: Reflections on ten years of experience on community psychology training in Italy', *Community Psychologist*, 25, 2, 15–16.

Francescato, D. and Putton, A. (1995), *Star meglio insieme oltre l'individualismo imparare a crescere a collaborare con gli altri*, Milan: Mondadori.

Francescato, D. and Tancredi, M. (1992), 'Methodologies of organisational change: the need for an integrated approach', in D. M. Hosking and N. Anderson (eds), *Organisational Change and Innovation: Psychological Perspectives and Practices in Europe*, London: Routledge.

Francescato, D., Leone, L. and Traversi, M. (1993), *Oltre la psicoterapia percorsi innovativi di psicologia di comunità*, Rome: Nis.

Francescato, D., Putton, A. and Cudini, S. (1986), *Star bene insieme a scuola: Strategie di educazione socioaffecttiva dalle materne alle medie*, Rome: Nis.

Francescato, D., Putton, A. and Cudini, S. (1995), 'Prevention in Italy: An overview of the field in prevention', *Human Services*, vol. 12, 1, 115–32; also in R. Hess and W. Stark (eds) (1995), 115–32.

Francescato, D., Putton, A., De Gennaro, L. and Locatelli, M. (1995), 'L'educazione socioaffecttiva nella scuola materna', *Eta evolutiva*, 50, 1–7.

Francescato, D., Putton, A., De Gennaro, L., Pirri, P. and Brauzzi, F. (1995), 'Ricerca intervento di educazione socioaffectiva nella scuola media inferiore', *Giornale italiano di psicologia*, 3, June, 1–9.

Ginsberg, B. and Chefter, M. (1990), *Politics by Other Means: The Declining Importance of Elections in America*, New York: Basic Books.

Gordon, T. (1974), *Teacher Effectiveness Training*, New York: Peter Weyden.

Hess, R. E. and Stark, W. (eds) (1995), *International Approaches to Prevention in Mental Health and Human Services*, New York: The Hawthorne Press.

Lang, P. (1994), 'Getting round to circle time: issues raised by research', Affective Education in Europe, seminar, Warwick University, 20–22 May 1994.

Levine, M. and Perkins, D. (1987), *Principles of Community Psychology: Perspectives and Applications*, New York: Oxford University Press.

Mansbridge, J. (1992), 'A deliberative theory of interest representation', in M. Petracca, *The Politics of Interests: Interest Groups Transformed*, Westview Press.

Mansbridge, J. (1994a), 'Public spirit', in H. Aron, T. Mann and T. Taylor, *Values and Public Policy*, Washington: The Brookings Institutions, 146–72.

Mansbridge, J. (1994b), 'Using power-fighting power', *Constellations*, vol. 1, 51–73.

Martin Gonzales, A. (1996), *Psicologia comunitaria: fundamentas y applicaciones*.

Orford, J. (1992), *Community Psychology: Theory and Practice*, Chichester: Wiley.

Pennisi, G. (1993), *Satrapi, mandarini e senzalavoro*, Rome: Ediesse.

Putton, A. (1993), 'L'educazione socioaffectiva: una strategia di prevenzione primaria nei contesti educativa', in D. Francescato, L. Leone, M. Traversi (eds), *Oltre la psicoterapia*, Rome: Nis.

CHAPTER 22

Students' perceptions of classroom climate: an evaluation of the effects of a PSE intervention

Isabel Menezes and Bártolo P. Campos

Project evaluation is generally an undervalued assignment in educational intervention, since practitioners tend to take into account only their perceptions of change or want to evaluate when the successes or failures are already there. The result is a general ignorance about the processes and elements that determine change and effectiveness, and an inability to replicate methodologies and results. Therefore there is a strong need to determine the effectiveness of intervention strategies by doing planned evaluations of project results (Illback *et al.*, 1990).

Some of the discomfort or even scepticism experienced by teachers with regard to project evaluation is related to the fact that evaluation outcomes are frequently presented as 'descriptions of the "way things really are" or "really work", or of some "true" state of affairs' (Guba and Lincoln, 1989, p. 8), objectively measured by experts who will ultimately judge the validity of their practice. The assumption of such a paradigm can sometimes result in disenfranchising teachers and other school agents, thus inhibiting their efforts in designing and implementing educational interventions. A more recent perspective, however, defies this positivistic perspective, emphasizing a 'responsive constructivist evaluation' (Guba and Lincoln, 1989, p. 38) that assumes the hermeneutic nature of evaluation and values an action orientation, so that the outcomes will eventually be useful for the teachers themselves.

In this chapter, we aim to describe a process of project evaluation of a PSE programme developed by a school involved in the Portuguese Curricular Reform (see Chapter 10 for a detailed description) that was implemented from 1991 to 1994. The evaluation process began in 1992 and involved the students that attended grades 7, 8, and 9 in two schools: the school where the PSE programme was being implemented (the PSE school), and a similar school (from the point of view of size, architecture, historical background, and geographical insertion) in which only 7-graders were experiencing the revised curricula (the 'other' school).

A PSYCHOLOGICAL PERSPECTIVE ON PSE

A main contribution of responsive constructivist evaluation is the idea that 'the findings are not "facts" in some ultimate sense but are, instead, literally *created* through an interactive process that *includes* the evaluator ... as well as the many stakeholders that are put at some risk by the evaluation. What emerges from this process is one or more *constructions* that are the realities of the case' (Guba and Lincoln, 1989, p. 8). And 'constructions are, quite literally, *created realities*' (*ibid.*, p. 143) that emerge, for the most part, from the participants' meaning-making systems. Thus, if evaluation is an interpretive endeavour a significant task is to clarify the theoretical assumptions that orient the evaluator in his or her hermeneutic efforts.

Assuming a psychological perspective on PSE implies asking a relevant question: What are the psychological dimensions of Personal and Social Education? It might be helpful to consider the basic motivations for addressing personal and social issues or affective themes in the curricula. Campos (1991) has proposed a typology with three basic motivations, namely:

- acquiring knowledge that is relevant for life, frequently translated into the curricula by the definition of cross-curricular themes
- developing a spiritual-moral-ethical self
- promoting competencies to deal with life problems, generally by the immersion within the various subjects of cross-curricular skills.

All these involve the development of psychological processes that are instrumental for the quality of action-in-context.

The understanding of the processes that underlie the construction of social knowledge is mandatory if we aim to develop our youngsters' knowledge of life; for instance, the existing research on socio-political reasoning (Adelson, 1971; Berti, 1988, 1994) demonstrates that young people reveal different levels of complexity when addressing social issues and that the mere inclusion of some of these issues in the school curriculum does not guarantee their full comprehension by the students. In a research project on political reasoning that we have developed, a young boy stresses the relevance of the 'Ministries' in governing the country; this relatively specific terminology seemed to indicate a quite abstract model of political functioning; but, when asked what the 'Ministries' were the picture was quite different: the 'Ministries' are buildings where officials are watching to see if the people are conforming to the existing laws; if they are not then the officials in the Ministry will send people a notice and make them pay a fine. Therefore, what emerges is a model of politics that is not only quite simple but of a bureaucratic nature, revealing, once more if necessary, that terminology acquisition does not imply understanding.

The development of a spiritual-moral-ethical self has been the object of intensive research on moral and interpersonal reasoning (e.g. Rest, 1986; Selman, 1976; Selman *et al.*, 1986) that has proved the relevance of processes such as social perspective taking (to name only one) in how children, young people and adults conceptualize issues of justice, interpersonal conflicts, etc. Finally, the relevance of psychological processes for managing conflicts, negotiating and deciding to take a stance has been demonstrated by several authors (e.g. Hopson and Scally, 1981; Weissberg et al., 1989).

Additionally, the developmental-ecological model of intervention, as well as existing research, reveals the significance of taking into account personal and transpersonal structures, thus understanding that human action is by definition an action-in-context and that change does not depend solely on the individual's idiosyncratic capacities but also on the opportunities, challenges and structure of his or her life contexts (see Campos et al., 1994; Orford, 1992; Sprinthall, 1991; Weissberg et al., 1989). The promotion of change has been shown to depend on

- the provision of meaningful, challenging and in-context experiences (role-taking vs. role-playing)
- balanced reflection over experience
- support, since 'growing is painful' (Sprinthall, 1991, p. 14)
- continuity, since episodic or discontinuous interventions do not create the necessary conditions for personal transformation.

Assuming this developmental-ecological paradigm, the evaluation of the PSE project focused on personal and transpersonal dimensions, namely self-concept, social perspective taking and political reasoning, and network orientation and perceptions of classroom environment, as well as teachers' perceptions of their work environment and conceptions about affective education. The evaluation involved all the students of grades 7, 8 and 9, in a total of 842 subjects, that were observed in various moments, at least twice, across a period of two years (1992–4). During this period, the evaluator was actively involved in the PSE school setting, in order to be able to describe, in detail, the process of implementing the PSE project. Additionally, the evaluator was explicitly seen as a resource of the school, in an intentional effort to develop a true partnership with the teachers (Guba and Lincoln, 1989; Kelly, 1968; Vincent and Trickett, 1983).

BRINGING PSE INTO PRACTICE: AN EXAMPLE

The implementation of the PSE intervention in the project school (referred to below as the 'PSE' school) occurred from 1991 to 1994. From 1992 onwards we were able to accompany this project, and to acknowledge some of its major characteristics, namely:

- a significant school involvement
- a collective feeling of 'this is it ...'
- a recognition of 'the need to change things'
- a collective sense of being involved in a new and challenging enterprise 'that will change things'
- a strong support of the school management and pedagogical boards
- concerns with the school ethos, 'towards democracy'
- conceptions of school change that appeal to a 'beyond classroom' perspective.

The PSE project included various strategies aiming to produce changes at the school level and at the classroom level. School level strategies include:

- redefining the school's regulations by a joint committee involving elected representatives of students, parents, teachers and staff
- reactivating the assembly of class representatives, involving all class representatives in a common meeting to discuss relevant problems
- organizing an in-service training course for the school's staff, on Educational Reform, problem-solving and conflicts negotiation
- promoting a contest for the students' lounge, with presentation of proposals for the creation of a students' space within the school.

Classroom level strategies comprise:

- promoting a more democratic and reflexive procedure for electing the class representative, namely by defining relevant criteria for choosing the 'right person for the job'
- involving the students in relevant school area projects (e.g. the relationship between the younger and the older students, the communication within the school) that imply: making enquiries and interviews within and outside the school; treating the data; and organizing and presenting the results to the school community, so that problems can be reflected on and ultimately solved.

Our aim was to evaluate the effects of these strategies on the students from the 'PSE' and the 'other' schools; as mentioned above, these groups vary according not only to their experience of the PSE project but also to the school curricula, 'traditional' (i.e. pre-Reform) or 'revised'. In the PSE school all groups receive the revised curriculum, while in the other school only those in Grade 7 do; students in Grade 8 and 9 still have the 'traditional' curriculum.

So far, the existing data (see Menezes and Campos, 1993a, 1993b and 1995) revealed that there is a tendency for students involved in the Reform experience in the PSE school to reveal positive effects in important areas of self-concept, to demonstrate a more positive perception of classroom climate in dimensions such as innovation and teacher support, and for students in the other school to show a more intense perception of teacher control. However, these differences become diluted with time. Results on teachers' perceptions of their work environment show that teachers in the PSE school have a more positive perception of their work climate than their colleagues in the other school; additionally, teachers in the PSE school have more positive perceptions of the school climate than their students have of the classroom climate, while teachers in the other school have more negative perceptions of the school climate than their students have of the classroom climate.

In this chapter we will produce a more in-depth, although still preliminary, analysis of the differences in the students' perceptions of classroom environment across time, in order to understand the short- and long-term effects of the PSE intervention.

PERCEPTIONS OF CLASSROOM ENVIRONMENT

According to Moos (1976, 1987), individual perceptions of the social climate of institutions are organized along three basic dimensions: relationship, goal orientation and system maintenance and change. The relationship dimension accounts for the quality of the interactions between the participants in the setting; the goal orientation dimension refers to how the setting is organized to achieve its aims; the system maintenance and change dimension designates the procedures used to guarantee the setting's stability and its permeability to innovation. Moos and collaborators have developed several questionnaires to observe perceptions of social climate in various settings, such as classrooms, families, prisons, hospitals, etc.

The Classroom Environment Scale (CES) has been produced by Moos and Trickett (1986) to analyse how students organize their perceptions of the classroom. The questionnaire involves nine scales that are directly related to the three basic dimensions defined above. The scales are the following: involvement, affiliation, teacher support, task orientation, competition, order and organization, rule clarity, teacher control and innovation (see Table 1).

Table 1: Exemplary items of the CES scales

CES scales	Exemplary items
Involvement	'students put a lot of energy into what they do here'
Affiliation	'there are groups of students who don't get along'
Teacher support	'the teacher goes out of his/her way to help the students'
Task orientation	'almost all class time is spent on the lesson for the day'
Competition	'students try hard to get the best grade'
Order and organization	'the teacher often has to tell the students to calm down'
Rule clarity	'rules in the class seem to change a lot'
Teacher control	'the teacher is not very strict'
Innovation	'what students do in class is very different on different days'

Existing research has revealed that positive perceptions of classroom environment have beneficial effects on adolescents' well-being and achievement (Cheung, 1995; Felner, Aber, Primavera and Cauce, 1985; Moos, 1979; Trickett and Moos, 1974). Yuen, Grace and Watkins (1994), for instance, verified that friendly and collaborative climates, with varied and challenging tasks, promoted students' achievement orientation, whereas competition and teacher control encouraged rote learning; Keyser and Barling (1981) found that the classroom climate can be a determinant of the students' sense of personal competence. Other studies have associated this construct with positive attitudes towards the curricular contents (Fouts and Myers, 1992; Fraser and Fisher, 1982; Haladyna, Olsen and Shaughnessy, 1982; Shaughnessy, Haladyna and Shaughnessy, 1983) or with the students' behaviour in the classroom (Brown, 1982; Short and Short, 1988). Educational innovation has been shown to enhance perceptions of teacher support, involvement and innovation, whereas traditional classes tend to reinforce perceptions of task orientation, competition and teacher control (Raviv, Raviv and Reisel, 1993). Teachers and students apparently tend to share perceptions of the ideal climate but to differ on their perceptions of the actual classroom climate (Raviv, Raviv and Reisel, 1990). Huang and Waxman (1995) verified that younger students generally have higher perceptions of involvement and satisfaction.

THE EVALUATION PROCEDURE

Samples and administration

The CES (Moos and Trickett, 1986) was administered to all the students in grades 7, 8 and 9, from the two schools selected: the PSE school, which was developing a project of PSE and experimenting with the 'revised' curriculum for all grades, and the other school that had the 'traditional' curriculum for grades 8 and 9, and the 'revised' curricula for grade 7. All the classes, with a total of 842 students, were observed on various occasions, at least twice, across a period of two years from 1992 to 1994 (Table 2).

This was because the PSE project had already been implemented for one year at the time of the beginning of the evaluation process; the multiple observations allow us to compare variations both within and between schools. However, for the sake of clarity, the groups will always be designated by the grade they were attending in 1992 (e.g. grade 7 '92, grade 8 '92 and grade 9 '92), even though grade 8 '92 students observed during 1993–4 were attending grade 9 by that time, and grade 7 '92 students observed in 1993–4 were also attending grade 8 by that time.

Table 2: Observation moments for the various classes

School	Classes	Dec. 1992	Jun. 1993	Dec. 1993	Jun. 1994
PSE school	Grade 7 '92	•		•	
	Grade 8 '92	•		•[1]	•
	Grade 9 '92	•	•		
Other school	Grade 7 '92	•		•	
	Grade 8 '92	•			•
	Grade 9 '92	•	•		

[1] Sub-group of grade 8

All the students completed the questionnaire on the classroom setting. To overcome the problems of a dichotomous procedure, the 'true' and 'false' options of the original version of the CES were substituted by a 6-point Likert scale, from 1, 'totally disagree', to 6, 'totally agree'.

Psychometric qualities of the questionnaire

Although the CES has been widely considered as a valid instrument for analysing the students' perceptions of the classroom environment (see Moos and Trickett, 1986), it is more and more common in educational research to stress the need for studying the validity of instruments in every administration. Recently, Trickett and colleagues (1993) also made relevant adaptations of the CES while using it with a population of disabled students. Moreover, our changes in the coding system could also imply some relevant modifications in the questionnaire. In fact, the consistency of the proposed theoretical dimensions is very low, as revealed by the Cronbach alpha (see Table 3).

Table 3: Internal consistency of the theoretical scales

Scales	Cronbach Alpha (Dec. 1992) N=842	Kuder-Richardson Moos and Trickett (1986) N=465
Involvement	.61	.85
Affiliation	.72	.74
Teacher support	.52	.84
Task orientation	.30	.84
Competition	.32	.67
Order and organization	.56	.85
Rule clarity	.45	.74
Teacher control	.46	.86
Innovation	.54	.80

Therefore, we decided to perform a factorial analysis to determine whether the perceptions of our sample were organized in an alternative and valid structure. Since the emerging factors were expected to be interrelated, the principal components factorial analysis used was an oblimin rotation. This procedure implied the revision of the theoretical scales and resulted in the elimination of 20 items (similarly to Trickett et al., 1993) that did not have a satisfactory saturation in any of the newly identified scales (Table 4).

Table 4: Revised scales of the CES and definitions

Revised scales	Definitions
Teacher support and consistency	The teacher demonstrates 'his/her interest in the students', is 'more a friend than an authority' but also 'assigns tasks so that everybody knows what to do', explains 'how to do class assignments', plans and defines things clearly and 'when he/she says that something should not be done, he/she means it'.
Order and organization	The general way in which the class is organized ('the class never starts on time') and how well-behaved students are during class ('students play a lot').
Student involvement and affiliation	Students appreciate and help each other, are able to work together, and are attentive to class matters.
Teacher autocratic control	The teacher is the class dictator, keeps changing the rules and does not trust the students; he/she can embarrass a student for not knowing the answer and students have to be careful with what they say and do.
Innovation	There is room for students' suggestions and new things are always being tried out; creativity is the motto.

In some cases, the scales are clearly similar to those identified by Moos and Trickett (1986) – even if the items that constitute them are different – but in others there are clear differences. These generally indicate that the students are less able to discriminate the proposed theoretical dimensions (for instance, mixing relationship and goal orientation and relationship and system maintenance and change dimensions), and that the teacher emerges as a central figure, around whom the students perceive the classroom climate. That is particularly the case in the teacher support and consistency and the teacher autocratic control scales, which appear to be the image of the 'good' and 'bad' teacher.

The consistency of these scales across the various administrations of the questionnaire also indicates the reliability of this organization (Table 5). Therefore, this revision of the CES scales will be used in analysing differences across the various groups and observation moments.

Table 5: Scale consistency (Cronbach alpha) across the various administrations

Scales	Dec./92 N=842	June/93 N=339	Dec./93 N=227	June/94 N=164
Teacher support and consistency	.8229	.8081	.8430	.6620
Order and organization	.7538	.7983	.8037	.8037
Student involvement and affiliation	.7675	.7340	.7379	.6810
Teacher autocratic control	.7206	.7529	.7654	.7124
Innovation	.7254	.7342	.7243	.6878

Results

As mentioned above, the groups are designated by the grade they were attending in 1992 even when referring to other moments of observation. As shown in Table 6, significant differences (p<.05) between students' classroom perceptions are as follows:

- In December 1992 there are *interaction effects* 'school by grade' with students' in lower grades revealing higher perceptions of teacher support and consistency and innovation; *grade effects* show that lower grade students have higher perceptions of teacher support and consistency, order and organization, and innovation; and *school effects* demonstrate higher perceptions of innovation in the PSE school and of teacher autocratic control in the other school.
- In June 1993 *school effects* reveal that the students' perceptions in the PSE school are higher in order and organization and innovation, while their colleagues in the other school perceive more teacher autocratic control.
- In December 1993 *school and grade effects* show higher perceptions of teacher support and consistency, student involvement and affiliation and innovation of the students in the other school; *school effects* also reveal higher perceptions of teacher support and consistency, student involvement and affiliation, order and organization and innovation of the students in the other school.
- In June 1994 there are no differences between the two schools.

Table 6: Means (x) and standard deviations (SD) of the various groups for the CES factors at the various observation moments

School Group	Factors	Dec. 1992			Jun. 1993			Dec. 1993			Jun. 1994		
		N	x	SD	N	x	SD	N	x	SD	N	x	SD
PSE													
Gr. 7 '92	TeacSC	104	4.689	.7504				84	4.519	.7333			
	O&O	104	2.695	.8442				84	2.585	.7412			
	StulAf	104	4.139	.9255				84	4.193	.8011			
	TeacAC	104	3.688	.8748				84	3.800	.8550			
	Inn	104	4.109	.6818				84	4.182	.6638			
Gr. 8 '92	TeacSC	128	4.561	.6531				39*	4.433	.6161	109	4.033	.5783
	O&O	128	2.604	.7004				39*	2.649	.7053	109	2.605	.7882
	StulAf	128	4.220	.6425				39*	4.250	.6748	109	4.092	.6913
	TeacAC	128	3.682	.7641				39*	3.539	.9585	109	3.692	.7917
	Inn	128	4.086	.6716				39*	3.686	.6196	109	3.704	.6876
Gr. 9 '92	TeacSC	197	4.411	.6112	179	4.307	.6013						
	O&O	197	2.513	.6255	179	2.686	.6363						
	StulAf	197	4.146	.7861	179	4.116	.7217						
	TeacAC	197	3.636	.7756	179	3.535	.7903						
	Inn	197	3.956	.6167	179	3.971	.5850						
Other													
Gr. 7 '92	TeacSC	129	4.841	.5856				104	4.741	.6303			
	O&O	129	2.549	.6977				104	2.898	.7414			
	StulAf	129	3.986	.8702				104	4.497	.6801			
	TeacAC	129	3.784	.7729				104	3.588	.7313			
	Inn	129	4.347	.6192				104	4.182	.6638			

Table 6 (contd.)

School Group	Factors	Dec. 1992			Jun. 1993			Dec. 1993			Jun. 1994		
		N	x	SD	N	x	SD	N	x	SD	N	x	SD
Gr. 8 '92	TeacSC	119	4.352	.7784							55	4.166	.4792
	O&O	119	2.600	.6400							55	2.472	.6277
	StulAf	119	4.151	.7942							55	4.241	.6688
	TeacAC	119	3.978	.6764							55	3.727	.7407
	Inn	119	3.747	.6941							55	3.570	.6912
Gr. 9 '92	TeacSC	169	4.337	.6614	160	4.230	.6491						
	O&O	169	2.392	.6352	160	2.381	.7090						
	StulAf	169	4.113	.7959	160	4.026	.7191						
	TeacAC	169	4.004	.6825	160	3.913	.6802						
	Inn	169	3.515	.6402	160	3.531	.7227						

* Sub-group of grade 8
TeacSC: teacher support and consistency; O&O: order and organization; StulAf: student involvement and affiliation; TeacAC: teacher autocratic control; Inn: innovation

The design also allows for across-moment comparisons between the various groups. These data lead to interesting conclusions regarding significant differences; we will mention only some of the most relevant:

- within the PSE school, 9 '92 graders in December 1992 show more positive perceptions of innovation than 8 '92 graders in December 1993 (it should be noted that this comparison allows us to analyse two groups attending the same grade, with the same age and permanence in the school)
- within the PSE school, 9 '92 graders in June 1993 show more positive perceptions of teacher support and consistency and innovation than 8 '92 graders in June 1994 (it should be noted that this comparison also allows us to analyse two groups attending the same grade, with the same age and permanence in the school)
- within the other school, no differences are detectable when comparing 9 '92 graders in June 1993 with 8 '92 graders in June 1994
- 7 '92 graders from the other school, which are the only group experiencing the revised curriculum, generally tend to have higher perceptions of teacher support and consistency and innovation (or at least one of these factors) when compared to all the other groups
- longitudinal data reveal that within the PSE school, 9 '92 graders in June 1993 show more positive perceptions of order and organization than in December 1992; 8 '92 graders show a decrease in perceptions of teacher support and consistency and innovation from December

1992 to June 1994; and there are no differences in the perceptions of 7 '92 graders

- longitudinal data reveal that within the other school, the perceptions of 9 '92 graders do not vary; the 8 '92 graders show a decrease in perceptions of teacher autocratic control from December 1992 to June 1994; and 7 '92 graders have a significant increase in perceptions of order and organization and student involvement and affiliation, and a significant decrease in perceptions of teacher autocratic control, from December 1992 to December 1993

- when comparing school differences in the students' perceptions across the various observation moments, the 9 '92 graders from the PSE school maintain their higher perceptions of innovation and lower perceptions of teacher autocratic control when compared to 9 '92 graders from the other school; similarly, the 7 '92 graders from the other school also maintain their higher perceptions of innovation; the perceptions of 8 '92 graders get diluted in the second observation period.

In spite of the complexity of these results, there seems to be a tendency for the groups that have been the first to experience the revised curricula in the two schools, that is 9 '92 graders from the PSE school and 7 '92 graders from the other school, to show the most positive and enduring effects. Additionally, the comparison between 8 '92 graders from the two schools reveals a tendency for a dilution effect across time that seems to result from a decrease in the perceptions of more positive climate characteristics (such as teacher support and consistency and innovation) for students in the PSE school, while their peers from the other school reveal a decrease in perceptions of more negative climate characteristics (teacher autocratic control).

TENTATIVE CONCLUSIONS

A major and most interesting finding of this research project is that the significant changes in students' perceptions of classroom environment as a result of the PSE project seem to become diluted as time goes by. This finding is consistent with other researches, which also detect a tendency for innovation effects to diminish after the first one or two years.

May this be due to the fact that innovation becomes routinized after some time, thus losing part of its novelty character? If this proved to be true, as the data on the 9 '92 graders from the PSE school and 7 '92 graders from the other school seem to indicate, the picture would be somewhat disappointing, since our experience from observing the two schools allows us to consider that there are important qualitative differences in the innovation the students experienced. Or could this be a result of a 'Hawthorne effect'? Maybe the students' acknowledgment of being the first group involved in a 'new' experience in the school could contribute to some of the changes. The effects of being involved in experimenting with the Curricular Reform for several years could, therefore, be somewhat perverse.

However, it is also true that there were important shifts in the educational policies during this period, which led teachers in the PSE school to express some disappointment, contrasting clearly with the 'high morale' of the beginning of the project. Could this have affected their attitudes and management of the classroom, and thus the perceptions of their students?

These tentative explanations clearly do not account effectively for the data we have so far. But the fact that time is a determining factor seems irrefutable. And the passing of time can probably produce in the practitioners a tendency to become less creative, innovative and reflective in implementing PSE programmes. This may be the most interesting speculation resulting from this study: the idea that innovative practices, to maintain a high level of effectiveness, must be conceived as a spiral process, always coming back to the beginning but with the renewed feeling of being there for the first time. Which, basically, is what personal and social development is all about.

REFERENCES

Adelson, J. (1971), 'The political imagination of the young adolescent', *Daedalus*, 100, 1013–50.

Berti, A. E. (1988), 'The development of political understanding in children between 6–15 years old', *Human Relations*, 41, 6, 437–46.

Berti, A. E. (1994), 'Children's understanding of the concept of the state', in M. Carretero and J. F. Voss (eds), *Cognitive and Instructional Processes in History and the Social Sciences*, New Jersey: Lawrence Erlbaum Associates.

Brown, E. (1982), 'The climates within classrooms: A partial function of roles', *Dissertation Abstracts International*, 43, 3354A.

Campos, B. P. (1991), 'Educação para a democracia e desenvolvimento psicológico', in *Educação e desenvolvimento pessoal e social*, Oporto: Afrontamento.

Campos, B. P., Costa, M. E. and Menezes, I. (1994), 'The social dimension of deliberate psychological education', in G. Musitu *et al.* (eds), Intervención comunitaría, Valencia: Set i Set Edic., 31–40.

Cheung, S.-K. (1995), 'Life events, classroom environment, achievement expectation, and depression among early adolescents', *Social Behavior and Personality*, 23(1), 83–92.

Felner, R., Aber, M., Primavera, J. and Cauce, A. (1985), 'Adaptation and vulnerability in high risk adolescents: An examination of environmental mediators', *American Journal of Community Psychology*, 13, 365–79.

Fouts, J. T. and Myers, R. E. (1992), 'Classroom environments and middle school students' views of science', *Journal of Educational Research*, 85(6), 356–61.

Fraser, B. and Fisher, D. (1982), 'Predicting students' outcomes from their perceptions of classrooms psychosocial environment', *American Educational Research Journal*, 19, 498–518.

Guba, E. G. and Lincoln, Y. S. (1989), *Fourth Generation Evaluation*, Newbury Park: Sage.

Haladyna, T., Olsen, R. and Shaughnessy, J. (1982), 'Relations of student, teacher, and learning environment variables to attitudes toward science', *Science Education*, 66, 671–87.

Hopson, B. and Scally, M. (1981), *Lifeskills Teaching*, London: McGraw Hill.

Huang, S.-Y. L. and Waxman, H. C. (1995), 'Motivation and learning-environment differences between Asian-American and White middle school students in mathematics', *Journal of Research and Development in Education*, 286(4), 208–19.

Illback, R. J., Zins, J. E., Maher, C. A. and Greenberg, R. (1990), 'An overview of principles and procedures of program planning and evaluation', in T. B. Gutkin and C. R. Reynolds (eds), *The Handbook of School Psychology*, 2nd edn, New York: Wiley, 799–820.

Kelly, J. G. (1968), 'Toward an ecological conception of preventive interventions', in J. N. Carter jr. (ed.), *Research Contribution from Psychology to Community Mental Health*, New York: Behavior Publications.

Keyser, V. and Barling, J. (1981), 'Determinants of children's self-efficacy beliefs in academic environment', *Cognitive Therapy and Research*, 5, 29–40.

Menezes, I. and Campos, B. P. (1993a), 'Effects of school programs of personal and social education on the psychological development of 8th graders', paper presented at the *Second International Conference of Psychological Intervention and Human Development: Educational and Community Intervention*, Valencia, July.

Menezes, I. and Campos, B. P. (1993b), 'Personal and social education in the schools: Is education really fostering psychological development?', paper presented at the seminar *Affective Education in Europe*, Warwick University, May.

Menezes, I. and Campos, B. P. (1995), 'Clima da escola: Um estudo comparativo das percepções de alunos e professores', in A. Estrela and J. Barroso (eds), *A escola. Um objecto de estudo*, Lisbon: AIPEL e FPCE-UL, October.

Moos, R. H. (1976), 'Conceptualizations of human environments', in H. Proshansky, W. Ittelson and L. Rivlin (eds), *Environmental Psychology: Man and his Physical Setting*, New York: Holt, Rinehart and Winston.

Moos, R. H. (1979), *Evaluating Educational Environments*, San Francisco: Jossey-Bass.

Moos, R. H. (1987), 'Person-environment congruence in work, school and health care settings', *Journal of Vocational Behavior*, 31, 231–47.

Moos, R. H. and Trickett, E. J. (1986), *Classroom Environment Scale Manual*, (2nd edn), Palo Alto: Consulting Psychologists Press.

Orford, J. (1992), *Community Intervention: Theory and Practice*, Chichester: Wiley.

Raviv, A., Raviv, A. and Reisel, E. (1990), 'Teachers and students: Two different perspectives? Measuring social climate in the classroom', *American Educational Research Journal*, 27(1), 141–57.

Raviv, A., Raviv, A. and Reisel, E. (1993), 'Environmental approach used for evaluating an educational innovation', *Journal of Educational*

Research, 86(6), 317–24.

Rest, J. (1986), *Moral Development: Advances in Research and Theory*, New York: Praeger.

Selman, R. L. (1976), 'Social-cognitive understanding: A guide to educational and clinical practice', in T. Lickona (ed.), *Moral Development and Behavior: Theory, Research and Social Issues*, New York: Holt, Rinehart and Winston.

Selman, R. L., Beardslee, W., Schultz, L. H., Krupa, M. and Podorefsky, D. (1986), 'Assessing interpersonal negotiation strategies: Toward the integration of structural and functional models', *Developmental Psychology*, 22, 4, 450–7.

Shaughnessy, J., Haladyna, T. and Shaughnessy, J. M. (1983), 'Relations of student, teacher, and learning environment variables to attitudes towards mathematics', *School Science and Mathematics*, 83, 21–37.

Short, P. M. and Short, R. J. (1988), 'Perceived classroom environment and student behavior in secondary schools', *Educational Research Quarterly*, 12(3), 35–9.

Sprinthall, N. A. (1991), 'Role taking programs for high school students: New methods to promote psychological development', in B. P. Campos (ed.), *Psychological Intervention and Human Development*, Oporto: Instituto de Consulta Psicológica, Formação e Desenvolvimento e Louvain-La-Neuve: Academia.

Trickett, E. J. and Moos, R. H. (1974), 'Personal correlates of contrasting environments: Student satisfaction in high school classrooms', *American Journal of Community Psychology*, 2, 1–12.

Trickett, E. J., Leone, P. E., Fink, C. M. and Braaten, S. L. (1993), 'The perceived environment of special education classrooms for adolescents: A revision of the Classroom Environment Scale', *Exceptional Children*, 59, 411–20.

Vincent, T. A. and Trickett, E. J. (1983), 'Preventive intervention and the human context: Ecological approaches to environment assesment and change', in R. D. Felner, L. A. Jackson, J. N. Moritsugu and S. S. Farber (eds), *Preventive Psychology*, New York: Pergamon.

Weissberg, R. P., Caplan, M. Z. and Sivo, P. (1989), 'A new conceptual framework for establishing school-based social competence promotion programs', in L. A. Bond and B. E. Compas (eds), *Primary Prevention and Promotion in the Schools*, Newbury Park, CA: Sage Publications, Inc.

Yuen, Y., Grace, C. and Watkins, D. (1994), 'Classroom environment and approaches to learning: An investigation of the actual and preferred perceptions of Hong-Kong secondary school students', *Instructional Science*, 22(3), 233–46.

PART 4

Endnote

Peter Lang

In my introductory chapter I drew attention to the existence of both common ground and significant variations in terms of the theory, policy and practice of affective education in Europe. The basis on which these two contrasting trends had been identified were my own investigations and discussion between representatives of the 16 European countries currently belonging to the European Affective Education Network (most of whom are represented in this book). In my introduction I also suggested that further work was needed to reach a detailed understanding of these parallels and differences.

Work which involves European countries in collaborative research in the affective area is likely to provide data from which such understanding can be developed. An illustration of the potential of such work is a current project in which researchers from 12 European countries and Israel are working together on a comparative project. The focus of their investigation is the attitudes to affective education held by key stake-holders in each country. The research involves two different questionnaires: one for teachers and one for pupils. The project is seen only as a first step and this, together with constraints of limited funding, has meant that data collection to date has used only a quantitative methodology. The questionnaire answers all involve ticking or circling existing prompts or scales. The questionnaires were designed to be amenable to statistical analysis using SPSS for Windows, many of the collaborators being familiar with the use of this package. The teachers' questionnaire was developed in draft at a research meeting in October 1996 attended by all participating researchers.

The questionnaire was divided into four sections. *Section One* asked for information about the respondents' school, their age and sex, the length of time they had been teaching, what subjects they taught and the age range of the pupils they taught. *Section Two* consisted of questions designed to generate data on the respondents' attitudes to the affective dimension of education in relation to themselves and their schools. *Section Three* asked how positive they felt about their work as a teacher and how positive they believed their colleagues felt. They were also asked to identify those things that made them feel the most positive and the most negative. *Section Four* asked them to identify the qualities they thought it was most important for schools to seek to promote in their pupils.

The questionnaire's development was undertaken with three important considerations in mind:

- The need for methodological consistency and statistical validity. There were a number of occasions during the discussions when those most expert in statistical techniques drew attention to actual or potential methodological and statistical flaws in the developing instrument. Although the resolution of some of these problems generated a heated debate, in the end they were all recast in a way that eliminated the problem to the satisfaction of the team.
- The importance of wording questions appropriately for all countries. Differences between the organization and culture of the education systems involved meant that the way a significant number of questions were expressed had to be thought through with some care. Although the principle which governed the development of the questionnaire was that every language version should be as far as possible identical in meaning, there were a number of questions where it was agreed that some latitude was needed in expression in different languages, as a literal translation from one context to another would lead to misunderstanding or ambiguity.
- The challenge of translation. At every stage all participants were exhorted to check carefully that there was no problem in terms of translation from English (the group working language) into their own language. Again there were a number of instances where it was found that words commonly found in English educational usage did not translate satisfactorily and alternative ways of expressing the particular process or concept had to be identified. Examples of this were: 'role' as used in 'the role of the teacher' and 'monitoring' as in 'monitoring pupil progress'. Perhaps the most surprising problem to arise at this stage was the fact that in modern Greek there is no one word for empathy, though one exists in classical Greek.

Directly after this first planning meeting this questionnaire was piloted in all the countries involved. In February 1997 a second meeting took place at which the feedback on the pilot was considered and the questionnaire revised accordingly. At this meeting a questionnaire for pupils was also produced. This questionnaire mirrored the teacher questionnaire as far as possible, thus pupils were asked their perspectives on the same issues as the teachers. These questionnaires were administered to samples of primary and secondary teachers and pupils in all the countries involved.

At a third meeting in October 1997 some preliminary analysis of data from questionnaires from ten of the collaborating European countries was undertaken. The analysis of these results showed that the majority of teachers in all the countries involved did not consider teaching to be the delivery of the academic curriculum alone. Although there were variations between countries and age groups, the general trend in the responses from teachers from all ten countries was that the affective education of students was one of their important responsibilities and to a lesser extent the responsibility of others. This was particularly true for aspects of personal and social development such as the promotion of effective communication skills, the preparation of students for responsible citizenship in a democracy and the raising of awareness with regard to issues of the environment, culture and equality. The only area where respondents saw the major responsibility as belonging to others was in connection with child abuse.

Most teachers in the sample reported a fair degree of job satisfaction. The factors reported as influencing their positive feelings varied considerably between countries. However, the majority involved good relationships with students, professional autonomy and professional recognition. Equally, absence of these factors was reported as making a significant contribution to lack of job satisfaction.

An interesting point was that in most countries students say they enjoy school more than teachers do. Additionally, although the students tend to rate academic concerns lower than teachers, students' scores are significantly higher than teachers' for responses related to teachers taking action in cases of abuse, teachers organizing extra-curricular activities for students, listening to their problems and mediating in cases of students being involved in disputes with other teachers. Both groups reported ambivalent feelings with regard to parental involvement in school life. Here it should be noted that students express a more negative attitude than teachers. There seems to be a high degree of agreement in terms of the qualities schools should seek to promote: responsibility, respect for others and fairness are seen as vital priorities by both students and teachers. The data analysis supported a finding already familiar from research into pupils' attitudes: there was a general tendency for younger students to report more positive attitudes than older students.

As a result of the work undertaken so far the collaborators believe that the following has been learnt. Whatever differences exist between the systems involved, it was possible to develop a questionnaire which all involved believed would make sense and be relevant to teachers and pupils in their own country. Although the development involved much debate and on occasions argument, the differences that were identified were not fundamental. Rather they involved issues such as differences in the ways subjects are categorized and variations in the age ranges of different levels of schooling. There were a number of issues relating to translation but these were overcome by replacing a single word with a short sentence in languages where there were no direct equivalents. The fact that at the level of practice, and from the diverse perspectives of those involved, a common understanding of the affective dimension exists was supported by the fact that in no country did teachers or pupils report problems connected with understanding or completing the questionnaire. The existence of 'common ground' mentioned in the introduction to this book is clearly confirmed.

At this stage of the analysis only limited significance can be given to any particular finding. Although specific conclusions are not yet possible, what has already emerged illustrates the possibilities of moving beyond general assumptions such as 'of course teachers in all countries will be concerned about the development and well-being of their pupils', to the development of a discourse and understanding specific to the practice of affective education in Europe.

I believe that such a European perspective would have an important contribution to make at a broader international level. I have already drawn attention to the distinction between generalists and specialists in the provision of the affective dimension of education (Lang, 1995, pp. 272–3). Although there are few education systems which are totally committed to one or other approach, it seems that it is the theories under-pinning specialist approaches which are the more influential in most parts of the world. A European perspective on affective education would certainly emphasize the generalist approach and go some way to redress-ing the imbalance.

A recent visit to China suggested the potential value of the develop-ment of a European alternative to what are mainly American models. Chinese educational thinking in relation to affective education, though considerably influenced by Confucianism, also draws heavily on American theory (specialist orientated), but the practice of affective education relies entirely on classroom teachers (generalists). Under such circumstances the European perspective advocated here, and to which this book is a con-tribution, could make an important input in the development of an affec-tive education appropriate to the needs of what is likely to be one of the world's most powerful and influential nations for the future.

Thus, though this book is intended partly as an overview of a current situation, it is also seen as an important starting point.

REFERENCE

Lang, P. (1995), 'International Perspectives on Pastoral Care (Affective Education)', in R. Best, P. Lang, C. Lodge and C. Watkins (eds), *Pastoral Care and Personal and Social Education: Entitlement and Provision*, London: Cassell.

PARTICIPANTS IN THE RESEARCH PROJECT

The following were the main collaborators in the research described above.

England	Peter Lang, Sean Neill, Chris Husbands: University of Warwick
Finland	Arja Puurula: University of Helsinki
Greece	Alkistis Kondoyianni, Rea Karageorgiou-Short, Maria Malikiosi-Loizos, Athena Sideri: University of Athens
Hungary	Katalin Horváth-Szabó, Pázmány Péter: Catholic University
Ireland	Maeve Martin: Maynooth University
Israel	Yaacov Katz: Bar-Ilan University

Italy	Emma Urgesi, Maria Teresa Crucillà: III University of Rome
Netherlands	Lennart Vriens: University of Utrecht
Northern Ireland	Ron Smith, Patricia Ward: North West Teachers Centre, Strathfoyle
Portugal	Isabel Menezes, Bártolo P. Campos: University of Oporto
Spain	Maria-José Bezanilla, Ana Martínez Pampliega, Manuel Marroquín, Aurelio Villa: University of Deusto

Index